Chad
a country study

Federal Research Division
Library of Congress
Edited by
Thomas Collelo
Research Completed
December 1988

On the cover: Two children help their father lift water from a well near Lake Chad.

DT
546.422
C48
1990

Second Edition, 1990; First Printing, 1990.

Library of Congress Cataloging-in-Publication Data

Chad: A Country Study.

   Area handbook series, DA Pam 550–159
   Research completed December 1988.
   Bibliography: pp. 223–234.
   Includes index.
   1. Chad. I. Collelo, Thomas, 1948-   . II. Area handbook of
Chad. III. Federal Research Division. Library of Congress.
IV. DA Pam 550–159.

DT546.422.C48   1990   916.743—dc20   89-600373

Headquarters, Department of the Army
DA Pam 550–159

For sale by the Superintendent of Documents, U.S. Government Printing Office
Washington, D.C. 20402

Foreword

This volume is one in a continuing series of books now being prepared by the Federal Research Division of the Library of Congress under the Country Studies—Area Handbook Program. The last page of this book lists the other published studies.

Most books in the series deal with a particular foreign country, describing and analyzing its political, economic, social, and national security systems and institutions, and examining the interrelationships of those systems and the ways they are shaped by cultural factors. Each study is written by a multidisciplinary team of social scientists. The authors seek to provide a basic understanding of the observed society, striving for a dynamic rather than a static portrayal. Particular attention is devoted to the people who make up the society, their origins, dominant beliefs and values, their common interests and the issues on which they are divided, the nature and extent of their involvement with national institutions, and their attitudes toward each other and toward their social system and political order.

The books represent the analysis of the authors and should not be construed as an expression of an official United States government position, policy, or decision. The authors have sought to adhere to accepted standards of scholarly objectivity. Corrections, additions, and suggestions for changes from readers will be welcomed for use in future editions.

Louis R. Mortimer
Acting Chief
Federal Research Division
Library of Congress
Washington, D.C. 20540

Foreword

Acknowledgments

The authors wish to thank individuals and private institutions who gave their time, research materials, and expertise to the production of this book. The authors are also grateful to members of the Federal Research Division staff who contributed directly to the preparation of the manuscript. These people include Richard F. Nyrop, who reviewed all drafts and served as liaison with the sponsoring agency; Martha E. Hopkins, who managed editing and production; Barbara Edgerton and Izella Watson, who provided word-processing support; and Helen C. Metz, who reviewed the text's French terminology.

Marilyn L. Majeska, Sharon Costello, Richard Kollodge, Lea Knott, and Michael Pleasants edited the manuscript; prepublication editorial review was performed by Beverly Wolpert; Shirley Kessell compiled the index. Diann J. Johnson of the Library of Congress Composing Unit prepared the camera-ready copy, under the supervision of Peggy Pixley.

Inestimable graphics support was provided by David P. Cabitto, assisted by Sandra K. Ferrell and Kimberly A. Lord; Ms. Lord also designed the cover artwork and the illustrations on the title page of each chapter. In addition, thanks are owed to Carolina E. Forrester, who reviewed the map drafts, and Harriett R. Blood, who prepared the topography and drainage map.

Finally, the authors acknowledge the generosity of the many individuals and public and private agencies who allowed their photographs to be used in this study. They are indebted especially to those who contributed original work not previously published.

Contents

List of Figures

Preface

Since the publication of the *Area Handbook for Chad* in 1972, Chadian society has experienced almost uninterrupted turmoil. The government in power in 1972, which was dominated by southern ethnic groups, fell to a military coup d'état in 1975. By 1978 an insurgent group, composed mostly of northerners, had displaced the military regime, and in 1982 a different rebel organization came to power. These years also saw the coming and going of foreign troops, most notably those of France and Libya. Adding to these politico-military machinations was a several-year-long drought that produced famine and a flow of refugees and rendered the economy dependent on the generosity of France and the international donor community.

Although *Chad: A Country Study* contains some material from the 1972 edition, it is basically a new book. Like its predecessor, this volume is an attempt to treat in a concise and objective manner the dominant social, political, economic, and military aspects of contemporary Chadian society. Sources of information included scholarly journals and monographs, official reports of governments and international organizations, foreign and domestic newspapers, and numerous periodicals. The authors have emphasized the use of foreign-language sources to a greater extent than in the past. Nevertheless, as a result of the warfare during the 1980s, up-to-date information on social and economic issues was scarce; little fieldwork had been done, and few government reports had been published.

Chapter bibliographies appear at the end of the book, and a brief annotated bibliographic note on sources recommended for further reading appears at the end of each chapter. Measurements are given in the metric system; a conversion table is provided to assist readers unfamiliar with metric measurements (see table 1, Appendix A). A glossary is included, and, to help readers identify numerous armies and militias, Appendix B, Principal Armed Factions, 1975–87, is provided.

To the extent possible, place-names follow the system adopted by the United States Board on Geographic Names; often these vary from conventional French usage. Because there is no standard to guide the spelling of proper names, the most common journalistic usages have been followed.

Country Profile

Formal Name: Republic of Chad.

Short Form: Chad.

Term for Citizens: Chadian(s).

Capital: N'Djamena.

Geography

Size: Approximately 1,284,000 square kilometers.

Topography: Northern third desert, with mountains in north and plateaus in northeast; central third broad, arid savanna with Lake Chad in west, massif in center, and highlands in east; southern third wooded and humid lowlands, intersected by rivers.

Climate: Northern Saharan zone generally hot and dry; central *sahelian* zone mostly dry with rainy season from June to early September; southern *soudanian* zone tropical with rainy season lasting from April to October.

Society

Population: Estimated at 5 million to 5.2 million in 1985, most of which concentrated in capital and southern third of country.

Education and Literacy: Education compulsory until age twelve, but only about 40 percent of primary-school-aged children attended in late 1980s. Overall literacy rate about 15 percent in 1982.

Health and Welfare: Years of civil strife, drought, and overall impoverishment have kept health care at low level. Few existing medical facilities concentrated in capital and major cities in south. Life expectancy in late 1970s about forty-three years for women and thirty-nine years for men.

Languages: French and Arabic official languages, Sara common in south, more than 100 others spoken.

Ethnic Groups: More than 200 distinct ethnic groups; Toubou common in north, Arabs in *sahelian* zone, Sara in *soudanian* zone.

Religion: More than half of population Muslim; rest adhere to traditional African religions or Christianity.

Economy

Gross Domestic Product (GDP): About US$817 million in 1986; US$160 per capita. In mid-1980s war, drought, famine, and low prices for cotton made Chad one of five poorest countries in world.

Agriculture: Contributed about 46 percent of GDP in 1986. Dominated by cotton grown in south. Approximately 83 percent of economically active population farmers or herders. Sorghum and millet major food crops.

Industry: Not well developed but contributed almost 18 percent of GDP in 1986. Employed only 5 percent of work force. Sector dominated by agribusiness. Mining, especially oil extraction, held some promise of development.

Imports: US$206.1 million in 1986, mainly manufactured goods and food, mostly from France and United States.

Exports: US$98.6 million in 1986, of which cotton constituted 43 percent. Remainder meat, fish, and animal products. Most exports went to other parts of Africa and Western Europe.

Fiscal Year: Calendar year.

Currency: African Financial Community (Communauté Financière Africaine) franc (CFA F), used by fourteen nations and freely convertible to French francs (FF). In December 1988, CFA F298 equaled US$1.

Transportation and Communications

Railroads: None. Closest rail terminals Ngaoundéré (Cameroon) and Maiduguri (Nigeria).

Roads: About 7,300 kilometers of partially maintained roads, of which 1,260 kilometers considered all-weather roads; no paved roads in 1987. About 24,000 kilometers of unimproved tracks.

Inland Waterways: Chari and Logone rivers principal branches of approximately 2,000-kilometer-long navigable system.

Ports: None. Closest port at Douala, Cameroon.

Airports: International airport at N'Djamena; smaller airfields at Abéché, Moundou, and Sarh; small dirt strips scattered throughout country.

Telecommunications: One of least developed systems in Africa. All international telecommunications passed through Paris.

Government and Politics

Government: Governmental system based on Fundamental Law of October 18, 1982, which served as interim constitution. Fundamental Law promulgated after Armed Forces of the North (Forces Armées du Nord—FAN) wrested control from incumbent government; in late 1980s, former FAN leaders still held many important positions. Fundamental Law gives president overriding authority for controlling all aspects of government. New constitution being drafted in 1989. In 1988 presidentially appointed Council of Ministers served as cabinet. No elected legislative body, but thirty-member National Advisory Council provided forum for limited debate. Judicial system based on French civil law but modified to include variety of customary and Islamic legal interpretations. In late 1980s, civil and military courts sometimes had overlapping jurisdictions.

Politics: Chadian Civil War and factionalism have dominated political events since mid-1960s. After its victory in 1982, Command Council of the Armed Forces of the North (Conseil de Commandement des Forces Armées du Nord—CCFAN) was dissolved and in June 1984 replaced by sole political party, National Union for Independence and Revolution (Union Nationale pour l'Indépendance et la Révolution—UNIR). UNIR, led by president, had fourteen-member Executive Bureau and eighty-member Central Committee. Party used mainly to integrate former government opponents into new regime. No elections planned as of late 1988.

Foreign Affairs: Since independence, external affairs governed by France, Chad's colonizer, and Libya, aggressive neighbor to north. Relations with France have wavered, but in late 1980s France provided some of Chad's air defense and other security needs, and French financial interests helped sustain economy. Libya has claimed and occupied Aozou Strip (see Glossary), aided several antigovernment rebel factions, and intervened militarily. In late 1988, relations with Libya were restored, so that Chad had amicable relations with all its neighbors. United States supported government and provided military and humanitarian assistance.

International Organizations: Member of African Development Bank, West African Economic Community, Conference of East and Central African States, European Community, Group of 77, World Bank, International Cotton Advisory Committee, Islamic Development Bank, International Telecommunications Satellite Organization, Interpol, Lake Chad Basin Commission, Nonaligned Movement, Organization of African Unity, Afro-Malagasy and

Mauritian Common Organization, Organization of the Islamic Conference, United Nations.

National Security

Armed Forces: In 1987 consisted of army of 28,000, air force of fewer than 200, and Presidential Guard of 3,600. Conscription for periods of one year or longer imposed erratically.

Military Units: Main army units included 3 operational infantry battalions and 127 infantry companies, with roughly 400 soldiers in each battalion and 100 to 150 in each company. Armored fighting vehicles organized into separate squadrons. Air force had no combat aircraft. Small inventory of aircraft provided marginal transport, reconnaissance, and counterinsurgency capabilities. Country divided into twelve military zones, plus separate military region in north.

Foreign Military Assistance: France traditional supplier of arms, matériel, and training. Since 1983 French aid supplemented by matériel and equipment from United States. Vast quantities of Libyan weaponry, aircraft, and vehicles—mostly of Soviet manufacture—captured in battle during 1987, some of which incorporated into Chadian stocks.

Defense Expenditures: According to Chadian government figures, defense costs were CFA F8.4 billion in 1986, or about 35 percent of annual government budget. Actual spending believed to be much higher, and official figure did not include all French contributions toward military expenses.

Internal Security Forces: National Security Police, known as Sûreté, served as national police force and municipal police in major towns. Security in rural areas performed by Territorial Military Police. Regular military police functions and rear area and route security carried out by National Military Police. Presidential Guard also assumed many internal security responsibilities.

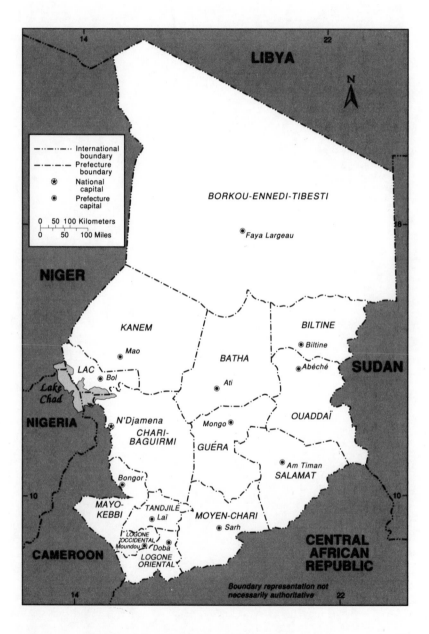

Figure 1. Administrative Divisions of Chad, 1988

Introduction

AN ARRAY OF MISFORTUNES has visited African states since the beginnings of the independence movement in the late 1950s. Of the many political ills, a few of the most traumatic have been neocolonialism, coups d'état, civil wars, governmental instability, and large-scale armed invasions. Some of the most egregious social afflictions have been poverty, illiteracy, ethnic and regional animosities, high mortality rates, and imbalanced population distribution. Dominant economic woes have included famine, drought, economic dependency, and overreliance on a single crop. Many African nations have experienced more than one of these troubles periodically. Few countries, however, have undergone all of them as extensively or as often as has Chad. In spite of its misfortunes, by the late 1980s Chad was exhibiting signs of stability that provided hope for some form of political, social, and economic recovery.

Landlocked in Africa's center, Chad has been simultaneously at the core of the region's evolution and in a zone dividing two geographic areas and cultural heritages. On the one hand, a great inland sea, of which Lake Chad is but a remnant, once supported a diversity of animal life and vegetation. In ancient times, people speaking three of Africa's four major language groups lived near its shores; some migrated to other regions of the continent while others remained. In more recent times, Chad has become a transition zone dividing the arid north from the tropical south. This geographic division coincides with social and cultural dichotomies.

As a result of years of voluntary or forced migrations, the people of Chad speak more than 100 distinct languages and comprise many different ethnic groups. Such diversity has enriched Chad's culture, permitting the admixture of traditions and life-styles. At the same time, it has promoted inter- and intraethnic strife, resulting in levels of violence ranging from clan feuds to full-scale civil war. Factionalism has become a keynote of Chad's recent history and has unquestionably impeded nation building.

Because of the area's centrality, Chad's history has been heavily influenced by the influx of foreigners. Some came for economic reasons, for example, to travel the trans-Saharan trade routes or to search for natural resources. Others came teaching the religion of Muhammad or of Christ. But some had more nefarious goals and invaded the region to capture slaves or to plunder weaker states.

Little is known about Chad before the beginning of the second millennium A.D. At about that time, the region gave birth to one of the great societies of Central Africa—the Kanem Empire, formed from a confederation of nomadic peoples. During the tenth century, Islam penetrated the empire, and later the king, or *mai*, became a Muslim. Kanem benefited from the rule of several effective *mais*. The most significant of these was Mai Dunama Dabbalemi, who reigned from about 1221 to 1259. By the end of the fourteenth century, internal struggles and external attacks had weakened the empire and forced it to uproot and move to Borno, an area to the southwest. The combined Kanem-Borno Empire peaked during the reign of Mai Idris Aluma, who ruled from about 1571 to 1603 and who is noted for his diplomatic, military, and administrative skills. By the early nineteenth century, unable to defend against Fulani invaders, Kanem-Borno was in decline, and by the end of the century it was overtaken by Arab invaders.

Another great empire was the kingdom of Bagirmi, which arose to the southeast of Kanem-Borno in the sixteenth century. This Islamic kingdom experienced periods of strength and weakness; when strong it aggressively expanded its territory, but when weak it was subjugated temporarily by neighboring states.

Wadai was a non-Muslim sultanate (or kingdom) that emerged to the northeast of Bagirmi in the sixteenth century as an offshoot of Darfur (Darfur Province in present-day Sudan). By the seventeenth century, it had converted to Islam, and around 1800 it began to expand under its sultan, Sabun. A later ruler, Muhammad Sharif, attacked Borno and eventually established Wadai's hegemony over Bagirmi. By the end of the nineteenth century, most of the great empires had been destroyed or were in eclipse.

The arrival of the French in the late 1800s had benefits and disadvantages for the indigenous population. By the early twentieth century, the French had stopped northern groups from slave raiding in the south, established a few schools, and initiated some development projects. The colonial administration, however, also dislocated villages and instituted mandatory cotton production quotas for farmers. Moreover, the French administration of Chad was conducted from faraway Brazzaville (in present-day Congo), and its efforts were concentrated in the south; throughout the colonial period, France's control of the central and northern areas was nominal.

This north-south distinction created a preindependence political system dominated by southerners, who were exposed more to French education and culture than were northerners. Following independence in 1960, this dominance persisted and created considerable resentment among central and northern groups, who felt that their interests were not adequately represented by the new government.

In the late 1980s, social differences based on region persisted. The sparsely populated, desert north was peopled mainly by Toubou, many of whom were nomadic. Semisedentary groups, several of which were of Arab descent, inhabited the semiarid central areas (called the Sahel—see Glossary). Islam was the major religion in these areas. The tropical south, also called the *soudanian* zone, was the most densely populated region and was home to darker skinned peoples, especially the Sara ethnic group. Here, agriculture was the principal means of livelihood, particularly the cultivation of cotton, although there was also some small-scale industry. Traditional African religions were prevalent in the south, but, because of earlier missionary efforts, so too were several Christian denominations. Termed *Le Tchad Utile* (Useful Chad) by the French, the south contained a disproportionate share of the educational and health facilities, as well as the majority of the development projects.

Throughout the colonial era and after independence, the Chadian economy has been based on agriculture. As such, it has been driven by the south, the only region with a climate suitable for the wide-scale production of cotton and foodstuffs (although livestock raising in the Sahel has also had some importance). At independence France left the colony with an economy retarded by exploitative policies. It was marked by insufficient development of infrastructure, overreliance on cotton and the whims of the international markets, and dependence on imports for industrial and consumer goods. By the late 1980s, warfare, drought, and famine had combined to keep the economy depressed, and international development organizations generally maintained that Chad was one of the poorest nations in the world. Indicative of this impoverishment was the fact that in 1988 Chad had a gross national product (GNP—see Glossary) per capita of only US$160 and no paved roads. According to some observers, Chad had become a ward of the international donor community.

The nation has been subjected to the machinations of a vast number of groups and organizations. Politically, Chadians have endured a series of authoritarian regimes, none of which has successfully limited factionalism. From 1960 until 1975, François Tombalbaye, a civilian, led the nation. His regime was characterized by southern domination of the administrative structure, although he made modest attempts at placating northern and central interests. As disaffection in these regions increased, in the late 1960s dissident groups formed an antigovernment coalition, the National Liberation Front of Chad (Front de Libération Nationale du Tchad—FROLINAT). Although never fully unified, this group or associated elements of it led the fight for greater northern and central representation in government.

By the early 1970s, Tombalbaye had alienated not only these groups but also even much of the south. Although he was wary of a French military presence after independence, the president readily embraced France's support in stemming violent discontent. Nonetheless, opposition grew, and in 1975 Tombalaye was killed in a military coup d'état. Another southerner, Félix Malloum, assumed power, but he had no more success than his predecessor in suppressing the burgeoning insurgencies and demands for greater regional participation. International intervention resulted in a peace accord between the government and the rebels and the formation of the Transitional Government of National Unity (Gouvernement d'Union Nationale de Transition—GUNT). For many observers, the establishment of GUNT was a watershed, marking the end of southern political domination. It did not, however, bring an end to strife.

The traditional north-and-central versus south split was transformed into an internecine argument among former opposition factions. GUNT's most important leaders were northerners Goukouni Oueddei and Hissein Habré, erstwhile allies in FROLINAT's Second Liberation Army. In command of separate factions, they battled one another for control of the capital, N'Djamena (see Civil Conflict and Libyan Intervention, ch. 5). With Libyan armed support, Goukouni evicted Habré's forces at the end of 1980. Under pressure from the Organization of African Unity (OAU) and other nations, in 1981 Goukouni asked the Libyan troops to leave; in their place, security was to be maintained by an OAU peacekeeping unit, the Inter-African Force (IAF). Seizing the initiative, Habré's regrouped and resupplied forces attacked from the northeast, and by 1982 his Armed Forces of the North (Forces Armées du Nord—FAN) had entered the capital, without any IAF interference, and sent Goukouni into exile.

Goukouni's defeat was only temporary. With massive Libyan military aid, by mid-1983 he was attacking from northern strongholds Habré's newly formed Chadian National Armed Forces (Forces Armées Nationales Tchadiennes—FANT). Concerned about Libyan leader Muammar al Qadhafi's intentions, France responded by dispatching a large force of troops and advisers. It also began a round-the-clock airlift of military supplies and established forward positions roughly along 16° north latitude. As a result of negotiations with Libya that required a mutual withdrawal of forces, French units were recalled in November 1984. Libya, however, failed to comply with these terms and reinforced its presence, especially in the Aozou Strip (see Glossary).

In 1986 the French redeployed to Chad. Habré's forces, which had also benefited since 1983 from weaponry provided by the United States, launched an offensive against the Libyan positions in late 1986 and early 1987 that resulted in the routing of Libyan troops and the capture of large amounts of Libyan military equipment.

By late 1988, a measure of calm had been restored to Chadian political life. Habré was attempting to consolidate his authority, but at the same time, he was mending some of the divisiveness that has hampered nation building (see Political Dynamics, ch. 4). He weathered a rebellion in the south in the late 1980s and brought many former opponents into high-ranking governmental positions. He sought to extend his regime through the National Union for Independence and Revolution (Union Nationale pour l'Indépendance et la Révolution—UNIR) and hoped to mobilize Chadians in rural areas.

These good intentions notwithstanding, the overwhelming majority of Chadians did not participate in the political process. The Fundamental Law of 1982, an interim constitution, vested paramount power in the president, who ruled almost without challenge. Although a committee was appointed to draft a permanent constitution, as of late 1988 there were no elected bodies, nor were any elections planned.

The evolution of Chad's armed forces mirrors the country's political transformation. Like the governmental structure of the 1960s, the army that was created after independence was dominated by southern groups. This fledgling force relied heavily on French matériel and—until Tombalbaye reconsidered this dependence—French military advisers. But neither the southern-dominated Chadian Armed Forces (Forces Armées Tchadiennes—FAT) nor the French units could deter the determined insurgents from the northern and central regions, most of whom fought under the FROLINAT banner. By 1978 FAT was in disarray, and it eventually splintered into minor factions.

Habré's FANT, formed in 1983, continued to provide national security in 1988, along with several French units. FANT was a conglomeration of FAN and smaller rebel armies that rallied to Habré's side in the 1980s (see The Armed Forces, ch. 5). Many former opposition leaders held positions of authority in the FANT organizational structure. In addition to 3 operational battalions and 127 infantry companies, FANT had a small air force.

Chad's internal security requirements were provided by the well-trained Presidential Guard and by several national and territorial police forces (see Internal Security and Public Order, ch. 5). Following the defection of many of Goukouni's followers to FANT in the late 1980s, the group that presented the most serious threat to Chad's security was the Democratic Revolutionary Council (Conseil Démocratique Révolutionnaire—CDR), which, under Libyan patronage, was active in the north. But Qadhafi's stated desire to normalize relations with Chad, enunciated in April 1988, inspired hopes that a period of genuine peace—a circumstance that the nation had not enjoyed during the previous two decades—might finally ensue.

December 13, 1988

* * *

After the research for this book was completed, several events occurred that greatly affected Chadian affairs. In November 1988, Habré convinced Acheikh ibn Oumar, the leader of the CDR, to join the government. In accordance with his policy of reconciliation with opponents, in March 1989 Habré appointed Oumar as minister of foreign affairs. Three high-ranking officials, reportedly members of the Zaghawa ethnic group who resented the large number of former regime opponents named to influential positions, unsuccessfully collaborated to assassinate Habré on the night of April 1, 1989. The three plotters were Minister of Interior Ibrahim Mahamat Itno, FANT commander in chief Hassane Djamouss, and Idris Deby, a high-ranking FANT officer; at one time, all of them had been very close advisers to the president.

According to one report, another grievance of the plotters was that Habré had been persecuting the Zaghawa while promoting the interests of the Daza, his own ethnic group. Indeed, a November 1988 report issued by the human rights organization Amnesty International criticized the government for arbitrary arrests and unreasonable detentions, lending credence to the plotters' claims.

In mid-June 1989, the fate of those involved in the coup attempt was unclear. Most accounts claimed that Itno had been arrested and that Djamouss and Deby had escaped capture; their whereabouts, however, were unknown, although some sources reported them to be in Sudan organizing an opposition army. Regardless of their circumstances, it was apparent in mid-1989 that Habré's policy of national reconciliation was not being carried out to the satisfaction of all of the factions in Chad, and the stability of the government remained uncertain.

June 16, 1989   Thomas Collelo

Chapter 1. Historical Setting

A bronze bracelet, believed to be from the Sao period

THE CONTEMPORARY ATTITUDES, institutions, and problems of Chad are the outgrowth of historical traditions and tendencies that have evolved over more than 1,000 years. The country is populated by diverse, yet in many cases, interrelated peoples whose evolution was characterized by intersecting migrations, splinterings, and regroupings. Most of the country's population groups originated in areas generally north and east of Chad's present-day boundaries.

Chad's geographic position along major trans-Saharan trade routes has also affected its historical development. In early times, trade consisted of goods and slaves seized in raids on groups in the south. Consolidations of small chiefdoms led to the evolution of a series of kingdoms and empires in the central region, of which the most important were Kanem-Borno, Bagirmi, and Wadai. The kingdoms and empires based their power on, and were ultimately subjected to, raids or the payment of tribute. Although there were early communities in both northern and southern Chad, most of the country's known history is focused on the Muslim peoples of the central region.

The political fortunes of the various kingdoms and empires were constantly affected by internal factionalism and external invasion— factors that still influenced political affairs in the 1970s and 1980s. Political disintegration was evident in both Borno and Bagirmi when the French arrived in the late nineteenth century. The rulers of Wadai resisted the French advance. The leaders of Borno and Bagirmi, however, regarded the French less as conquerors than as a counterbalance to the ascendant Wadai.

The French declared the central portion of the country officially pacified in 1924 and had begun administering much of the non-Muslim south before that. In many respects, the nomadic northern groups have never been subjugated, and turmoil in the north persisted in the 1980s.

After 1905 the central and northern areas were administered as a territory in the federation of French Equatorial Africa (Afrique Equatoriale Française—AEF; see Glossary). French interest, however, focused on other territories in the federation, and until after World War II, the French presence had little impact on the life of the average inhabitant. The French limited implementation of their administrative policy primarily to urban areas and their compulsory agricultural programs to what constitutes the south of present-day Chad. Participation by the local population in the colonial administration was marginal, and until the mid-1950s the educational opportunities prerequisite for such participation were practically nonexistent.

After World War II, representative institutions were introduced, and the growth of party politics began. Political groupings reflected domestic political developments in France and traditional ethnic factionalism in Chad. Short-lived political coalitions and party splinterings were commonplace. When Chad achieved independence in 1960, southerners—the group most exposed to the French administrators—dominated political life. These southerners were led by President François Tombalbaye, who made only halfhearted efforts at regional integration in government and who generally repressed opposition. Within five years of having taken office, Tombalbaye's heavy-handed approach had alienated a large segment of the population, especially northerners and easterners, and had spurred rebellions. The most prominent of the northern rebel groups was the National Liberation Front of Chad (Front de Libération Nationale du Tchad—FROLINAT), an umbrella organization formed in 1966. Over the years, FROLINAT went through a series of transformations and fragmentations. Nonetheless, by the mid-1970s rebel activity, in conjunction with Tombalbaye's political ineptitude, helped bring about the government's downfall. Tombalbaye was killed in 1975 during a military coup d'état led by Félix Malloum.

The new government, however, had no more success than its predecessor in halting rebel activity. In 1979 Hissein Habré, a northern rebel leader, ousted Malloum. Throughout the 1980s, the quest for political control changed from a north-south struggle to a primarily northern intraregional conflict. The turmoil of the late 1970s and 1980s had international and domestic aspects, as Libya, France, the United States, and many African nations became involved in the Chadian imbroglio. By early 1988, stability had been restored, but inter- and intraethnic differences, as well as regional divisions, continued to threaten Chad's progress toward national integration.

Prehistory

The territory now known as Chad possesses some of the richest archaeological sites in Africa. During the seventh millennium B.C., the northern half of Chad was part of a broad expanse of land, stretching from the Indus River in the east to the Atlantic Ocean in the west, in which ecological conditions favored early human settlement. Rock art of the ''Round Head'' style, found in the

Ennedi region, has been dated to before the seventh millennium B.C. and, because of the tools with which the rocks were carved and the scenes they depict, may represent the oldest evidence in the Sahara of Neolithic industries. Many of the pottery-making and Neolithic activities in Ennedi date back further than any of those of the Nile Valley to the east.

In the prehistoric period, Chad was much wetter than it is today, as evidenced by large game animals depicted in rock paintings in the Tibesti and Borkou regions. Recent linguistic research suggests that all of Africa's languages south of the Sahara Desert (except Khoisan) originated in prehistoric times in a narrow band between Lake Chad and the Nile Valley (see Languages and Ethnic Groups, ch. 2). The origins of Chad's peoples, however, remain unclear. Several of the proven archaeological sites have been only partially studied, and other sites of great potential have yet to be mapped.

Era of Empires, A.D. 900–1900

Toward the end of the first millennium A.D., the formation of states began across central Chad in the *sahelian* zone between the desert and the savanna. For almost the next 1,000 years, these states, their relations with each other, and their effects on the peoples who lived in "stateless" societies along their peripheries dominated Chad's political history. Recent research suggests that indigenous Africans founded most of these states, not migrating Arabic-speaking groups, as was believed previously. Nonetheless, immigrants, Arabic-speaking or otherwise, played a significant role, along with Islam, in the formation and early evolution of these states (see Islam, ch. 2).

Most states began as kingdoms, in which the king was considered divine and endowed with temporal and spiritual powers. All states were militaristic (or they did not survive long), but none was able to expand far into southern Chad, where forests and the tsetse fly complicated the use of cavalry. Control over the trans-Saharan trade routes that passed through the region formed the economic basis of these kingdoms. Although many states rose and fell, the most important and durable of the empires were Kanem-Borno, Bagirmi, and Wadai, according to most written sources (mainly court chronicles and writings of Arab traders and travelers).

Kanem-Borno

The Kanem Empire originated in the ninth century A.D. to the northeast of Lake Chad (see fig. 2). It was formed from a confederation of nomadic peoples who spoke languages of the Teda-Daza (Toubou) group (see Languages and Ethnic Groups, ch. 2). One

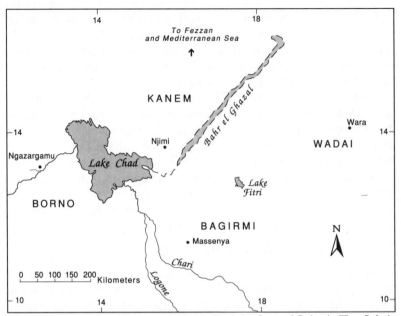

Source: Based on information from Anders J. Bjørkelo, *State and Society in Three Sudanic Kingdoms,* Bergen, Norway, 1976, 5.

Figure 2. Empires of the Chad Region

theory, based on early Arabic sources, suggests that the dominance of the Zaghawa people bound the confederation together. But local oral traditions omit the Zaghawa and refer instead to a legendary Arab, Sayf ibn Dhi Yazan—believed by some to have been a Yemeni—who assumed leadership of the Magoumi clan and began the Sayfawa dynastic lineage. Historians agree that the leaders of the new state were ancestors of the Kanembu people. The leaders adopted the title *mai,* or king, and their subjects regarded them as divine.

One factor that influenced the formation of states in Chad was the penetration of Islam during the tenth century. Arabs migrating from the north and east brought the new religion. Toward the end of the eleventh century, the Sayfawa king, Mai Humai, converted to Islam. (Some historians believe that it was Humai rather than Sayf ibn Dhi Yazan who established the Sayfawa lineage as the ruling dynasty of Kanem.) Islam offered the Sayfawa rulers the advantages of new ideas from Arabia and the Mediterranean world, as well as literacy in administration. But many people resisted the new religion in favor of traditional beliefs and practices. When

Humai converted, for example, it is believed that the Zaghawa broke from the empire and moved east. This pattern of conflict and compromise with Islam occurs repeatedly in Chadian history.

Prior to the twelfth century, the nomadic Sayfawa confederation expanded southward into Kanem (the word for "south" in the Teda language). By the thirteenth century, Kanem's rule expanded. At the same time, the Kanembu people became more sedentary and established a capital at Njimi, northeast of Lake Chad. Even though the Kanembu were becoming more sedentary, Kanem's rulers continued to travel frequently throughout the kingdom to remind the herders and farmers of the government's power and to allow them to demonstrate their allegiance by paying tribute.

Kanem's expansion peaked during the long and energetic reign of Mai Dunama Dabbalemi (ca. 1221–59). Dabbalemi initiated diplomatic exchanges with sultans in North Africa and apparently arranged for the establishment of a special hostel in Cairo to facilitate pilgrimages to Mecca. During Dabbalemi's reign, the Fezzan region (in present-day Libya) fell under Kanem's authority, and the empire's influence extended westward to Kano, eastward to Wadai, and southward to the Adamawa grasslands (in present-day Cameroon). Portraying these boundaries on maps can be misleading, however, because the degree of control extended in ever-weakening gradations from the core of the empire around Njimi to remote peripheries, from which allegiance and tribute were usually only symbolic. Moreover, cartographic lines are static and misrepresent the mobility inherent in nomadism and migration, which were common. The loyalty of peoples and their leaders was more important in governance than the physical control of territory.

Dabbalemi devised a system to reward military commanders with authority over the people they conquered. This system, however, tempted military officers to pass their positions to their sons, thus transforming the office from one based on achievement and loyalty to the *mai* into one based on hereditary nobility. Dabbalemi was able to suppress this tendency, but after his death, dissension among his sons weakened the Sayfawa Dynasty. Dynastic feuds degenerated into civil war, and Kanem's outlying peoples soon ceased paying tribute.

By the end of the fourteenth century, internal struggles and external attacks had torn Kanem apart. Between 1376 and 1400, six *mais* reigned, but Bulala invaders (from the area around Lake Fitri to the east) killed five of them. This proliferation of *mais* resulted in numerous claimants to the throne and led to a series of internecine wars. Finally, around 1396 the Bulala forced Mai Umar Idrismi to abandon Njimi and move the Kanembu people to Borno on the western edge of Lake Chad. Over time, the intermarriage of the Kanembu and Borno peoples created a new people and language, the Kanuri.

But even in Borno, the Sayfawa Dynasty's troubles persisted. During the first three-quarters of the fifteenth century, for example, fifteen *mais* occupied the throne. Then, around 1472 Mai Ali Dunamami defeated his rivals and began the consolidation of Borno. He built a fortified capital at Ngazargamu, to the west of Lake Chad (in present-day Niger), the first permanent home a Sayfawa *mai* had enjoyed in a century. So successful was the Sayfawa rejuvenation that by the early sixteenth century the Bulala were defeated and Njimi retaken. The empire's leaders, however, remained at Ngazargamu because its lands were more productive agriculturally and better suited to the raising of cattle.

Kanem-Borno peaked during the reign of the outstanding statesman Mai Idris Aluma (ca. 1571–1603). Aluma (also spelled Alooma) is remembered for his military skills, administrative reforms, and Islamic piety. His main adversaries were the Hausa to the west, the Tuareg and Toubou to the north, and the Bulala to the east. One epic poem extols his victories in 330 wars and more than 1,000 battles. His innovations included the employment of fixed military camps (with walls); permanent sieges and "scorched earth" tactics, where soldiers burned everything in their path; armored horses and riders; and the use of Berber camelry, Kotoko boatmen, and iron-helmeted musketeers trained by Turkish military advisers. His active diplomacy featured relations with Tripoli, Egypt, and the Ottoman Empire, which sent a 200-member ambassadorial party across the desert to Aluma's court at Ngazargamu. Aluma also signed what was probably the first written treaty or cease-fire in Chadian history. (Like many cease-fires negotiated in the 1970s and 1980s, it was promptly broken.)

Aluma introduced a number of legal and administrative reforms based on his religious beliefs and Islamic law (sharia). He sponsored the construction of numerous mosques and made a pilgrimage to Mecca, where he arranged for the establishment of a hostel to be used by pilgrims from his empire. As with other dynamic politicians, Aluma's reformist goals led him to seek loyal and competent advisers and allies, and he frequently relied on slaves who had been educated in noble homes. Aluma regularly sought advice from a council composed of heads of the most important clans. He required major political figures to live at the court, and he reinforced political alliances through appropriate marriages (Aluma himself was the son of a Kanuri father and a Bulala mother).

Kanem-Borno under Aluma was strong and wealthy. Government revenue came from tribute (or booty, if the recalcitrant people had to be conquered), sales of slaves, and duties on and participation in trans-Saharan trade. Unlike West Africa, the Chadian region did not have gold. Still, it was central to one of the most convenient trans-Saharan routes. Between Lake Chad and Fezzan lay a sequence of well-spaced wells and oases, and from Fezzan there were easy connections to North Africa and the Mediterranean Sea. Many products were sent north, including natron (sodium carbonate), cotton, kola nuts, ivory, ostrich feathers, perfume, wax, and hides, but the most important of all were slaves. Imports included salt, horses, silks, glass, muskets, and copper.

Aluma took a keen interest in trade and other economic matters. He is credited with having the roads cleared, designing better boats for Lake Chad, introducing standard units of measure for grain, and moving farmers into new lands. In addition, he improved the ease and security of transit through the empire with the goal of making it so safe that "a lone woman clad in gold might walk with none to fear but God."

The administrative reforms and military brilliance of Aluma sustained the empire until the mid-1600s, when its power began to fade. By the late 1700s, Borno rule extended only westward, into the land of the Hausa. Around that time, Fulani people, invading from the west, were able to make major inroads into Borno. By the early nineteenth century, Kanem-Borno was clearly an empire in decline, and in 1808 Fulani warriors conquered Ngazargamu. Usman dan Fodio led the Fulani thrust and proclaimed a jihad (holy war) on the irreligious Muslims of the area. His campaign eventually affected Kanem-Borno and inspired a trend toward Islamic orthodoxy. But Muhammad al Kanem contested the Fulani advance. Kanem was a Muslim scholar and non-Sayfawa warlord who had put together an alliance of Shuwa Arabs, Kanembu, and other seminomadic peoples. He eventually built a capital at Kukawa (in present-day Nigeria). Sayfawa *mais* remained titular monarchs until 1846. In that year, the last *mai*, in league with Wadai tribesmen, precipitated a civil war. It was at that point that Kanem's son, Umar, became king, thus ending one of the longest dynastic reigns in regional history.

Although the dynasty ended, the kingdom of Kanem-Borno survived. But Umar, who eschewed the title *mai* for the simpler designation *shehu* (from the Arabic "shaykh"), could not match his father's vitality and gradually allowed the kingdom to be ruled by advisers (*wazirs*). Borno began to decline, as a result of administrative disorganization, regional particularism, and attacks by the militant Wadai Empire to the east. The decline continued under Umar's sons, and in 1893 Rabih Fadlallah, leading an invading army from eastern Sudan, conquered Borno.

Bagirmi and Wadai

In addition to Kanem-Borno, two other states in the region, Bagirmi and Wadai, achieved historical prominence. The kingdom of Bagirmi emerged to the southeast of Kanem-Borno in the sixteenth century. Under the reign of Abdullah IV (1568–98), Islam was adopted, and the state became a sultanate, using Islamic judicial and administrative procedures. Later, a palace and court were constructed in the capital city of Massenya.

Bagirmi's political history was a function of its strength and unity in relation to its larger neighbors. Absorbed into Kanem-Borno during the reign of Aluma, Bagirmi broke free later in the 1600s, only to be returned to tributary status in the mid-1700s. During periods of strength, the sultanate became imperialistic. It established control over small feudal kingdoms on its peripheries and entered into alliances with nearby nomadic peoples. Early in the nineteenth century, Bagirmi fell into decay and was threatened militarily by the nearby kingdom of Wadai. Although Bagirmi resisted, it accepted tributary status in order to obtain help from Wadai in putting down internal dissension. When Rabih Fadlallah's forces burned Massenya in 1893, the twenty-fifth sultan, Abd ar Rahman Gwaranga, sought and received protectorate status from the French.

Located northeast of Bagirmi, Wadai was a non-Muslim kingdom that emerged in the sixteenth century as an offshoot of the state of Darfur (in present-day Sudan). Early in the seventeenth century, the Maba and other small groups in the region rallied to the Islamic banner of Abd al Karim, who led an invasion from the east and overthrew the ruling Tunjur group. Abd al Karim established a dynasty and sultanate that lasted until the arrival of the French. During much of the eighteenth century, Wadai resisted reincorporation into Darfur.

In about 1800, during the reign of Sabun, the sultanate of Wadai began to expand its power. A new trade route north—via Ennedi, Al Kufrah, and Benghazi—was discovered, and Sabun outfitted royal caravans to take advantage of it. He began minting his own coinage and imported chain mail, firearms, and military advisers from North Africa. Sabun's successors were less able than he, and Darfur took advantage of a disputed political succession in 1838 to put its own candidate in power in Wara, the capital of Wadai. This tactic backfired, however, when Darfur's choice, Muhammad

Sharif, rejected Darfur's meddling and asserted his own authority. In doing so, he gained acceptance from Wadai's various factions and went on to become Wadai's ablest ruler.

Sharif conducted military campaigns as far west as Borno and eventually established Wadai's hegemony over Bagirmi and kingdoms as far away as the Chari River. In Mecca, Sharif had met the founder of the Sanusiyya Islamic brotherhood, a movement that was strong among the inhabitants of Cyrenaica (in present-day Libya) and that was to become a dominant political force and source of resistance to French colonization (see Islam, ch. 2). Indeed, the militaristic Wadai opposed French domination until well into the twentieth century.

Arrival of the French and Colonial Administration

European interest in Africa generally grew during the nineteenth century. By 1887 France, motivated by the search for wealth, had driven inland from its settlements on central Africa's west coast to claim the territory of Ubangi-Chari (present-day Central African Republic). It claimed this area as a zone of French influence, and within two years it occupied part of what is now southern Chad. In the early 1890s, French military expeditions sent to Chad encountered the forces of Rabih Fadlallah, who had been conducting slave raids (*razzias*) in southern Chad throughout the 1890s and had sacked the settlements of Kanem-Borno, Bagirmi, and Wadai. After years of indecisive engagements, French forces finally defeated Rabih Fadlallah at the Battle of Kousséri in 1900.

Two fundamental themes dominated Chad's colonial experience with the French: an absence of policies designed to unify the territory and an exceptionally slow pace of modernization. In the French scale of priorities, the colony of Chad ranked near the bottom; it was less important than non-African territories, North Africa, West Africa, or even the other French possessions in Central Africa. The French came to perceive Chad primarily as a source of raw cotton and untrained labor to be used in the more productive colonies to the south. Within Chad there was neither the will nor the resources to do much more than maintain a semblance of law and order. In fact, even this basic function of governance was often neglected; throughout the colonial period, large areas of Chad were never governed effectively from N'Djamena (called Fort-Lamy prior to September 1973).

Chad was linked in 1905 with three French colonies to the south—Ubangi-Chari, Moyen-Congo (present-day Congo), and Gabon. But Chad did not receive separate colony status or a unified administrative policy until 1920. The four colonies were administered

11

together as French Equatorial Africa under the direction of a governor general stationed in Brazzaville. The governor general had broad administrative control over the federation, including external and internal security, economic and financial affairs, and all communications with the French minister of the colonies. Lieutenant governors, also appointed by the French government, were expected to implement in each colony the orders of the governor general. The central administration in Brazzaville tightly controlled the lieutenant governors despite reformist efforts toward decentralization between 1910 and 1946. Chad's lieutenant governor had greater autonomy because of the distance from Brazzaville and because of France's much greater interest in the other three colonies.

The lines of control from Brazzaville, feeble as they may have been, were still stronger than those from N'Djamena to its hinterland. In the huge Borkou-Ennedi-Tibesti Prefecture, the handful of French military administrators soon reached a tacit agreement with the inhabitants of the desert; as long as caravan trails remained relatively secure and minimal levels of law and order were met, the military administration (headquartered in Faya Largeau) usually left the people alone (see fig. 1). In central Chad, French rule was only slightly more substantive. In Ouaddaï and Biltine prefectures, endemic resistance continued against the French and, in some cases, against any authority that attempted to suppress banditry and brigandage. The thinly staffed colonial administration provided only weak supervision over arid Kanem Prefecture and the sparsely populated areas of Guéra and Salamat prefectures. Old-fashioned *razzias* continued in the 1920s, and it was reported in 1923 that a group of Senegalese Muslims on their way to Mecca had been seized and sold into slavery. Unwilling to expend the resources required for effective administration, the French government responded with sporadic coercion and a growing reliance on indirect rule through the sultanates.

France managed to govern effectively only the south, but until 1946 administrative direction came from Bangui in Ubangi-Chari rather than N'Djamena. Unlike northern and central Chad, a French colonial system of direct civilian administration was set up among the Sara, a southern ethnic group, and their neighbors. Also, unlike the rest of Chad, a modest level of economic development occurred in the south because of the introduction in 1929 of large-scale cotton production (see Cotton, ch. 3). Remittances and pensions to southerners who served in the French military also enhanced economic well-being.

But even the advantages of more income, schools, and roads failed to win popular support for the French in the south. In addition

A view of Faya Largeau, a former French outpost
Courtesy Michael R. Saks

to earlier grievances, such as forced porterage (which claimed thousands of lives) and village relocation, southern farmers resented the mandatory quotas for the production of cotton, which France purchased at artificially low prices. Government-protected chiefs further abused this situation. The chiefs were resented all the more because they were generally the artificial creations of the French in a region of previously stateless societies. This commonality of treatment and the colonial organizational framework began to create during this period a sense of Sara ethnicity among persons whose collective identities had previously been limited to small kinship groups.

Although France had put forth considerable effort during the conquest of Chad, the ensuing administration of the territory was halfhearted. Officials in the French colonial service resisted assignments to Chad, so posts often went to novices or to out-of-favor officials. One historian of France's empire has concluded that it was almost impossible to be too demented or depraved to be considered unfit for duty in Chad. Still, major scandals occurred periodically, and many of the posts remained vacant. In 1928, for example, 42 percent of the Chadian subdivisions lacked official administrators.

An event occurred in 1935 that was to have far-reaching consequences throughout the 1970s and 1980s. In that year, the French colonial administration negotiated a border adjustment with Italy, Libya's colonial master. The adjustment would have relocated the Libyan-Chad boundary about 100 kilometers south across the Aozou Strip (see Glossary). Although the French legislature never ratified the agreement, the negotiations formed part of the basis of Libya's claim to the area decades later.

Decolonization Politics

In 1940 Chad became internationally prominent when its lieutenant governor, Félix Eboué, led the rest of the AEF federation to support the Free French under Charles de Gaulle rather than the government of Vichy France. Chad became the base for Colonel Jacques Leclerc's conquest of the Fezzan (1940-43), and the entire episode became the basis of an enduring sentimental bond between the France of de Gaulle's generation and Chad. More funds and attention flowed to Chad than ever before, and Eboué became the governor general of the entire AEF in November 1941.

Born in French Guiana of mixed African and European parentage, Eboué was keenly interested in the problems of cultural dislocation resulting from unchecked modernization in Africa. He worked to return authority to authentic traditional leaders while training them in modern administrative techniques. He recognized a place for African middle-class professionals in cities, but he opposed the migration of workers to cities, supporting instead the creation of integrated rural industries where workers could remain with their families. When Eboué died in 1944, the AEF lost a major source of progressive ideas, and Chad lost a leader with considerable influence in France.

French voters rejected many of the progressive ideas of Eboué and others after the war ended. Nevertheless, the constitution that was approved in 1946 granted Chad and other African colonies the right to elect a territorial assembly with limited powers. The Assembly in turn elected delegates to the French General Council of all the AEF (see Preindependence Factions, ch. 4). The position of governor general was redesignated high commissioner, and each territory gained the right to elect representatives to French parliamentary bodies, including the National Assembly, the Council of the Republic, and the Assembly of the French Union. The African peoples became French citizens, and the colonies were designated overseas territories of France. But the real locus of authority remained in Paris, and French personnel continued to dominate the AEF's administration. No formal attempt was made to train Chadian Africans for civil service positions before 1955.

Until the early 1950s, political forces originating in France dominated the development of politics in Chad. Local elections were won largely by members of the Chadian Democratic Union (Union Démocratique Tchadienne—UDT), which was associated with a political party in France, the Assembly of French People. The UDT represented French commercial interests and a bloc of traditional leaders composed primarily of Muslim and Ouaddaïan nobility. Chad's European community initiated the practice of using the civil service for partisan political ends; African civil servants who were identified with organizations opposed to the UDT soon found themselves dismissed or transferred to distant posts. For example, François Tombalbaye (later to become president) lost his job as a teacher and ended up making bricks by hand because of his union activities and his role in the opposition Chadian Progressive Party (Parti Progressiste Tchadien—PPT).

Nonetheless, by 1953 politics were becoming less European dominated, and the PPT was emerging as the major rival of the UDT. The leader of the PPT was Gabriel Lisette, a black colonial administrator born in Panama and posted to Chad in 1946. Elected as a deputy to the French National Assembly, Lisette was later chosen as secretary general of the African Democratic Assembly (Rassemblement Démocratique Africain—RDA), an interterritorial, Marxist-oriented party considered quite radical at the time. The PPT originated as a territorial branch of the RDA and rapidly became the political vehicle of the country's non-Muslim intellectuals. Traditional rulers perceived the PPT to be antithetical to their interests and recognized that the local territorial assembly could adversely affect their revenue and power. These factors persuaded traditional rulers to become more active in the UDT, which, because of internal divisions, had changed its name in the late 1950s to the Chadian Social Action (Action Sociale Tchadienne—AST).

Although party names changed frequently and dramatic factional schisms occurred throughout the 1950s, electoral competition was essentially between three political blocs: the UDT [AST], the PPT, and the allies of Ahmed Koulamallah from Chari-Baguirmi and Kanem prefectures. A clever politician and charismatic leader of the Tijaniyya Islamic brotherhood in Chad, Koulamallah campaigned in different times and places as a member of the Bagirmi nobility (he was an estranged son of the sultan), a radical socialist leader, or a militant Muslim fundamentalist. As a result, politics in the 1950s was a struggle between the south, which mostly supported the PPT, and the Muslim *sahelian* belt, which favored the UDT [AST]. Koulamallah played a generally disruptive role in the middle.

15

In 1956 the French National Assembly passed the *loi cadre* (enabling act), which resulted in greater self-rule for Chad and other African territories. Electoral reforms expanded the pool of eligible voters, and power began to shift from the sparsely settled northern and central Chadian regions toward the more densely populated south. The PPT had become less militant, winning the support of chiefs in the south and members of the French colonial administration, but not that of private French commercial interests. The PPT and allied parties won forty-seven of the sixty-five seats in the 1957 elections, and Lisette formed the first African government in Chad. He maintained a majority for only about a year, however, before factions representing traditional chiefs withdrew their support from his coalition government.

In September 1958, voters in all of Africa's French territories took part in a referendum on the Fifth Republic's constitution, drawn up under de Gaulle. For a variety of political and economic reasons, most of Chad's political groups supported the new constitution, and all voted for a resolution calling for Chad to become an autonomous republic within the French community. The three other AEF territories voted similarly, and in November 1958 the AEF was officially terminated. Coordination on such issues as customs and currency continued among the four territories through written agreements or on an ad hoc basis. Nonetheless, some Chadians supported the creation of an even stronger French federation, rather than independence. The leading proponent of this proposal was Barthélemy Boganda of Ubangi-Chari, but his death in 1959 and the vigorous opposition of Gabon resulted in political independence on a separate basis for all four republics.

After Lisette's coalition crumbled in early 1959, two other alliances governed briefly. Then in March the PPT returned to power, this time under the leadership of Tombalbaye, a union leader and representative from Moyen-Chari Prefecture. Lisette, whose power was undermined because of his non-African origins, became deputy prime minister in charge of economic coordination and foreign affairs. Tombalbaye soon consolidated enough political support from the south and north to isolate the opposition into a collection of conservative Muslim leaders from central Chad. The latter group formed a political party in January 1960, but its parliamentary representation steadily dropped as Tombalbaye wooed individual members to the PPT. By independence in August 1960, the PPT and the south had clearly achieved dominance, but Tombalbaye's political skills made it possible for observers to talk optimistically about the possibility of building a broad-based coalition of political forces.

A monument to Colonel Jacques Leclerc, a French war hero, and
Emil Gentil, founder of Fort-Lamy
Courtesy Michael R. Saks

Tombalbaye Era, 1960–75

Tombalbaye faced a task of considerable magnitude when Chad became a sovereign state. His challenge was to build a nation out of a vast and diverse territory that had poor communications, few known resources, a tiny market, and a collection of impoverished people with sharply differing political traditions, ethnic and regional loyalties, and sociocultural patterns. The colonial powers that had created the country's boundaries had done little to promote economic interdependence, political cooperation, or cross-cultural understanding. Chadians who had hoped that the country's first president might turn out to be a state builder like the thirteenth century's Dabbalemi or the sixteenth century's Aluma were soon disappointed. During its first fifteen years, Chad under Tombalbaye experienced worsening economic conditions, eventual alienation of the most patient of foreign allies, exacerbation of ethnic and regional conflict, and grave weakening of the state as an instrument of governance.

Tombalbaye's Governance: Policies and Methods

At the outset, Tombalbaye demonstrated an autocratic style along with a distrust of the institutions of democracy. One week before

17

the country gained independence, Tombalbaye purged Lisette from his own party, declared Lisette a noncitizen while he was traveling abroad, and barred him from returning to Chad. This "coup by telegram" was the first in an extensive series of Tombalbaye's increasingly authoritarian actions to eliminate or neutralize opponents.

To increase his power and freedom of action, Tombalbaye declared a ban on all political parties except the PPT in January 1962, and in April he established a presidential form of government. When serious rioting occurred in 1963 in N'Djamena and Am Timan, the government declared a state of emergency and dissolved the National Assembly. And, as part of a major campaign against real and imagined political opponents, Tombalbaye created a special criminal court. By the end of the year, the country's prisons contained a virtual "who's who" of Chadian politicians. In June 1964, a new National Assembly granted Tombalbaye complete control over all appointments to the Political Bureau of the PPT, which by then was the sole source of political authority. With the PPT, government, and upper echelons of the civil service stocked with loyalists, and with opposition leaders in prison, exile, or completely co-opted, Tombalbaye was in full command of the country.

An effort to Africanize the civil service and security forces as rapidly as possible complemented Tombalbaye's drive for personal power. Between 1960 and 1963, the number of French officials in the central government administration declined from ninety-five to thirty (although the total number of French personnel increased as technical advisers were hired for development programs), and by the end of 1962 the entire territorial administrative structure was in Chadian hands. In addition, units of Chad's national army replaced French military forces in Borkou-Ennedi-Tibesti Prefecture and in Abéché, a process formally completed on January 23, 1965.

Africanization was not entirely popular among Chad's farmers and herders, despite their deep resentment of French colonial rule. A decline in the quality of government service was immediately apparent, in part because of the usual difficulties of transition, but also because many of the newly hired and promoted Chadians were less experienced and less adequately trained than their departing French counterparts. Increasing the discontent, Tombalbaye imposed an additional tax in 1964, under the euphemism of a "national loan." On top of that action, some government administrators were allegedly forcing citizens in rural areas to make payments at three times the official taxation rates. Reports of corruption and other abuses of authority grew as Chad's new officials became aware of both the increased pressures and the decreased constraints on public servants.

Because the great majority of the country's Western-educated and French-speaking citizens were southerners, the policy of Africanization often represented a "southernization" of the Chadian government. What appeared to some Western observers to be progress in African self-government was perceived by those from the northern and central areas to be an increasingly blatant seizure of power by southerners. To many in northern and central Chad, the southern Chadians were simply another set of foreigners, almost as alien and arrogant as the departing French. Tombalbaye's failure to establish hiring and training policies geared to achieving greater ethnic and regional balance in public administration was one of his most serious shortcomings. Another was his lack of success—or lack of interest—in reaching power-sharing agreements with key leaders in the Saharan and *sahelian* regions.

Dissatisfaction with these failures was expressed violently, and the government response was just as violent. When Muslims rioted in N'Djamena in September 1963 following the arbitrary arrests of three Muslim leaders, the government reacted swiftly and repressively. A little more than a year later, an altercation at a public dance in the northern town of Bardaï prompted a Sara deputy prefect to order the inhabitants of an entire village to march to prison, where many were stripped and all were insulted. Many were arbitrarily fined for such offenses as wearing beards or turbans. Included among the targets of abuse was Oueddei Kichidemi, the *derde,* or spiritual head, of the Teda people, a Toubou group. Explosive confrontations such as this occurred repeatedly as the inexperienced southerners, who understood little and cared less for the customs of the peoples they governed, replaced experienced French administrators.

By this time, just five years after independence, the possibility of armed conflict was growing. Politicians throughout Chad increasingly used traditional loyalties and enmities to decry opposition and solidify popular support for their positions. In view of Chad's historical legacy of conflict, some historians have argued that even the most competent leader with the most enlightened set of policies would have eventually faced secessionist movements or armed opposition. Tombalbaye, however, hastened the onset of civil conflict by quickly squandering his legitimacy through repressive tactics and regional favoritism.

Rebellion in Eastern and Northern Chad

On November 1, 1965, frustration with what was perceived as government mismanagement and tax collection abuses erupted in riots in the town of Mangalmé in Guéra Prefecture. Five hundred persons died, including the local deputy to the National Assembly and nine other government officials. From Mangalmé and nearby Batha Prefecture, the rebellion spread to Ouaddaï and Salamat prefectures, where in February 1967 the prefect and deputy prefect were killed. In August 1968, a major mutiny in Aozou among the Toubou-dominated National and Nomad Guard highlighted the continuing unrest in the north (see Origins and Early Development, ch. 5). In the same year, antigovernment activities and tracts began to appear in Chari-Baguirmi Prefecture, only about 100 kilometers from N'Djamena. Travel became unsafe in much of central Chad, and governmental authority in the north was reduced by 1969 to the garrison towns of Faya Largeau, Fada, Bardaï, and Ounianga Kébir.

In addition to historical causes and what Tombalbaye himself was later to call "maladministration," the country's Arabic-speaking neighbors abetted rebellion in the northern and central regions of Chad. In Sudan and Libya, numerous self-styled "liberation fronts" appeared in the mid-1960s, printing manifestos and claiming leadership over rebellious groups inside Chad. The most prominent of these fronts, the National Liberation Front of Chad (Front de Libération Nationale du Tchad—FROLINAT), was formed in June 1966 in Nyala in southwestern Sudan. Personality, philosophical, and ethnic differences soon led to the front's fragmentation, with one group moving to Khartoum and another, which retained the FROLINAT designation, establishing offices in Algiers and Tripoli.

The influence of external assistance to the rebels during this period was minimal. Prior to 1976, Chad's uprisings were disorganized and uncoordinated among dissident groups. Most observers attribute the rebels' success more to the ineptitude of Chad's government and national army than to outside assistance.

After FROLINAT's eastern region field commander, Ibrahim Abatcha, died in combat in February 1968, four contenders for leadership emerged. Within two years, two of them reportedly had been assassinated and one had fled to Sudan; the fourth, Abba Siddick, became FROLINAT's new secretary general in 1970. But in 1971, when Siddick called for greater cooperation among various groups under the FROLINAT banner, he encountered vigorous opposition in the north from Goukouni Oueddei, son of Oueddei

Kichidemi, and Hissein Habré, one of the leaders of the Armed Forces of the North (Forces Armées du Nord—FAN). Goukouni and Habré broke with Siddick, who managed to retain only nominal control over FROLINAT's First Liberation Army in east-central Chad (see Appendix B).

Tombalbaye's initial response to the increasing antigovernment activities was to attempt to crush them. When the government's forces proved woefully inadequate for the task, Tombalbaye swallowed his pride and called in the French under provisions of military treaties signed in 1960.

Confronted by the unpopularity of such a step, the French government joined many Chadian intellectuals in calling for a broad range of economic and political reforms by Chad's government. Desperate for French assistance, Tombalbaye reluctantly accepted the thirty-three member Administrative Reform Mission (Mission de Réforme Administrative—MRA), which arrived in 1969 with authority to retrain the army, reorganize the civil service, and recommend the abolition of unpopular laws and taxes. The most significant political reform was the full restoration to Chad's major sultans of their previous judicial authority. The government also allowed them to resume their function as tax collectors in exchange for 10 percent of the revenue. This action, which Tombalbaye implemented grudgingly, temporarily undermined rebel activities across central Chad.

Liberalization continued in the late 1960s and early 1970s. Following the 1969 presidential elections, in which Tombalbaye ran unopposed, some 600 political prisoners were released, including a number of prominent Muslims. In April 1971, Tombalbaye, addressing the Seventh Congress of the PPT, admitted for the first time that he had made mistakes and that there were some shortcomings associated with his policies. He promised a campaign of national reconciliation, and a few weeks later he formed a government that included a greater proportion of Muslims and northerners. In June Tombalbaye freed another 1,500 political prisoners and toured rebel regions in the north, where he promised, among other things, government-subsidized salt and sugar for the nomads of Zouar and Bardaï.

These reforms and French assistance contributed to the relative calm of 1970 and 1971. French military forces provided extensive and effective assistance in containing rebellious activities in central Chad. By June 1971, overt rebellion had been reduced for the most part to isolated pockets in the Tibesti region. The French government, under domestic pressure, began to withdraw its forces from Chad.

Fall of the Tombalbaye Government

Tombalbaye's reform efforts ceased abruptly in August 1971. In that month, he claimed to have quashed a coup involving some recently amnestied Chadians who allegedly received support from Libyan leader Muammar al Qadhafi. Tombalbaye severed relations with Libya and invited anti-Qadhafi elements to establish bases in Chad. In retaliation, Qadhafi recognized FROLINAT, offered (for the first time formally) an operational base in Tripoli to Siddick, and increased the flow of supplies to the Chadian rebels.

Domestic calm deteriorated further when students conducted a strike in N'Djamena in November 1971. Although easily contained, the strike demonstrated the growing politicization and disaffection of young members of the southern elite and reflected their increased awareness of the army's political potential. Tombalbaye then replaced the chief of staff, General Jacques Doumro, who was a favorite of the students, with Colonel Félix Malloum.

In June 1972, a band of Libyan-trained saboteurs was captured while attempting to smuggle guns and explosives into the capital. These arrests coincided with a serious financial crisis, a worsening drought, bitter government infighting, and civil unrest in the capital. These events convinced Tombalbaye to abandon his policy of national reconciliation. He incarcerated more than 1,000 real or suspected ''enemies of the state.'' In an indication of his growing distrust of the previously secure south, Tombalbaye detained hundreds of southerners and removed two key southern cabinet ministers. He also effected a dramatic diplomatic about-face designed to obtain economic assistance from the Arab world while undermining FROLINAT. To enhance ties to the Arab world, Tombalbaye broke Chad's relations with Israel in September 1972. A few months later, Tombalbaye secured an initial pledge of CFA F23 billion (for value of the CFA franc—see Glossary) from Libya. In 1973 other Arab capitals promised aid. In addition, Chad withdrew from the Afro-Malagasy and Mauritian Common Organization (Organisation Commune Africaine, Malgache, et Mauricienne—OCAMM) a moderate alliance of French-speaking African states.

Tombalbaye's strategy to create difficulties for FROLINAT was successful. When Qadhafi began restricting deliveries of military supplies and food to the rebels, fighting for the limited supplies erupted between FROLINAT's First Liberation Army and FAN (at that time also called the Second Liberation Army). The Second Liberation Army lost control of Ennedi and retreated into northern Borkou and Tibesti. In April 1974, however, it struck back by seizing three European hostages, including a French archaeologist at Bardaï.

By this time, the Tombalbaye presidency was rapidly unraveling, as greater attention focused on the real and suspected threats from within the government. In June 1973, Tombalbaye arrested Malloum, the head of the women's wing of the PPT, and a score of other party officials, mostly from the south. These individuals were held on charges of "political sorcery" in what came to be known as the "Black Sheep Plot" because of their alleged involvement in animal sacrifices. Moreover, when Outel Bono, a widely admired liberal politician, was assassinated in Paris while organizing a new political party in August, many believed that Tombalbaye's government was behind the murder. Also that month, Tombalbaye decided to replace the PPT with a new party, the National Movement for the Cultural and Social Revolution (Mouvement National pour la Révolution Culturelle et Sociale—MNRCS).

To deflect domestic criticism, Tombalbaye embarked on a campaign to promote *authenticité,* or "Chaditude." This effort was aimed at expunging foreign practices and influences. To shore up his support from Chad's expanding urban elite, Tombalbaye Africanized the names of several places (Fort-Lamy and Fort-Archambault became N'Djamena and Sarh, respectively) and ordered civil servants to use indigenous names in place of their European ones; he changed his first name to Ngarta. In addition, his policies induced many foreign missionaries to repatriate. His strident attacks on the French government were also popular. Tombalbaye lashed out specifically at Jacques Foccart, the powerful secretary general to the French Presidency for African Affairs, who was labeled an "evil genius" and formally condemned in a National Assembly resolution as the source of some "fourteen plots" against the government of Chad.

To restore his sagging support among Sara traditionalists in the rural south, Tombalbaye came out in favor of the harsh physical and psychological *yondo* initiation rites for all southern males between sixteen and fifty, making them compulsory for any non-Muslim seeking admission to the civil service, government, and higher ranks of the military (see Classical African Religions, ch. 2). From mid-1973 to April 1974, an estimated 3,000 southern civil servants, including two cabinet ministers and one colonel, went through the *yondo* ordeal. Because the rites were perceived as anti-Christian and essentially borrowed from one Sara subgroup, resistance to the process exacerbated antagonisms along clan and religious lines. Therefore, rather than encouraging greater southern support,

Tombalbaye's action created disaffection among civil servants, army officers, and students.

The worsening drought in the early 1970s also affected Chad's degenerating political situation. Throughout 1974 international criticism of Chad's handling of drought-relief efforts reached a new peak, as government insensitivity and overt profiteering became obvious.

In response to its economic crisis, the government launched Operation Agriculture, which involved a massive volunteer cotton-planting effort on virgin lands. The project increased production somewhat, but at the expense of major economic dislocations and greater southern resentment, particularly from people in cities and towns who were rounded up by the military to "volunteer" for agricultural labor.

By early 1975, many observers believed that Tombalbaye had eroded his two main bases of support—the south and the armed forces. Only intra-Sara divisions and concern over the possible loss of southern influence in government had prevented any well-organized anti-Tombalbaye movement. In addition, throughout the early 1970s Tombalbaye's criticism of the army's mediocre performance in the field had angered the officer corps and dissipated its loyalty. Other military grievances included frequent purges and reshufflings of the top ranks. In March 1975, Tombalbaye ordered the arrest of several senior military officers as suspects in yet another plot. On April 13, 1975, several units of N'Djamena's gendarmerie, acting under the initial direction of junior military officers, killed Tombalbaye during a mutiny.

Civil War and Northern Dominance, 1975–82

Malloum's Military Government, 1975–78

The coup d'état that terminated Tombalbaye's government received an enthusiastic response in N'Djamena. Malloum emerged as the chairman of the new Supreme Military Council (Conseil Supérieur Militaire—CSM). His government contained more Muslims from northern and eastern Chad, but ethnic and regional dominance still remained very much in the hands of southerners. The successor government soon overturned many of Tombalbaye's more odious policies. For example, the CSM attempted to distribute external drought-relief assistance more equitably and efficiently and devised plans to develop numerous economic reforms, including reductions in taxes and government expenditures.

Neither reformers nor skilled administrators, the new military leaders were unable to retain for long the modicum of authority,

President Tombalbaye marching in a parade celebrating the tenth
anniversary of independence
Courtesy Michael R. Saks
Fountain in Sultan Kasser Plaza in N'Djamena
Courtesy Michael R. Saks

legitimacy, and popularity that they had gained through their over-throw of the unpopular Tombalbaye. The expectations of most urban Chadians far exceeded the capacity of the new government—or possibly any government—to satisfy them. It soon became clear, moreover, that the new leaders (mostly southern military officers) saw themselves as caretakers rather than innovators, and few of Tombalbaye's close associates were punished. Throughout its tenure, the CSM was unable to win the support of the capital's increasingly radicalized unions, students, and urban dwellers. The government suspended the National Union of Chadian Workers (Union Nationale de Travailleurs du Tchad—UNTT) and pro-hibited strikes, but labor and urban unrest continued from 1975 through 1978. On the first anniversary of the formation of the CSM, Malloum was the target of a grenade attack that injured several top officials and spectators. A year after that, in March 1977, the CSM executed summarily the leaders of a short-lived mutiny by several military units in N'Djamena.

The fundamental failures of Malloum's government, however, were most evident in its interactions with France, Libya, and FROLINAT. In his first few months in office, Malloum persuaded a few eastern rebel elements to join the new government. In the north, the *derde* (Oueddei Kichidemi) returned from exile in Libya in August 1975. But his son, Goukouni Oueddei, refused to respond to his entreaties or those of the government and remained in opposi-tion. When the Command Council of the Armed Forces of the North (Conseil de Commandement des Forces Armées du Nord—CCFAN), a structure set up in 1972 by Habré and Goukouni to represent northern elements in FROLINAT, continued to refuse negotiations with the CSM over the release of the hostage French archaeologist, France began dealing directly with the rebels. Mal-loum's government reacted to this embarrassment by demanding the departure of 1,500 French troops, at a time in late 1975 when Chad's military situation was beginning to worsen. Throughout 1976 and 1977, the military balance of power shifted in favor of FROLINAT as Libya provided the rebels with substantially more weaponry and logistical support than ever before. Faya Largeau was placed under siege twice in 1976, and then in June 1977 Bardaï fell to the CCFAN.

The sharp increase in Libyan activity also brought to a head the power struggle within the CCFAN between Goukouni and Habré. In 1971 Habré had left his position as a deputy prefect in the Tom-balbaye government to join Goukouni's rebels. Goukouni and Habré, ambitious Toubou leaders from two different and competing clans, became bitter rivals, first within the CCFAN and later within all of Chad. In the CCFAN, the key issues dividing the men were relations with Libya and the handling of the hostage affair. Habré opposed vigorously all Libyan designs on the Aozou Strip and favored retaining the French hostage even after most of the ransom demands had been met. Goukouni felt that priority should go to the conflict with the CSM, for which Libyan assistance could be decisive, and that the kidnapping had already achieved more than enough. Habré finally split with him in 1976, taking a few hundred followers to fight in Batha and Biltine prefectures and retaining for his group the name FAN (see Appendix B). Goukouni and his followers prevailed (the CCFAN released the hostage to French authorities in January 1977).

As the military position of the CSM continued to decline in 1977, Malloum's political overtures to the rebel groups and leaders became increasingly flexible. In September Malloum and Habré met in Khartoum to begin negotiations on a formal alliance. Their efforts culminated in a carefully drafted agreement, the Fundamental Charter, which formed the basis of the National Union Government of August 1978. Malloum was named president of the new government, while Habré, as prime minister, became the first significant insurgent figure to hold an executive position in a postcolonial government.

Habré's ascension to power in N'Djamena was intended to signal to Goukouni and other rebel leaders the government's willingness to negotiate seriously following its reversals on the battlefield in 1978. In February Faya Largeau fell to FROLINAT, and with it roughly half the country's territory. Shortly thereafter, Malloum flew to Sabha in southern Libya to negotiate a cease-fire, but even as it was being codified in March, FROLINAT's position was hardening. Goukouni claimed that all three liberation armies were now united under his leadership in the new People's Armed Forces (Forces Armées Populaires—FAP) and that their objective remained the overthrow of the "dictatorial neocolonial regime imposed by France on Chad since August 11, 1960." FAP continued to advance toward the capital until it was halted near Ati in major battles with French military forces and units of the Chadian Armed Forces (Forces Armées Tchadiennes—FAT; see Appendix B). It was Malloum's hope that the FROLINAT leadership would soften its terms, or possibly undergo renewed fragmentation.

Civil War and Multilateral Mediation, 1979–82

From 1979 to 1982, Chad experienced unprecedented change and spiraling violence. Southerners finally lost control of what remained of the Chadian government, while civil conflicts became significantly more internationalized. In early 1979, the fragile Malloum-Habré alliance collapsed after months of aggressive actions by Habré, including demands that more northerners be appointed to high government offices and that Arabic be used in place of French in broadcasting. Appealing for support among the large communities of Muslims and Arabs in N'Djamena, Habré unleashed his FAN on February 12. With the French garrison remaining uninvolved, FAN sent Malloum into retirement (under French protection) and drove the remnants of FAT toward the south. On February 22, Goukouni and FAP entered the capital. By this time, most of the city's Sara population had fled to the south, where attacks against Muslims and nonsoutherners erupted, particularly in Sarh, Moundou, and throughout Moyen-Chari Prefecture. By mid-March more than 10,000 were said to have died as a result of violence throughout the south.

In early 1979, Chad became an open arena of unrestrained factional politics. Opportunistic power seekers sought to gather followers (often using sectarian appeals) and to win support from Chad's African neighbors. Between March 10 and August 21, four separate conferences took place in the Nigerian cities of Kano and Lagos, during which Chad's neighbors attempted to establish a political framework acceptable to the warring factions. Chad's neighbors, however, also used the meetings to pursue interests of their own, resulting in numerous externally generated complications and a growing number of factions brought into the process. For example, at one point, Qadhafi became so angry with Habré that the Libyan sent arms to Colonel Wadel Abdelkader Kamougué's anti-Habré faction in the south, even though Kamougué was also anti-Libyan. At the second conference in Kano, both Habré and Goukouni were placed under what amounted to house arrest so Nigeria could promote the chances of a Kanembu leader, Mahmat Shawa Lol. In fact, Nigerian support made Lol the Chadian titular head of state for a few weeks, even though his Third Liberation Army was only a phantom force, and his domestic political support was insignificant. Within Chad the warring parties used the conferences and their associated truces to recover from one round of fighting and prepare for the next.

The final conference culminated in the Lagos Accord of August 21, 1979, which representatives of eleven Chadian factions signed and the foreign ministers of nine other African states witnessed. The Lagos Accord established the procedures for setting up the Transitional Government of National Unity (Gouvernement d'Union Nationale de Transition—GUNT), which was sworn into office in November. By mutual agreement, Goukouni was named president, Kamougué was appointed vice-president, and Habré was named minister of national defense, veterans, and war victims. The distribution of cabinet positions was balanced between south (eleven portfolios), north, center, and east (thirteen), and among protégés of neighboring states. A peacekeeping mission of the Organization of African Unity (OAU), to be drawn from troops from Congo, Guinea, and Benin, was to replace the French. This force never materialized in any effective sense, but the OAU was committed to GUNT under the presidency of Goukouni.

GUNT, however, failed. Its major participants deeply mistrusted each other, and they never achieved a sense of coherence. As a result, the various factional militias remained armed. By January 1980, a unit of Habré's army was attacking the forces of one of the constituent groups of GUNT in Ouaddaï Prefecture. Shortly thereafter, N'Djamena plunged into another cycle of violence, and by the end of March 1980 Habré was openly defying the government, having taken control of a section of the capital. The 600 Congolese troops of the OAU peacekeeping force remained out of the fray, as did the French, while units of five separate Chadian armies prowled the streets of N'Djamena. The battles continued throughout the summer, punctuated by more OAU mediation efforts and five formal cease-fires.

It became evident that the profound rivalry between Goukouni and Habré was at the core of the conflict. By mid-1980 the south—cut off from communication and trade with N'Djamena and defended by a regrouped, southern army—had become a state within a state. Colonel Kamougué, the strongman of the south, remained a prudent distance away from the capital and waited to negotiate with whichever northerner emerged as the winner.

In 1980 the beleaguered Goukouni turned to Libya, much as he had done four years earlier. With the French forces having departed in mid-May 1980, Goukouni signed a military cooperation treaty with Libya in June (without prior approval of the all-but-defunct GUNT). In October he requested direct military assistance from Qadhafi, and by December Libyan forces had firm control of the capital and most other urban centers outside the south. Habré fled to Sudan, vowing to resume the struggle.

Although Libyan intervention enabled Goukouni to win militarily, the association with Qadhafi created diplomatic problems for GUNT. In January 1981, when Goukouni and Qadhafi issued a joint communiqué stating that Chad and Libya had agreed to ''work for the realization of complete unity between the two countries,'' an international uproar ensued. Although both leaders later denied any intention to merge their states politically, the diplomatic damage had been done.

Throughout 1981 most of the members of the OAU, along with France and the United States, encouraged Libyan troops to withdraw from Chad. One week after the "unity communiqué," the OAU's committee on Chad met in Togo to assess the situation. In a surprisingly blunt resolution, the twelve states on the committee denounced the union goal as a violation of the 1979 Lagos Accord, called for Libya to withdraw its troops, and promised to provide a peacekeeping unit, the Inter-African Force (IAF). Goukouni was skeptical of OAU promises, but in September he received a French pledge of support for his government and the IAF.

But as Goukouni's relations with the OAU and France improved, his ties with Libya deteriorated. One reason for this deterioration was that the economic assistance that Libya had promised never materialized. Another, and perhaps more significant, factor was that Qadhafi was strongly suspected of helping Goukouni's rival within GUNT, Acyl Ahmat, leader of the Democratic Revolutionary Council (Conseil Démocratique Révolutionnaire—CDR). Both Habré and Goukouni feared Acyl because he and many of the members of the CDR were Arabs of the Awlad Sulayman tribe. About 150 years earlier, this group had migrated from Libya to Chad and thus represented the historical and cultural basis of Libyan claims in Chad (see Languages and Ethnic Groups, ch. 2).

As a consequence of the Libya-Chad rift, Goukouni asked the Libyan forces in late October 1981 to leave, and by mid-November they had complied. Their departure, however, allowed Habré's FAN—reconstituted in eastern Chad with Egyptian, Sudanese, and, reportedly, significant United States assistance—to win key positions along the highway from Abéché to N'Djamena. Habré was restrained only by the arrival and deployment in December 1981 of some 4,800 IAF troops from Nigeria, Senegal, and Zaire.

In February 1982, a special OAU meeting in Nairobi resulted in a plan that called for a cease-fire, negotiations among all parties, elections, and the departure of the IAF; all terms were to be carried out within six months. Habré accepted the plan, but Goukouni rejected it, asserting that Habré had lost any claim to legitimacy when he broke with GUNT. When Habré renewed his military advance toward N'Djamena, the IAF remained essentially neutral, just as the French had done when FROLINAT marched on Malloum three years earlier. FAN secured control of the capital on June 7. Goukouni and other members of GUNT fled to Cameroon and eventually reappeared in Libya. For the remainder of the year, Habré consolidated his power in much of war-weary Chad

and worked to secure international recognition for his government.

* * *

Little research material was available in English on the historical background of Chad or the central Sudanic region. For earlier
historical periods, *The Cambridge History of Africa* offers a comprehensive survey, along with maps and bibliographic references. Principal sources include the contributions of Nehemia Levtzion in
Volume 2 of the Cambridge series and H.J. Fisher in Volumes
3 and 4, as well as *African History* by Philip Curtin and others, for
nineteenth-century material in particular. The published thesis *State
and Society in Three Central Sudanic Kingdoms* by Anders J. Bjørkelo,
although not widely available, contains extensive analysis and
interpretation. A detailed examination of Kanem-Borno is presented
in *Pages d'histoire du Kanem,* by Jean-Claude Zeltner.

Dennis D. Cordell's *Dar al-Kuti and the Last Years of the Trans-
Saharan Slave Trade,* although not specifically about Chad, is
especially useful for its regional perspective and its analysis of
nineteenth-century developments. Cordell also provides useful perspectives on the culture of the Sara people.

No standard English work on the colonial experience in Chad
is readily available, and the most frequently cited French source,
Jacques Le Cornec's *Histoire politique du Tchad de 1900 à 1962,* is
dated. Brian Weinstein's biography of Félix Eboué surveys the
human dimension of the colonial era. Samuel Decalo's *Historical
Dictionary of Chad* is also a valuable reference work.

Chad's recent history is analyzed in the works of Decalo, René
Lemarchand, and William J. Foltz. Other important references
include *Conflict in Chad* by Virginia M. Thompson and Richard
Adloff and *A State in Disarray,* by Michael P. Kelley. French works
on recent history include *Le Frolinat et les révoltes populaires du Tchad,
1965–1976* by Robert Buijtenhuijs and *Tchad-Libye: La querelle des
frontières* by Bernard Lanne. (For further information and complete
citations, see Bibliography.)

Chapter 2. The Society and Its Environment

A bee-hived shaped mud hut, sometimes found in areas of Mayo-Kebbi Prefecture

GEOGRAPHIC VARIATION, ETHNIC and linguistic diversity, and religious differences have presented serious obstacles to nation building in Chad. A range of environments has contributed to the evolution of a variety of life-styles and social structures, including nomadic societies in the Sahara Desert in the north, semi-nomadic (or semisedentary) peoples in the Sahel (see Glossary) in the center, and agricultural communities in the *soudanian* south. With three of Africa's four major language families represented within its borders, Chad's peoples do not share broad cultural characteristics, as do, for example, the Bantu peoples of countries in central, eastern, and southern Africa. Religion also divides Chad's people among followers of classical African religions, Islam, and Christianity. Ethnic differences often overlay and intensify these divisions.

Preoccupied with assuring the country's survival, successive Chadian governments have had little motivation or resources to deal with urgent social and economic problems. Up-to-date population data—necessary for reliable development planning—are lacking; however, a census scheduled for 1989 promised to remedy this problem partially.

Other challenges include providing adequate education and health care. Starting in the mid-1960s, civil strife has undermined the Chadian goal of universal primary school education. It has also brought the exile of much of the country's intellectual community and the flight of foreign personnel who had staffed institutions of higher learning. Health care has fared even more poorly than has education. Although the number of medical facilities of all kinds seems to have grown between the early 1970s and the early 1980s, the number of trained personnel has not kept pace. And once again, the violence of war and discontent with the government in rural areas have provoked the closing of many facilities and the flight of their staffs.

Physical Setting

Located in north-central Africa, Chad stretches for about 1,800 kilometers from its northernmost point to its southern boundary. Except in the far northwest and south, where its borders converge, Chad's average width is about 800 kilometers. Its area of 1,284,000 square kilometers is roughly equal to the combined areas of Idaho, Wyoming, Utah, Nevada, and Arizona. Chad's neighbors include

Libya to the north, Niger and Nigeria to the west, Sudan to the east, Central African Republic to the south, and Cameroon to the southwest.

Chad exhibits two striking geographical characteristics. First, the country is landlocked. N'Djamena, the capital, is located more than 1,100 kilometers northeast of the Atlantic Ocean; Abéché, a major city in the east, lies 2,650 kilometers from the Red Sea; and Faya Largeau, a much smaller but strategically important center in the north, is in the middle of the Sahara Desert, 1,550 kilometers from the Mediterranean Sea. These vast distances from the sea have had a profound impact on Chad's historical and contemporary development. The second noteworthy characteristic is that the country borders on very different parts of the African continent: North Africa, with its Islamic culture and economic orientation toward the Mediterranean Basin; West Africa, with its diverse religions and cultures and its history of highly developed states and regional economies; Northeast Africa, oriented toward the Nile Valley and Red Sea region; and Central or Equatorial Africa, some of whose people have retained classical African religions while others have adopted Christianity, and whose economies were part of the great Zaire River system. Although much of Chad's distinctiveness comes from this diversity of influences, since independence the diversity has also been an obstacle to the creation of a national identity.

The Land

Although Chadian society is economically, socially, and culturally fragmented, the country's geography is unified by the Lake Chad Basin (see fig. 3). Once a huge inland sea (the Paleochadian Sea) whose only remnant is shallow Lake Chad, this vast depression extends west into Nigeria and Niger. The larger, northern portion of the basin is bounded within Chad by the Tibesti Mountains in the northwest, the Ennedi Plateau in the northeast, the Ouaddaï Highlands in the east along the border with Sudan, the Guéra Massif in central Chad, and the Mandara Mountains along Chad's southwestern border with Cameroon. The smaller, southern part of the basin falls almost exclusively in Chad. It is delimited in the north by the Guéra Massif, in the south by highlands 250 kilometers south of the border with Central African Republic, and in the southwest by the Mandara Mountains.

Lake Chad, located in the southwestern part of the basin at an altitude of 282 meters, surprisingly does not mark the basin's lowest point; instead, this is found in the Bodele and Djourab regions in the north-central and northeastern parts of the country, respectively.

This oddity arises because the great stationary dunes (*ergs*) of the Kanem region create a dam, preventing lake waters from flowing to the basin's lowest point. At various times in the past, and as late as the 1870s, the Bahr el Ghazal Depression, which extends from the northeastern part of the lake to the Djourab, acted as an overflow canal; since independence, climatic conditions have made overflows impossible.

North and northeast of Lake Chad, the basin extends for more than 800 kilometers, passing through regions characterized by great rolling dunes separated by very deep depressions. Although vegetation holds the dunes in place in the Kanem region, farther north they are bare and have a fluid, rippling character. From its low point in the Djourab, the basin then rises to the plateaus and peaks of the Tibesti Mountains in the north. The summit of this formation—as well as the highest point in the Sahara Desert—is Emi Koussi, a dormant volcano that reaches 3,414 meters above sea level. The basin's northeastern limit is the Ennedi Plateau, whose limestone bed rises in steps etched by erosion.

East of the lake, the basin rises gradually to the Ouaddaï Highlands, which mark Chad's eastern border and also divide the Chad and Nile watersheds. Southeast of Lake Chad, the regular contours of the terrain are broken by the Guéra Massif, which divides the basin into its northern and southern parts.

South of the lake lie the floodplains of the Chari and Logone rivers, much of which are inundated during the rainy season. Farther south, the basin floor slopes upward, forming a series of low sand and clay plateaus, called *koros*, which eventually climb to 615 meters above sea level. South of the Chadian border, the *koros* divide the Lake Chad Basin from the Ubangi-Zaire river system.

Water Systems

Permanent streams do not exist in northern or central Chad. Following infrequent rains in the Ennedi Plateau and Ouaddaï Highlands, water may flow through depressions called *enneris* and wadis. Often the result of flash floods, such streams usually dry out within a few days as the remaining puddles seep into the sandy clay soil. The most important of these streams is the Batha, which in the rainy season carries water west from the Ouaddaï Highlands and the Guéra Massif to Lake Fitri.

Chad's major rivers are the Chari and the Logone and their tributaries, which flow from the southeast into Lake Chad. Both river systems rise in the highlands of Central African Republic and Cameroon, regions that receive more than 1,250 millimeters of rainfall annually. Fed by rivers of Central African Republic, as well

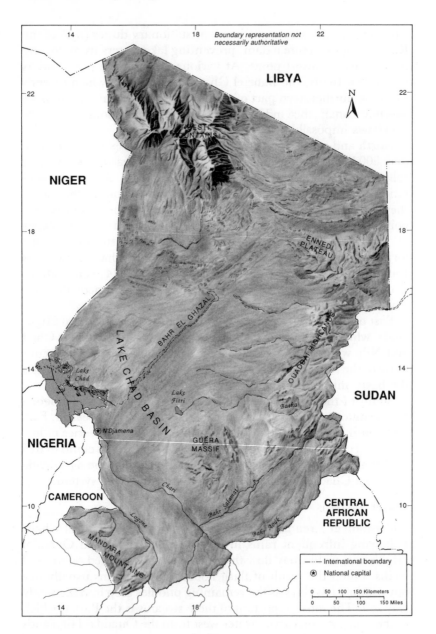

Figure 3. Topography and Drainage

as by the Bahr Salamat, Bahr Aouk, and Bahr Sara rivers of southeastern Chad, the Chari River is about 1,200 kilometers long.

From its origins near the city of Sarh, the middle course of the Chari makes its way through swampy terrain; the lower Chari is joined by the Logone River near N'Djamena. The Chari's volume varies greatly, from 17 cubic meters per second during the dry season to 340 cubic meters per second during the wettest part of the year.

The Logone River is formed by tributaries flowing from Cameroon and Central African Republic. Both shorter and smaller in volume than the Chari, it flows northeast for 960 kilometers; its volume ranges from five to eighty-five cubic meters per second. At N'Djamena the Logone empties into the Chari, and the combined rivers flow together for thirty kilometers through a large delta and into Lake Chad. At the end of the rainy season in the fall, the river overflows its banks and creates a huge floodplain in the delta.

The seventh largest lake in the world (and the fourth largest in Africa), Lake Chad is located in the *sahelian* zone, a region just south of the Sahara Desert. The Chari River contributes 95 percent of Lake Chad's water, an average annual volume of 40 billion cubic meters, 95 percent of which is lost to evaporation. The size of the lake is determined by rains in the southern highlands bordering the basin and by temperatures in the Sahel. Fluctuations in both cause the lake to change dramatically in size, from 9,800 square kilometers in the dry season to 25,500 at the end of the rainy season. Lake Chad also changes greatly in size from one year to another. In 1870 its maximum area was 28,000 square kilometers. The measurement dropped to 12,700 in 1908. In the 1940s and 1950s, the lake remained small, but it grew again to 26,000 square kilometers in 1963. The droughts of the late 1960s, early 1970s, and mid-1980s caused Lake Chad to shrink once again, however. The only other lakes of importance in Chad are Lake Fitri, in Batha Prefecture, and Lake Iro, in the marshy southeast.

Climate

The Lake Chad Basin embraces a great range of tropical climates from north to south, although most of these climates tend to be dry. Apart from the far north, most regions are characterized by a cycle of alternating rainy and dry seasons. In any given year, the duration of each season is determined largely by the positions of two great air masses—a maritime mass over the Atlantic Ocean to the southwest and a much drier continental mass. During the rainy season, winds from the southwest push the moister maritime system north over the African continent where it meets and slips under the continental mass along a front called the "intertropical convergence zone." At the height of the rainy season, the front may reach as far as Kanem Prefecture. By the middle of the dry season, the intertropical convergence zone moves south of Chad, taking the rain with it. This weather system contributes to the formation of three major regions of climate and vegetation.

Saharan Region

The Saharan region covers roughly the northern third of the country, including Borkou-Ennedi-Tibesti Prefecture along with the northern parts of Kanem, Batha, and Biltine prefectures (see fig. 1). Much of this area receives only traces of rain during the entire year; at Faya Largeau, for example, annual rainfall averages less than thirty millimeters. Scattered small oases and occasional wells provide water for a few date palms or small plots of millet and garden crops. In much of the north, the average daily maximum temperature is about 32°C during January, the coolest month of the year, and about 45°C during May, the hottest month. On occasion, strong winds from the northeast produce violent sandstorms. In northern Biltine Prefecture, a region called the Mortcha plays a major role in animal husbandry. Dry for nine months of the year, it receives 350 millimeters or more of rain, mostly during July and August. A carpet of green springs from the desert during this brief wet season, attracting herders from throughout the region who come to pasture their cattle and camels. Because very few wells and springs have water throughout the year, the herders leave with the end of the rains, turning over the land to the antelopes, gazelles, and ostriches that can survive with little groundwater.

Sahelian Region

The semiarid *sahelian* zone, or Sahel, forms a belt about 500 kilometers wide that runs from Lac and Chari-Baguirmi prefectures eastward through Guéra, Ouaddaï, and northern Salamat prefectures to the Sudanese frontier. The climate in this transition zone between the desert and the southern *soudanian* zone is divided into a rainy season (from June to early September) and a dry period (from October to May). In the northern Sahel, thorny shrubs and acacia trees grow wild, while date palms, cereals, and garden crops are raised in scattered oases. Outside these settlements, nomads tend their flocks during the rainy season, moving southward as forage and surface water disappear with the onset of the dry part of the year. The central Sahel is characterized by drought-resistant grasses and small woods. Rainfall is more abundant there than in the Saharan region. For example, N'Djamena records a maximum

Villagers drawing water from a wood-lined well
Courtesy United Nations (Uri Golani)

annual average rainfall of 580 millimeters, while Ouaddaï Prefecture receives just a bit less. During the hot season, in April and May, maximum temperatures frequently rise above 40°C. In the southern part of the Sahel, rainfall is sufficient to permit crop production on unirrigated land, and millet and sorghum are grown (see Agriculture, ch. 3). Agriculture is also common in the marshlands east of Lake Chad and near swamps or wells. Many farmers in the region combine subsistence agriculture with the raising of cattle, sheep, goats, and poultry.

Soudanian Region

The humid *soudanian* zone includes the southern prefectures of Mayo-Kebbi, Tandjilé, Logone Occidental, Logone Oriental, Moyen-Chari, and southern Salamat. Between April and October, the rainy season brings between 750 and 1,250 millimeters of precipitation. Temperatures are high throughout the year. Daytime readings in Moundou, the major city in the southwest, range from 27°C in the middle of the cool season in January to about 40°C in the hot months of March, April, and May.

The *soudanian* region is predominantly savanna, or plains covered with a mixture of tropical or subtropical grasses and woodlands. The growth is lush during the rainy season but turns brown and dormant during the five-month dry season between November and March. Over a large part of the region, however, natural vegetation has yielded to agriculture.

Population

In the late 1980s, demographic data for Chad were very incomplete. One of the most important demographic techniques is projection from one set of data to anticipate the evolution of the population, but the lack of a national census in Chad has made applying such a technique difficult. In addition, population projections assume that the population has evolved with regularity since the last collection of data. In Chad, domestic conflict, foreign military occupation of part of its territory, and serious famines, from 1968 through 1973 and in the early 1980s, have disrupted the regular change of the population. As a result, many population estimates were probably inaccurate. In 1988 most population estimates continued to be based on projections from partial studies made in 1964 and 1968 by the National Institute of Economic and Statistical Studies (Institut National des Etudes Statistiques et Economiques—INSEE) in France and by the Chadian government. These survey data, projected forward, were the major reference sources for the Chadian government and for many international agencies and foreign governments. Two organizations, the Sahel Institute (Institut du Sahel—INSAH) and the Population Reference Bureau (PRB), gave different figures for Chad's population in 1985. The first organization estimated the population at almost 5 million; the second, at 5.2 million. In the late 1980s, cognizant of the need for demographic data for planning, the Ministry of Planning and Reconstruction and the United Nations Economic Commission for Africa began planning the first national census for 1989.

Estimates of total population acquire greater meaning when the processes behind them are examined more closely. Population change is the sum of two sets of additions and two sets of subtractions. First, there are additions through births. In mid-1987 the PRB estimated Chad's birthrate at 43 live births per 1,000 inhabitants annually (the world average was 28 in 1987). The same organization suggested that, on average, Chadian women gave birth to 5.9 children over their reproductive years, a slightly lower number than the 6.3 average for Africa women as a whole.

Second, there are additions through immigration. Although ethnic, political, and economic ties connect most regions of Chad with neighboring states, such links probably have not brought a large number of permanent immigrants. By the late 1980s, Chadians who had fled the civil strife in the southern and central parts of the country during the late 1970s and early 1980s apparently had returned in large numbers. Nonetheless, overall immigration probably has not exceeded emigration.

Subtractions for population decrease also are calculated for two sets of events. First, there are subtractions through deaths. In the mid-1980s, the PRB estimated Chad's mortality rate at 23 deaths annually per 1,000 inhabitants—one of the highest mortality rates in the world (the global average stood at 10 in 1987). Civilian and military deaths, resulting from warfare, poor health conditions, and drought undoubtedly have contributed to this high mortality rate. The yearly infant mortality rate (the number of children per 1,000 births who die before age one) was also extremely high in Chad, estimated by INSAH and the PRB at 155 and 143, respectively. Among children, a second peak in mortality occurs after weaning (from about one and one-half to two years of age), when they are deprived of their mothers' natural immunities. High mortality rates are indicative of short life expectancies. In Chad, INSAH estimated the life expectancy for a female born in the period 1975–80 at 43.4 years; for a male, it was even lower—38.5 years.

Emigration is the second form of subtraction. Although the data for Chad were partial, labor migration and refugee flight were the two major types of emigration. In recent decades, some of the old labor migration streams have continued, such as that to Sudan, and newer ones have joined them, such as those to Nigeria and the oil-rich countries of the Middle East during the petroleum boom of the 1970s and early 1980s.

Since independence, refugee flight has been a major component of emigration. In the late 1960s, troubles in eastern and southeastern Chad provoked emigration to Sudan. Patterns of flight have shifted with shifts in the theater of conflict. Following the battles of N'Djamena in 1979 and 1980, many residents sought refuge across the Chari River in neighboring Cameroon. Violence against southerners in N'Djamena brought further emigration, and the de facto partitioning of the country during the early 1980s brought retribution against northern merchants living in the southern cities of Moundou and Sarh. Although some of these people later returned to their homes within Chad, others sought refuge in Cameroon, Nigeria, and Central African Republic; some members of the bourgeoisie and intelligentsia fled to Western Europe. In the 1980s, the conflict shifted north, where the Chadian and Libyan armies clashed repeatedly. These campaigns marked a major escalation in violence and probably provoked flight as well (see Civil Conflict and Libyan Intervention, ch. 5).

As a population, Chadians were quite young (see fig. 4). The PRB estimated that 44 percent of the population was younger than fifteen in 1987. Only 2 percent of the population was older than sixty-four. These percentages are best appreciated as components of what is called the dependency ratio—the combined percentage of people less than fifteen and more than sixty-four, who, because they are considered only marginally productive, must be supported by the remainder of the population. Although some social scientists and development analysts challenge this conventional definition, pointing out that in rural Africa and urban shantytowns children may indeed add to the household income, most demographers agree that the measure is nonetheless a good general indicator of the dependency burden. In Chad, then, the 46 percent of the population less than fifteen and more than sixty-four essentially had to be supported by the other 54 percent. Although this ratio was not the highest in Africa, the level of dependency was difficult for Chadian society to bear, in part because poor health and inadequate nutrition already took such a high toll among the working population, and because mechanization had not raised productivity.

In terms of the sex structure of the population, the 1964 INSAH survey calculated that there were 90 males for every 100 females; in urban centers, the male percentage of the population rose slightly, to 96 for every 100 women. A small part of this imbalance may be attributed to higher male mortality rates, but male labor migration is probably a much more important factor. The absence of a census or more recent demographic surveys made it impossible to determine if the Chadian Civil War had affected the sex ratio.

In the late 1980s, Chad had a low population density of about 3.8 people per square kilometer. The population was also very unevenly distributed because of contrasts in climate and physical environment. The Saharan zone was the least densely populated. In 1982 it was estimated to have a population density of 0.15 per square kilometer. Most inhabitants of the region lived in its southern reaches, south of 16° north latitude.

The *sahelian* zone had a population density of seven persons per square kilometer in 1971. Within the region, broad spectrums of rainfall and environment and the diverse life-styles that accompany them have resulted in widely varying population densities, from very low among the nomads in the northern regions to much higher among the agricultural populations in the south.

The highest population densities—about thirteen people per square kilometer—occurred in the *soudanian* zone. In 1971 almost 45 percent of the total Chadian population lived in this region.

Chad was quite rural. The PRB placed the urban population of Africa at 31 percent in 1985, whereas Chad's urban population was estimated at only 22 percent. Although the urban population remained relatively small, urbanization accelerated in the 1980s. Whereas in 1971 only seven centers had more than 10,000 inhabitants, INSAH estimated that by 1978 nine cities had populations of more than 20,000. From a total of 132,502 enumerated in the urban census of 1968, N'Djamena's population grew to 150,000 in 1971, nearly doubling to 280,000 in 1978. Although much of the population abandoned the city during the battles of 1979 and 1980, most people returned over the next several years. In 1983 the Chadian government predicted that urban growth would continue at an annual rate of 7.8 percent for the capital and 4.6 percent for secondary cities such as Moundou, Sarh, and Abéché.

Languages and Ethnic Groups

The people of Chad speak more than 100 different languages and divide themselves into many ethnic groups. It is important to note, however, that language and ethnicity are not the same. Moreover, neither element can be tied to a particular physical type. The commonly held image that Africa is populated by discrete ethnic groups (or "tribes") who live isolated from each other, guarding their languages and customs jealously and intermarrying only

45

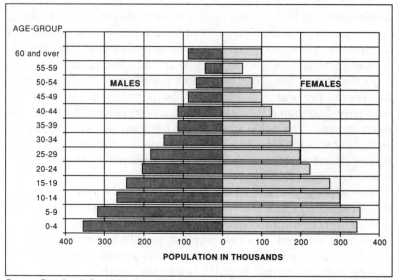

AGE-GROUP

60 and over
55-59
50-54   MALES   FEMALES
45-49
40-44
35-39
30-34
25-29
20-24
15-19
10-14
5-9
0-4

400   300   200   100   0   100   200   300   400

POPULATION IN THOUSANDS

Source: Based on information from Chad, Ministry of Planning and Reconstruction, *Tchad: Relance économique en chiffres*, N'Djamena, Chad, 1983, 15.

Figure 4. Population Distribution by Age and Sex, 1982

with each other, is a stereotype that hinders understanding of the dynamics of African societies. In Chad, European conquest and administration intensified feelings of ethnic separateness by drawing local boundaries along perceived ethnic lines. The Europeans also appointed chiefs and other local African authorities who had little legitimacy over the groups they were to lead. In general, the French favored southerners over northerners and settled populations over nomads. This bias continued after independence and has been an important element in internecine conflict.

Although the possession of a common language shows that its speakers have lived together and have a common history, peoples also change languages. This is particularly so in Chad, where the openness of the terrain, marginal rainfall, frequent drought and famine, and low population densities have encouraged physical and linguistic mobility. Slave raids among non-Muslim peoples, internal slave trade, and exports of captives northward from the ninth to the twentieth centuries also have resulted in language changes.

Anthropologists view ethnicity as being more than genetics. Like language, ethnicity implies a shared heritage, partly economic, where people of the same ethnic group may share a livelihood, and partly social, taking the form of shared ways of doing things and

A seminomadic family of the Daza ethnic group
Courtesy UNICEF (Maggie Murray-Lee)

organizing relations among individuals and groups. Ethnicity also involves a cultural component made up of shared values and a common worldview. Like language, ethnicity is not immutable. Shared ways of doing things change over time and alter a group's perception of its own identity.

Not only do the social aspects of ethnic identity change but the biological composition (or gene pool) also may change over time. Although most ethnic groups emphasize intermarriage, people are often proscribed from seeking partners among close relatives—a prohibition that promotes biological variation. In all groups, the departure of some individuals or groups and the integration of others also changes the biological component.

The Chadian government has avoided official recognition of ethnicity. With the exception of a few surveys conducted shortly after independence, little data were available on this important aspect of Chadian society. Nonetheless, ethnic identity was a significant component of life in Chad.

Chad's languages fall into ten major groups, each of which belongs to either the Nilo-Saharan, Afro-Asiatic, or Congo-Kordofanian language family. These represent three of the four major language families in Africa; only the Khoisan languages of southern Africa are not represented. The presence of such different languages suggests that the Lake Chad Basin may have been an important point of dispersal in ancient times.

Nilo-Saharan Languages

Similarities of language do not imply other congruences. Nilo-Saharan language speakers, for example, display a variety of lifestyles. Nomads in the Sahara, semisedentary and sedentary peoples in the Sahel, and sedentary populations in the *soudanian* zone all may speak Nilo-Saharan languages.

Central Saharan Languages

The distribution and numbers of Central Saharan language speakers probably have changed dramatically since independence. The Chadian Civil War and the Chadian-Libyan conflict have disrupted life in the northern part of the country. Also, the rise to power of two heads of state from the far north, Goukouni Oueddei and Hissein Habré, may have inspired the migration of northerners to the national capital and a greater integration of the region into the life of the country.

Teda and Daza are related languages in the Central Saharan group. Teda is spoken by the Toubou people of the Tibesti Mountains and by some inhabitants of nearby oases in northeastern Niger and southwestern Libya. Daza speakers live south of the Toubou in Borkou Subprefecture and Kanem Prefecture, between the Tibesti Mountains and Lake Chad (see fig. 5).

Despite their shared linguistic heritage, the Toubou and the Daza do not think of themselves as belonging to a common group. Moreover, each is further divided into subgroups identified with particular places. Among the Toubou, the Teda of Tibesti are the largest subgroup. Daza speakers separate themselves into more than a dozen groups. The Kreda of Bahr el Ghazal are the largest. Next in importance are the Daza of Kanem. Smaller and more scattered subgroups include the Charfarda of Ouaddaï; the Kecherda and Djagada of Kanem; the Doza, Annakaza, Kokorda, Kamadja, and Noarma of Borkou; and the Ounia, Gaeda, and Erdiha of Ennedi.

About one-third of the Teda are nomads. The remainder, along with all of the Daza, are seminomadic, moving from pasture to pasture during eight or nine months each year but returning to permanent villages during the rains. In general, the Teda herd camels and live farther north, where they move from oasis to oasis. The Daza often herd camels, but they also raise horses, sheep, and goats. Their itineraries take them farther south, where some have acquired cattle (whose limited capacity to endure the heat and harsh environment of the northern regions has altered patterns of transhumance). Some cattle owners leave their animals with herders in the south when they return north; others choose to remain in the south and entrust their other animals to relatives or herders who take them north.

Kanembu is the major language of Lac Prefecture and southern Kanem Prefecture. Although Kanuri, which derived from Kanembu, was the major language of the Borno Empire, in Chad it is limited to handfuls of speakers in urban centers. Kanuri remains a major language in southeastern Niger, northeastern Nigeria, and northern Cameroon.

In the early 1980s, the Kanembu constituted the greatest part of the population of Lac Prefecture, but some Kanembu also lived in Chari-Baguirmi Prefecture. Once the core ethnic group of the Kanem-Borno Empire, whose territories at one time included northeastern Nigeria and southern Libya, the Kanembu retain ties beyond the borders of Chad (see Kanem-Borno, ch. 1). For example, close family and commercial ties bind them with the Kanuri of northeastern Nigeria. Within Chad, many Kanembu of Lac and Kanem prefectures identify with the Alifa of Mao, the governor of the region in precolonial times.

Baele (also erroneously called Bideyat) is the language of the Bideyat of Ennedi Subprefecture and the Zaghawa of Biltine Prefecture. Despite this similarity, the Zaghawa and the Bideyat exhibit diverse life-styles. Some Zaghawa live in a centralized sultanate, with a ruling family of Dadjo origin; these Zaghawa are semisedentary and prominent in local and regional commerce. Other Zaghawa, however, living primarily in the south, are nomads. The Bideyat also are nomadic.

Ouaddaïan Languages

The origins of Ouaddaïan languages remain obscure, although their distribution implies origins farther east, an interpretation supported by oral traditions. Speakers of Ouaddaïan languages may have moved westward to avoid Arab immigration from the east. Another theory suggests that speakers of Ouaddaïan languages once were continuously distributed throughout the region but subsequently lost ground as the population accepted Arabic.

Although some authorities separate Tama, Dadjo, and Mimi, others consider them to be part of a larger Ouaddaïan group, a linguistic archipelago stretching from western Sudan to central Chad. In Chad they are found in Biltine, Ouaddaï, and Guéra prefectures.

Tama languages are spoken in Biltine and northern Ouaddaï Prefectures, and include Tama, Marari (Abou Charib), Sungor,

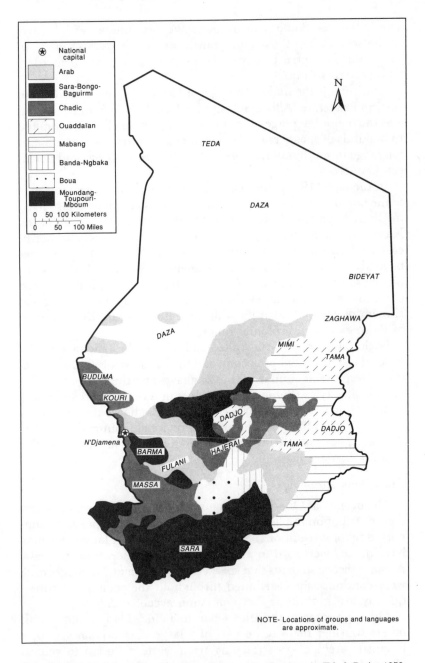

Source: Based on information from Jean Cabot, *Atlas Practique du Tchad,* Paris, 1972, 36–37.

Figure 5. Ethnolinguistic Map

Kibet, Mourro, and Dagel. The Tama speakers, who live in eastern Biltine Prefecture near the Sudanese border, are the largest of these groups. Although they live in the arid Sahel, crop rotation has allowed them to settle in permanent villages. The Tama live in cantons of several thousand people, each administered by a canton chief. For several centuries, central authority has been vested in sultans believed to be of Dadjo origin, who are enthroned in ceremonies at the ruins of Nir, the precolonial capital.

The Marari and Abou Charib, sedentary peoples sharing a Tama language, live south and west, respectively, of the Tama in Ouaddaï Prefecture. Although they speak a Tama language, their traditions suggest descent from the Tunjur, migrants from Sudan who once ruled the sultanate of Wadai (see Bagirmi and Wadai, ch. 1). To the west of the Tama and northwest of the Marari and Abou Charib are the Sungor, another sedentary population. The Sungor consider themselves to be of Yemeni ancestry, a popular and prestigious Islamic pedigree among Muslims of the region. Despite speaking a Tama language, Sungor society and customs most resemble those of the Maba.

The Dadjo language has eastern and western dialects. Once the rulers of the sultanate of Wadai, the Dadjo people were separated into two groups during the fifteenth century. At that time, the Tunjur conquered Wadai, and some Dadjo people fled west. The eastern Dadjo remained in southern present-day Ouaddaï Prefecture and, following defeat by the Tunjur, founded a new sultanate with its capital at Goz Béïda. Their descendants are primarily farmers. The western Dadjo live among the Hajerai peoples of northern Guéra Prefecture. Cognizant of their common origin, the eastern and western groups permit intermarriage.

Mimi is the least frequently spoken Ouaddaïan language. Mimi speakers who live in the plains use Arabic to communicate with their neighbors; Mimi speakers who live in the mountains generally speak Zaghawa with other highland dwellers.

Mabang Languages

Mabang languages are concentrated in the highlands of Ouaddaï Prefecture, but they are also spoken in Biltine and Salamat prefectures. Maba is the major language of the group. Maba speakers are semisedentary farmers who combine millet cultivation during the rainy season with herding during the drier parts of the year. For the last several decades, many Maba laborers have migrated to Sudan. The core ethnic group of the sultanate of Wadai, the Maba played a central role in that state even after conquest by rulers from the east in the seventeenth century. Wadai sultans frequently

51

took Maba women as first wives, and the first dignitary of the court usually was also Maba.

Massalit, another major Mabang language, is spoken by people who live east of the Maba along the Sudan border. Complemented by a far larger Massalit population in Sudan, the Chadian Massalit are farmers who rely on passing animal herds to fertilize their fields.

Massalat speakers are found farther west and are divided into two groups, one in eastern Batha near Ouaddaï Prefecture, and the other in northern Guéra Prefecture. Once part of the larger Massalit community, the Massalat have diverged from the main group. The two languages are sufficiently different that linguists classify Massalat in a separate subgroup. In addition, the Massalat physically and culturally resemble the Dadjo more closely than they do their relatives to the east.

Runga is spoken over a large part of Salamat Prefecture and in a small part of Central African Republic. Many Runga speakers are farmers who grow millet, sorghum, peanuts, and cotton. In the nineteenth century, the Runga were ruled by sultans from a capital in the Salamat region. Herders of Wadai, the Runga also founded Dar al Kuti, the most important precolonial state in northern Central African Republic. Extensive slave raiding by the Sudanese warlord Rabih Fadlallah in the 1890s decimated the Runga in Chad; as late as the 1960s, they numbered only about 12,000.

Other Mabang languages spoken by much smaller populations include Marfa, Karanga, and Kashméré, found in the highlands north of Abéché; Koniéré, spoken in a small region just east of Abéché; and Bakhat, a language of restricted distribution, found west of Abéché.

Sara-Bongo-Baguirmi Languages

Classified in the Chari-Nile subfamily of the Nilo-Saharan languages, Sara-Bongo-Baguirmi languages are scattered from Lake Chad to the White Nile in southwestern Sudan. Unlike Central Saharan languages, when mapped out they form a patchwork quilt rather than a solid band.

Kouka, Bilala, and Medogo, languages spoken around Lake Fitri in southwestern Batha Prefecture, are the northernmost members of this subgroup. These languages are mutually comprehensible, and the peoples who use them are thought to be descendants of the core ethnic groups of the precolonial sultanate of Yao (a state founded by the Bulala, who ruled a vast region extending as far west as Kanem in the fifteenth century). The Kouka, Bilala, and

A young woman prepares a meal in a village in Chari-Baguirmi
Prefecture
Courtesy Audrey Kizziar

Medogo populations intermarry and share institutions for the mediation of disputes. The groups farm and raise animals, which they sometimes entrust to neighboring Arabs. Their similarities are so striking that they are sometimes classed together as the Lisi.

Barma is spoken in Chari-Baguirmi Prefecture by the Baguirmi, the core population of another precolonial state. Today the Baguirmi are concentrated in and around Massenya, a city southeast of N'Djamena named for their precolonial capital. The Baguirmi identify themselves as either river Barmi or land Barmi. The land Barmi farm millet, sorghum, beans, sesame, peanuts, and cotton. The river Barmi fish along carefully demarcated stretches of the Chari and Bahr Ergig rivers. Arabic loanwords are numerous in Barma, a product of the Baguirmi's adoption of Islam and their interaction with neighboring Arab pastoralists over a long period of time. Long-standing economic ties with the West have also prompted the incorporation of a Kanuri commercial vocabulary.

Kenga, found among the Hajerai in Guéra Prefecture, is closely related to Barma. Although its speakers are said to have played a prominent role in the foundation of the Bagirmi Empire, today they resemble their highland neighbors more closely than their more distant linguistic relatives.

53

Sara languages of southern Chad constitute the quilt's largest patch, stretching from Logone Occidental Prefecture to eastern Moyen-Chari Prefecture. Linguists divide Sara languages into five subgroups. Sara languages seem to have drifted into southern Chad from the northeast. Eventually, Sara speakers left behind the northern languages of the group as they made their way to the richer hunting grounds and agricultural land south of the Chari River. This must have occurred very long ago, however, because the Sara languages and those of the northern members of the group are mutually unintelligible. Moreover, Sara oral traditions record only short-range migrations of Sara speakers in the south, suggesting that movement from the north happened earlier.

Boua

Boua languages are distributed along the middle Chari River in Moyen-Chari Prefecture and in central Guéra Prefecture. Like the Sara, they are divided into five subgroups: Boua proper, Neillim, Tounia, Koke, and Fanian or Mana. Only a few thousand people speak Boua languages, but it is believed that their ancestors preceded Sara-speaking settlers in the Chari Valley. Several centuries ago, all the Boua subgroups may have lived farther north in Guéra Prefecture. Under pressure from slave raiders along the Islamic frontier, some Boua speakers probably migrated southward. Although speakers of Boua proper submitted to neighboring slave raiders from the Bagirmi Empire, they in turn raided their Neillim neighbors to the southeast. Similarly, the Neillim attacked the Tounia to their southeast. The Tounia sought refuge among the Kaba (a Sara subgroup) on the site of the present-day city of Sarh.

Afro-Asiatic Languages

Two major Afro-Asiatic language are represented in Chad. Chadic languages stretch from the western borders of Nigeria to Ouaddaï Prefecture, and Arabic-speaking populations are scattered throughout the Sahel.

Chadic Languages

Most speakers of Chadic languages, including the 20 million speakers of Hausa, the major Chadic language, live west of Chad. The peculiar east-west distribution of Chadic along the southern fringe of the Sahara from western Nigeria to eastern Chad has led some experts to suggest that ancestral Chadic languages were spoken by peoples living along the southern shores of the Paleochadian Sea. The first cluster of languages is closely associated with water— the lake, the delta, the Chari and Logone rivers, and their adjacent floodplains. Water also is important to the economies of most of the populations speaking these languages. In the second cluster, Chadic speakers are descended from refugee populations who perhaps sought shelter in the highlands when the contraction of the sea and the increased aridity of the region allowed the penetration of more aggressive herding populations.

Within Chad, the Chadic languages are distributed in two patterns. The first extends from Lake Chad south along the Chari and Logone rivers to Mayo-Kebbi Prefecture. Individual languages fall into five groups, arrayed from north to southeast.

Buduma-Kouri is spoken by two groups of lake people who intermarry despite some social differences. The Buduma, who believe that they are the original inhabitants of Lake Chad, live on its northern islands and shores. In the past, the Buduma spent much of their time fishing on lake islands. In recent times, however, their economic activities have diversified to include farming and herding. Active in commerce between Chad and Nigeria, the Buduma raise cattle whose very large and hollow horns serve as flotation devices that permit their owners to "herd" them in the lake itself. The lake has long protected the Buduma, allowing them to maintain a separate identity. Despite centuries of contact with Islamic states around the lake, for example, they maintained their own religion until the early twentieth century.

The Kouri, who speak the same language, live on the shores and islands of the southern part of Lake Chad. Devout Muslims, the Kouri believe that they are descendants of Muslim migrants from Yemen and that they are related to the Kanembu, whose medieval empire sponsored the spread of Islam in the region. Kouri economic activities resemble those of the Buduma; however, the absence of polders (see Glossary) along this part of the lakeshore has led the Kouri to confine farming to small plots around their villages. Although they confine their herds to the islands during the dry season, they may entrust them to neighboring Kanembu for pasturing during the rains.

Kotoko is spoken along the lower Chari and Logone rivers by peoples thought to be descendants of the legendary Sao (see Prehistory, ch. 1). Divided into small states with fortified cities as their capitals, the Kotoko consider themselves "owners of the land" by virtue of their long residence, and other peoples in the region recognize this claim. For example, neighboring Arabs pay tribute for the right to farm and herd. The Kotoko also have a monopoly over fishing and water transport. Rights to the waters of the Logone and Chari rivers are divided among the cities, each of which has a "chief of the waters," whose communications with the water spirits determine the opening of the fishing season. Non-Kotoko must pay for the right to fish. Outnumbered in their own lands by Bororo and Arab herders, only about 7,000 Kotoko lived in Chad in the late 1960s; three times as many lived across the Logone in Cameroon. Strife in Chad—particularly the troubles in N'Djamena in 1979 and 1980—probably has accelerated the emigration of the Kotoko from Chad.

Massa languages, including Massa, Moussey, Marba, and Dari, are centered in southern Chari-Baguirmi and Mayo-Kebbi prefectures. The Massa proper farm, herd, and fish in floodplains of the middle Chari. Repeatedly through their history, the Massa suffered raids from their Muslim neighbors—the Kanuri of the Borno Empire, the Barmi of the Bagirmi Empire, and the Fulani of Cameroon. The Massa survived these military onslaughts, in part because their villages, which crown the hills in the Chari floodplain, afforded protection for much of the year. Having survived these threats, in recent years the Massa ironically have adopted Muslim dress and have superimposed some features of Fulani political structure on their local "chiefs of the lands." The other speakers of Massa languages resemble the Massa proper. Estimated to number 120,000 in the late 1970s, the largest group among them is the Moussey, who live in and around Gounou Gaya in Mayo-Kebbi Prefecture.

The last cluster of Chadic languages in this first distribution encompasses Nachéré, Lélé, Gablai, and Guidar spoken primarily in Tandjilé Prefecture and with outlying languages that include Gabri (in Tandjilé Prefecture) and Toumak, Somrai, Ndam, Miltou, and Saraoua (in Moyen-Chari Prefecture). This cluster of languages forms a transition zone between the Massa and the Sara languages. The numbers of speakers of these languages are small, probably because their peoples have been absorbed by more numerous neighbors through intermarriage or emigration.

The second Chadic language distribution comprises two clusters. The first brings together the languages spoken by the Hajerai, the mountain peoples of Guéra Prefecture. These peoples are descended from refugees from the surrounding plains who sought shelter in the mountains when invaded by raiders from neighboring centralized states. Despite the presence of non-Chadic languages (such as Kenga, which is part of the Sara-Bongo-Baguirmi group), most Hajerai speak Chadic languages, such as Djongor, Dangaleat, Bidyo, Mogoum, Sokoro, Barain, and Saba. The Hajerai groups share important religious institutions, such as the *margai* cult of place spirits; at the same time, they maintain separate identities and refuse to intermarry (see Classical African Religions, this ch.). All have traditions of fierce independence. The Hajerai were among the earliest supporters of rebellion against the Chadian national government in the 1960s.

Moubi languages of Ouaddaï Prèfecture make up the second cluster of this second distribution of Chadic languages. The Moubi are a sedentary people who live south of the Massalit. They grow millet, sorghum, sesame, beans, cotton, and peanuts. In recent years, they have also adopted cattle herding, a practice borrowed from the Missiriye Arab herders who regularly cross their lands and with whom the Moubi have long exchanged goods and services. Like the Hajerai, the Moubi have resisted the government since shortly after independence.

Arabic

There are about thirty different dialects of Arabic in Chad. The Arabs divide themselves into three major "tribes": the Juhayna, the Hassuna, and the Awlad Sulayman. In this context, tribe refers to a group claiming descent from a common ancestor. The Juhayna, who began arriving from Sudan in the fourteenth century, are by far the most important. The Hassuna, who migrated to Chad from Libya, live in Kanem Prefecture. The Awlad Sulayman also hail from Libya, but they arrived in the nineteenth century, well after the others. Most of the Arabs are herders or farmers.

Among Arabic herdsmen, life-styles vary considerably. The different needs of camels, cattle, goats, and sheep result in different patterns of settlement and movement. In addition to herding, many Arabic speakers earn their livelihoods as small and middle-level merchants. In N'Djamena and in towns such as Sarh and Moundou, Arabic speakers dominated local commerce up until the 1970s; however, because of the anti-Muslim violence in the south in the late 1970s, many moved to central or nothern Chad.

Despite the diversity of dialects and the scattered distribution of Arabic-speaking populations, the language has had a major impact on Chad. In the Sahel, Arab herdsmen and their wives frequent local markets to exchange their animals, butter, and milk for agricultural products, cloth, and crafts. Itinerant Arab traders and settled merchants in the towns play major roles in local and regional economies. As a result, Chadian Arabic (or Turku) has became a lingua franca, or trade language. Arabic also has been important because it is the language of Islam and of the Quran, its holy book. Quranic education has stimulated the spread of the language and enhanced its stature among the non-Arab Muslims of Chad.

Not all Arabic speakers are of Arab descent. The assimilation of local peoples (both free and slave) into Arabic groups has affected both the dialects and the customs of Arabic speakers in Chad. Non-Arabs also have adopted the language. To cite two examples, the Yalna and the Bandala are of Hajerai and Ouaddaïan origin, respectively, and were probably originally slaves who adopted the Arabic language of their masters. Among the Runga, who were not slaves, Arabic is also widely spoken.

Congo-Kordofanian Languages

Moundang-Toupouri-Mboum

Classified as belonging to the Niger-Congo subfamily of the Congo-Kordofanian family, languages in the Moundang-Toupouri-Mboum groups are spoken by a variety of populations in Mayo-Kebbi and Logone Oriental prefectures. These languages may be divided into seven subgroups: Moundang, Toupouri, Mboum/Laka, Kera, Mongbai, Kim, and Mesme. Speakers of Moundang, Toupouri, and Mboum/Laka are by far the most numerous of this group. Despite belonging to the same language group, these three populations have very different social structures, life-styles, and myths of origin.

Moundang is spoken by more than 100,000 people in Mayo-Kebbi Prefecture; numerous Moundang speakers also live in Cameroon. The Moundang people raise millet for food and cotton for sale. They also own cattle, which are used for marriage payments, religious sacrifices, and payment of fines. Bororo herders live in the same region and often take care of Moundang livestock.

On the broadest level, the Moundang still belong to a kingdom founded two centuries ago. Although the French colonial administration and the independent Chadian governments undermined the military power of the *gon lere* (king), he continued to wield influence in the 1980s from his capital at Léré. On a smaller scale, clan institutions remain important. Associated with particular territories, taboos, totem animals, and marriage rules, clan government, which predates the kingdom, is much less centralized. In some respects, the two sets of institutions act as checks on each other. For example, the clans allow the king to organize manhood initiation ceremonies, central to the maintenance of Moundang identity; however, the councils of elders of each clan may offer advice to the ruler.

In the nineteenth century, the Moundang suffered frequent attacks by Fulani invaders from the west. They were never subjugated, but the close contact has resulted in the adoption of Fulani principles of political organization and dress.

Mboum/Laka speakers live in southern Logone Oriental Prefecture. About 100,000 Mboum/Laka speakers lived in Chad in the 1980s; a larger population lived across the border in Cameroon and Central African Republic. Sedentary farmers, the Mboum and the Laka probably were pushed east and south by the expansion of the Fulani over the past two centuries.

The Toupouri language and people are found in Mayo-Kebbi Prefecture around the town of Fianga. Almost all of their land is cultivated, and productivity is enhanced by the use of animal fertilizer and double cropping. During the rainy season, the Toupouri raise sorghum. *Berebere,* a kind of millet, is grown in the drier part of the year. Cattle and fish provide additional food resources. Numbering about 100,000, the Toupouri live in the most densely populated part of Chad; some cantons reach densities of twelve people per square kilometer. Overcrowding has promoted emigration, primarily to N'Djamena and Nigeria.

Fulani

Fulani speakers are not very numerous in Chad. Part of the West Atlantic subfamily of the Congo-Kordofanian family of languages, Fulani (called Peul by the French) first appeared in the Senegal River Valley in West Africa. Population growth and the vagaries of climate encouraged the eastward drift of Fulani-speaking herders through the Sahel. Some Fulani speakers adopted Islam and became very important actors in the spread of the religion and the rise of Muslim states west of Chad. Many of these people settled, taking up village or urban life and abandoning nomadism. Other Fulani speakers, however, remained loyal to their pre-Islamic faith and their nomadic life-style.

Fulani speakers arrived in Chad only in the past two centuries. In the mid-1960s, about 32,000 Fulani lived in Kanem, southern Batha, and northern Chari-Baguirmi prefectures, where they raised mainly cattle and sheep. Many of the Fulani are fervent Muslims, and some are teachers of the Quran.

Related to the Fulani ethnically and linguistically—but refusing contact—are the nomadic Bororo of western Chad. In the dry season, the Bororo pasture their animals around wells and pools in northern Mayo-Kebbi Prefecture near Bongor. After the first major rains, they leave for Kanem Prefecture, north of Lake Chad.

Banda-Ngbaka

Also members of the Niger-Congo subfamily of the Congo-

Kordofanian languages, Banda-Ngbaka languages are located in Guéra, Salamat, and Moyen-Chari prefectures. Subgroups include Sango, Bolgo, Goula, and Goula Iro. Although not spoken as a first language in Chad, Sango has been particularly important because it served as a trade language during the colonial era. Although most Banda-Ngbaka languages are found farther south in Central African Republic, the presence of these subgroups in Chad suggests that Banda-Ngbaka speakers were once much more numerous in Chad. Bolgo, found with Hajerai and Goula languages in the vicinity of Lake Iro and Lake Mamoun, is spoken by refugee populations. Populations speaking these languages are very diverse. Although the Goula speak a Banda-Ngbaka language, for example, their culture resembles that of the Sara.

Social Structure

The variety and number of languages in Chad are mirrored by the country's diversity of social structures. The colonial administration and independent governments have attempted to impose a "national" society on the citizenry, but for most Chadians the local or regional society remains the most important reference point outside the immediate family.

This diversity of social structure has several dimensions. For example, some social structures are small in scale, while others are huge. Among the Toubou and the Daza, some clans group only a hundred individuals. At the other extreme are the kingdoms and sultanates—found among the peoples of Ouaddaï Prefecture, the Moundang of Mayo-Kebbi Prefecture, the Barmi of Chari-Baguirmi Prefecture, and the Kanembu of Kanem Prefecture, among others—which bring together thousands or even tens of thousands of people. Although these social units have enjoyed only limited formal legal recognition since the colonial epoch, they remain important institutions whose authority is recognized by their people.

Chadian social structures also differ in the way they locate people in their physical environment. Despite a sense of territory, even among such highly mobile peoples as the Toubou and Daza, the bond between an individual clan and its land is less specific than the link between the inhabitants of a densely settled farming village and its fields.

Diverse social structures foster variety in the relationships among members of a group and between people and their territory. Whereas a Toubou or a Daza is aware of her or his clan identity, she or he often lives as an individual among people of other clans. Among seminomadic Arabs of the Sahel, people identify most closely with the *kashimbet,* or "threshold of the house," a residential unit made up of an elder male or group of males, their wives, and descendants. Although the *kashimbet* does not preclude mobility, people reside most of the time with their kin.

These three diversities—scale, relationships with the environment, and social links among group members—are highly conditioned by the environment and the way the society exploits it. Accordingly, the three major patterns of social structure correspond closely with the three major geographical regions of the country (see Physical Setting, this ch.).

The remainder of this section examines a representative society from each region: the Toubou and Daza nomads of the Sahara, the Arab semisedentary herders of the *sahelian* zone, and the Sara farmers of the *soudanian* region.

Toubou and Daza: Nomads of the Sahara

Toubou and Daza life centers on their livestock (their major source of wealth and sustenance) and on the scattered oases where they or their herders cultivate dates and grain. In a few places, the Toubou and Daza (or more often members of the Haddad group who work for them) also mine salt and natron, a salt like substance used for medicinal purposes and for livestock (see Mining, ch. 3).

The Toubou family is made up of parents, children, and another relative or two. Although the husband or father is the head of the household, he rarely makes decisions without consulting his wife. When he is absent, his wife often takes complete charge, moving family tents, changing pastures, and buying and selling cattle. Although Toubou men may have several wives, few do. Families gather in larger camps during the months of transhumance. Camp membership is fluid, sometimes changing during the season and almost never remaining the same from one season to the next.

After the family, the clan is the most stable Toubou institution. Individuals identify with their clan, which has a reputed founder, a name, a symbol, and associated taboos. Clans enjoy collective priority use of certain palm groves, cultivable land, springs, and pastures; outsiders may not use these resources without clan permission. Social relations are based on reciprocity, hospitality, and assistance. Theft and murder within the clan are forbidden, and stolen animals must be returned.

Within the overall context of clan identity, however, Toubou and Daza society is shaped by the individual. Jean Chapelle, a well-known observer of Chadian societies, notes that "it is not society that forms the individual, but the individual who constructs the society most useful" for him or her. Three features of Toubou social structure make this process possible. The first is residence. In general, clan members are scattered throughout a region; therefore, an individual is likely to find hospitable clans people in most settlements or camps of any size. A second factor is the maintenance of ties with the maternal clan. Although the maternal clan does not occupy the central place of the paternal clan, it provides another universe of potential ties.

Marriage creates a third set of individual options. Although relatives and the immediate family influence decisions about a marriage partner, individual preference is recognized as important. In addition, once a marriage is contracted between individuals of two clans, other clan members are forbidden to change it. The Toubou proscribe marriage with any blood relative less than four generations removed—in the words of the Toubou recorded by Chapelle, "when there are only three grandfathers."

The ownership of land, animals, and resources takes several forms. Within an oasis or settled zone belonging to a particular clan, land, trees (usually date palms), and nearby wells may have different owners. Each family's rights to the use of particular plots of land are recognized by other clan members. Families also may have privileged access to certain wells and the right to a part of the harvest from the fields irrigated by their water. Within the clan and family contexts, individuals also may have personal claims to palm trees and animals. Toubou legal customs are based on restitution, indemnification, and revenge. Conflicts are resolved in several settings. Murder, for example, is settled directly between the families of the victim and the murderer. Toubou honor requires that someone from the victim's family try to kill the murderer or a relative; such efforts eventually end with negotiations to settle the matter. Reconciliation follows the payment of the *goroga,* or blood price, usually in the form of camels.

Despite shared linguistic heritage, few institutions among the Toubou and the Daza generate a broader sense of identity than the clan. Regional divisions do exist, however. Among the Toubou, there are four such subgroups, the Teda of Tibesti Subprefecture being the largest. There are more than a dozen subgroups of Daza: the Kreda of Bahr el Ghazal are the largest; next in importance are the Daza of Kanem Prefecture. During the colonial period (and since independence), Chadian administrations have conferred legality and legitimacy on these regional groupings by dividing the Toubou and Daza regions into corresponding territorial units called cantons and appointing chiefs to administer them (see Regional Government, ch. 4).

Only among the Toubou of the Tibesti region have institutions evolved somewhat differently. Since the end of the sixteenth century, the *derde* (spiritual head) of the Tomagra clan has exercised authority over part of the massif and the other clans who live there. He is selected by a group of electors according to strict rules. The *derde* exercises judicial rather than executive power, arbitrating conflict and levying sanctions based on a code of compensations.

Since the beginning of the civil conflict in Chad, the *derde* has come to occupy a more important position. In 1965 the Chadian government assumed direct authority over the Tibesti Mountains, sending a military garrison and administrators to Bardaï, the capital of Tibesti Subprefecture. Within a year, abuses of authority had roused considerable opposition among the Toubou (see Tombalbaye's Governance: Policies and Methods, ch. 1). The *derde*, Oueddei Kichidemi, recognized but little respected up to that time, protested the excesses, went into exile in Libya, and, with the support of Toubou students at the Islamic University of Al Bayda, became a symbol of opposition to the Chadian government. This role enhanced the position of the *derde* among the Toubou. After 1967 the *derde* hoped to rally the Toubou to the National Liberation Front of Chad (Front de Libération Nationale du Tchad—FROLINAT). Moral authority became military authority shortly thereafter when his son, Goukouni Oueddei, became one of the leaders of the Second Liberation Army of FROLINAT. Goukouni has since become a national figure; he played an important role in the battles of N'Djamena in 1979 and 1980 and served as head of state for a time. Another northerner, Hissein Habré of the Daza Annakaza, replaced Goukouni in 1982.

Arabs: Semisedentary Peoples of the Sahel

The Arabs of Chad are semisedentary (or seminomadic) peoples who herd their camels, horses, cattle, goats, and sheep on the plains of the Sahel. Except in the extreme north, they live among sedentary peoples, and in the region around N'Djamena some Arabs have adopted a more settled existence. In the rainy season, Arab groups spread out through the region; in the dry season, they live a more settled existence, usually on the dormant agricultural lands of their sedentary neighbors. They leave the far north to the Toubou, avoid the mountains of Ouaddaï and Guéra prefectures, and move south of 10° north latitude only in times of extreme drought.

The Arabs were not state builders in Chad, a role played instead by the Maba in Wadai, the Barma in Bagirmi, and the Kanembu in Kanem-Borno (see Era of Empires, A.D. 900–1900, ch. 1). The

Arabs exercised great influence over all three empires, however, either by conquest (in the case of Wadai) or by converting their rulers to Islam (in the cases of Bagirmi and Kanem). As with nomads and seminomads elsewhere, the possession of camels and horses translated into military potential that commanded the respect of the settled states. For example, the Awlad Sulayman of Kanem, despite their small numbers, gained fame and fortune during the second half of the nineteenth century by playing the increasingly aggressive empire of Wadai against weaker Kanem-Borno. In the decade after 1900, they used the same tactic to enhance and enrich themselves at the expense of the French and the Sanusiyya, a Muslim religious order of Libyan origin with political and economic interests in the Lake Chad Basin.

Chadian Arabs are divided into three "tribes": the Juhayna, the Hassuna, and the Awlad Sulayman. Members of each tribe believe themselves to be descended from a common ancestor. Among the smaller social units, belief in a shared genealogy (rather than common residence or a common faith) provides a major ideological rationale for joint action.

As is true for the Toubou, the basic Arab social unit is the *kashimbet*, a minimal lineage made up of several generations of men, their wives, and children or grandchildren reckoned through the male line. Members of the same *kashimbet* live near each other and more or less follow the same route during migration. Each *kashimbet* is headed by an elder male, or shaykh. This aspect of the social structure is visible in the disposition of tents (or houses among the more sedentary Arabs of N'Djamena). The residence of the shaykh is often at the center of the camp or settlement, with the woven straw tents or adobe houses of his relatives arrayed around it in concentric circles. The area is surrounded by a fence or some other boundary that defines the *zariba*, or walled camp. Within the *kashimbet*, loyalty is generally intense, institutionalized relationships being reinforced by bonds of common residence and personal acquaintance.

Kinship bonds also provide the ideological basis for broader units. Led by the head of the senior lineage, who is more a "first among equals" than a chief, the shaykhs of neighboring *kashimbets* sometimes meet to decide matters of common interest, such as the date of the annual migration. The shaykhs' leader, or *lawan*, may also deal with outsiders on their behalf. He concludes contracts with farmers to allow Arabs to pass the dry season on agricultural lands and levies tribute on strangers who wish to use the group's pastures and wells.

Unlike what is found in Toubou society, marriage among the Arabs strengthens kinship ties. First, marriage is more a family than an individual concern; senior males from each family make initial contacts and eventually negotiate the marriage contract. An ideal union reinforces the social, moral, and material position of the group. Second, parallel cousin marriage (that is, union between the children of brothers or male relatives more removed), is preferred. This custom encourages the duplication of bonds within the group rather than the creation of a far-flung network of more tenuous, individual alliances, as occurs among the Toubou. Finally, the marriage ceremony is itself a community affair. Among the Toubou, marriage is associated with the feigned "stealing" of the bride from her family, whose members respond with grief and anger, but marriage among the Arabs is an expression of solidarity. The ceremony is celebrated by a *faqih* (Muslim religious leader), and a joyous procession of neighbors, relatives, and friends escorts the bride to the house of her husband.

Despite their wide distribution and numerous contacts with sedentary peoples, Arabs have never played a preponderant role in Chadian affairs. During the colonial period, they resisted the French, who attempted to impose a territorially defined administration but who ultimately governed through the Arabs' kin-based social structures. This inability of the colonial authorities to penetrate and change Arab social and political institutions allowed the Arabs to resist Western education and employment in the emerging capitalist economy. Their pastoral life-style also saved them from the forced cultivation of commercial crops that so disrupted the societies of their sedentary neighbors.

Since independence the Arabs have remained on the margins of Chadian national life. The government, dominated by southerners, suspected the Arabs of a major role in the civil strife of the late 1960s. In the Sahel, however, settled non-Arab peoples (such as the Moubi and Hajerai of Guéra Prefecture) have played a much more important role in resisting central power. Although it is true that the Arabs have opposed the government at times, they also have rallied to it. Such a pattern suggests that the Arabs have followed their time-honored prescription of keeping the state off balance to ensure maximum freedom of action.

Sara: Sedentary Peoples of the Soudanian Zone

The essential social unit of Sara society is the lineage. Called the *qir ka* among the eastern Sara, *qin ka* among those of the center, and *qel ka* among the western subgroups, the term actually refers to the male ancestor from whom members of the lineage believe they descend. Within the context of the *qir ka,* an individual identifies patrilineally. Legal identity and rights to land are determined by membership in the patrilineage. The mother's lineage, however, is not disregarded; it may offer shelter and support, when the individual is cut off from the paternal lineage, or benefit from certain kinds of labor obligations.

Although the basic social group is the lineage, the basic residential unit is the village. In general, local government takes two forms. If the villagers all belong to the same lineage, the village is governed by lineage institutions whereby the elders make important decisions, preside over important cultural rites (such as manhood initiation), and play an important role in agricultural rituals. If villagers are divided among several lineages, however, elders from the different groups may meet together to resolve common problems. In such encounters, elders of the lineage that first settled the territory preside as "first among equals."

During the colonial era, the French superimposed a territorially based administration over precolonial Sara social and political institutions. On the local level, this took the form of the canton (or county). The canton was headed by a chief named by the central government, who in turn named "village chiefs." Although candidates for such positions existed among the traditional Sara authorities, the French generally preferred to appoint collaborators who had no independent base of support. Apart from creating new political structures, the French also sought to reorganize Sara society spatially. They forced people to regroup in more compact villages along roads, causing lineages to abandon traditional lands. Despite considerable initial resistance, the colonial administration eventually succeeded in imposing these new settlement patterns and new chiefs, thus undermining Sara political and social structures. Since independence, efforts by the Chadian government to centralize authority have continued. Nonetheless, Sara institutions have retained influence, and the Sara have added new structures to reinforce Sara solidarity.

Religion

The separation of religion from social structure in Chad represents a false dichotomy, for they are perceived as two sides of the same coin. Three religious traditions coexist in Chad—classical African religions, Islam, and Christianity. None is monolithic. The first tradition includes a variety of ancestor and/or place-oriented religions whose expression is highly specific. Islam, although characterized by an orthodox set of beliefs and observances, also is expressed in diverse ways. Christianity arrived in Chad much more recently with the arrival of Europeans. Its followers are divided into Roman Catholics and Protestants (including several denominations); as with Chadian Islam, Chadian Christianity retains aspects of pre-Christian religious belief.

The number of followers of each tradition in Chad is unknown. Estimates made in 1962 suggested that 35 percent of Chadians practiced classical African religions, 55 percent were Muslims, and 10 percent were Christians. In the 1970s and 1980s, this distribution undoubtedly changed. Observers report that Islam has spread among the Hajerai and among other non-Muslim populations of the Saharan and *sahelian* zones. However, the proportion of Muslims may have fallen because the birthrate among the followers of classical religions and Christians in southern Chad is thought to be higher than that among Muslims. In addition, the upheavals since the mid-1970s have resulted in the departure of some missionaries; whether or not Chadian Christians have been numerous enough and organized enough to have attracted more converts since that time is unknown.

Classical African Religions

Classical African religions regard the world as a product of a complex system of relationships among people, living and dead, and animals, plants, and natural and supernatural phenomena. This religious tradition is often called "animism" because of its central premise that all things are "animated" by life forces. The relationships among all things are ordered and often hierarchical. Human societies reflect this order, and human survival and success require that it be maintained. Antisocial acts or bad luck signal that this harmony has been upset, leading to efforts to restore it through ritual acts, such as prayers, sacrifices, libations, communions, dances, and symbolic struggles. Such intervention, it is believed, helps ward off the chaos that adversely affects people and their souls, families and communities, and crops and harvests.

Ancestors play an important role in Chadian classical religions. They are thought to span the gap between the supernatural and natural worlds. They connect these two worlds specifically by linking living lineage members with their earliest forebears. Because of their proximity, and because they once walked among the living, ancestors are prone to intervene in daily affairs. This intervention is particularly likely in the case of the recently deceased, who are thought to spend weeks or months in limbo between the living and the dead. Many religious observances include special rituals to propitiate these spirits, encourage them to take their leave with serenity, and restore the social order their deaths have disrupted.

Spirits are also numerous. These invisible beings inhabit a parallel world and sometimes reside in particular places or are associated with particular natural phenomena. Among the Mbaye, a Sara subgroup, water and lightning spirits are thought to bring violent death and influence other spirits to intervene in daily life. The sun spirit, capable of rendering service or causing harm, also must be propitiated. Spirits may live in family groups with spouses and children. They are also capable of taking human, animal, or plant forms when they appear among the living.

The supernatural powers that control natural events are also of major concern. Among farming peoples, rituals to propitiate such powers are associated with the beginning and end of the agricultural cycle. Among the Sara, the new year begins with the appearance of the first new moon following the harvest. The next day, people hunt with nets and fire, offering the catch to ancestors. Libations are offered to ancestors, and the first meal from the new harvest is consumed.

Among the more centralized societies of Chad, the ruler frequently is associated with divine power. Poised at the apex of society, he or (more rarely) she is responsible for good relations with the supernatural forces that sanction and maintain the social order. For example, among the Moundang, the *gon lere* of Léré is responsible for relations with the sky spirits. And among the Sara Madjingay, the *mbang* (chief) of the village of Bédaya controls religious rituals that preserve and renew the social order. Even after the coming of Islam, the symbols of such authority reinforced the rulers of nominally Islamic states such as Wadai, Kanem-Borno, and Bagirmi.

Finally, most classical African religions involve belief in a supreme being who created the world and its inhabitants but who then retired from active intervention in human affairs. As a result, shrines to a high god are uncommon, and people tend to appeal to the lesser spirits; yet the notion of a supreme being may have helped the spread of Christianity. When missionaries arrived in southern Chad, they often used the local name of this high god to refer to the Christian supreme being. Thus, although a much more interventionist spirit, the Christian god was recognizable to the people. This recognition probably facilitated conversion, but it may also have ironically encouraged syncretism (the mixing of religious traditions), a practice disturbing to many missionaries and to Protestants in particular. Followers of classical African religions would probably not perceive any necessary contradiction between accepting the Christian god and continuing to believe in the spirits just described.

Because order is thought to be the natural, desirable state, disorder is not happenstance. Classical African religions devote considerable energy to the maintenance of order and the determination of who or what is responsible for disorder. In the case of illness, for example, it is of the greatest importance to ascertain which spirit or which person is responsible for undermining the natural order; only then is it possible to prescribe a remedy. In such circumstances, people frequently take their cases to ritual specialists, who divine the threats to harmony and recommend appropriate action. Such specialists share their knowledge only with peers. Indeed, they themselves have probably acquired such knowledge incrementally as they made their way through elaborate apprenticeships.

Although classical African religions provide institutionalized ways of maintaining or restoring community solidarity, they also allow individuals to influence the cosmic order to advance their own interests. Magic and sorcery both serve this end. From society's standpoint, magic is positive or neutral. On the one hand, magicians try to influence life forces to alter the physical world, perhaps to bring good fortune or a return to health. Sorcerers, on the other hand, are antisocial, using sorcery (or "black magic") to control or consume the vital force of others. Unlike magicians, whose identity is generally known, sorcerers hide their supernatural powers, practicing their nefarious rites in secret. When misfortune occurs, people often suspect that sorcery is at the root of their troubles. They seek counsel from diviners or magicians to identify the responsible party and ways to rectify the situation; if the disruption is deemed to threaten everyone, leaders may act on behalf of the community at large. If discovered, sorcerers are punished.

The survival of any society requires that knowledge be passed from one generation to another. In many Chadian societies, this transmission is marked by ritual. Knowledge of the world and its forces is limited to adults; among the predominantly patrilineal societies of Chad, it is further limited to men in particular. Rituals often mark the transition from childhood to adulthood. However, they actively "transform" children into adults, teaching them what adults must know to assume societal responsibilities.

Although such rites differ among societies, the Sara *yondo* may serve as a model of male initiation ceremonies found in Chad. The *yondo* takes place at a limited number of sites every six or seven years. Boys from different villages, usually accompanied by an elder, gather for the rites, which, before the advent of Western education with its nine-month academic calendar, lasted several months. In recent decades, the *yondo* has been limited to several weeks between academic years.

The *yondo* and its counterparts among other Chadian societies reinforce male bonds and male authority. Women are not allowed to witness the rite. Their initiated sons and brothers no longer eat with them and go to live in separate houses. Although rites also mark the transition to womanhood in many Chadian societies, such ceremonies are much shorter. Rather than encouraging girls to participate in the larger society, they stress household responsibilities and deference to male authority.

Islam

Tenets of Islam

"Islam" means submission to the will of God, and a Muslim is one who submits. In A.D. 610, Muhammad, an Arabian merchant of Mecca, revealed the first in a series of revelations granted him by God (Allah, in Arabic) through the archangel Gabriel. Later known simply as the Prophet, Muhammad denounced the polytheism of his fellow Meccans and preached a new order that would reinforce community solidarity. His censure of the emerging individualistic, mercantile society in Mecca eventually provoked a split in the community. In A.D. 622, Muhammad and his followers fled northwest to Yathrib, a settlement that has since come to be known simply as Medina, or "the city." This journey (called the *hijra*, or the flight) marks the beginning of the Islamic Era. The Muslim lunar calendar begins with this event, so that its year 1 corresponds to A.D. 622. (However, the solar and Muslim calendars are separated by more than 622 years; a lunar year has an average of 354 days and thus is considerably shorter than the 365-day solar year.) In Medina, the Prophet continued his preaching. Eventually defeating his detractors in battle, Muhammad became the temporal and spiritual leader of most of Arabia by the time of his death in A.D. 632.

In the decades after his death, Muhammad's followers collected his revelations into a single book of recitations called the Quran. During the same period, some of his close associates collected and codified the Prophet's sayings, as well as accounts of his behavior, to serve as guides for future generations. These compilations are called the *hadith*, or "sayings," which, along with the Quran, are central to Islamic jurisprudence.

The *shahada* (or profession of faith) states the central belief of Islam: "There is no god but God (Allah), and Muhammad is his Prophet." This simple testimony is repeated on many ritual occasions. When recited with conviction, it signals conversion.

Muslim children at a Quranic school
Courtesy United Nations

The duties of a Muslim form the five pillars of the faith. These are recitation of the *shahada,* daily prayer (*salat*), almsgiving (*zakat*), fasting (*sawm*), and, if possible, making the pilgrimage to Mecca (*hajj*).

Islam in Chad

Islam became a dynamic political and military force in the Middle East in the decades immediately following Muhammad's death. By the late seventh century A.D., Muslim conquerors had reached North Africa and moved south into the desert. Although it is difficult to date the arrival and spread of Islam in Chad, by the time Arab migrants began arriving from the east in the fourteenth century, the faith was already widespread. Instead of being the product of conquest or the imposition of political power, Islamization in Chad was gradual, the effect of the slow spread of Islamic civilization beyond its political frontiers.

Islam in Chad has adapted to its local context in many ways. For one thing, despite the presence of a large number of Arabs, Arabic is not the maternal language of the majority of Chadian Muslims. As a result, although many Chadian Muslims have attended Quranic schools, they often have learned to recite Quranic verses without understanding their meaning. Hence, perhaps even more than among those who understand Arabic, the recitation of

71

verse has taken on a mystical character among Chadian Muslims. Islam in Chad also is syncretic. Chadian Muslims have retained and combined pre-Islamic with Islamic rituals and beliefs. Moreover, Islam in Chad was not particularly influenced by the great mystical movements of the Islamic Middle Ages or the fundamentalist upheavals that affected the faith in the Middle East, West Africa, and Sudan. Beginning in the Middle East in the thirteenth century, Muslim mystics sought to complement the intellectual comprehension of Islam with direct religious experience through prayer, contemplation, and action. The followers of these mystics founded brotherhoods (*turuq*; sing., *tariqa*), which institutionalized their teachers' interpretations of the faith. Such organizations stimulated the spread of Islam and also provided opportunities for joint action, for the most part, which was not the case in Chad, where only two brotherhoods exist. Perhaps as a result of prolonged contact with West African Muslim traders and pilgrims, most Chadian Muslims identify with the Tijaniyya order, but the brotherhood has not served as a rallying point for unified action. Similarly, the Sanusiyya, a brotherhood founded in Libya in the mid-nineteenth century, enjoyed substantial economic and political influence in the Lake Chad Basin around 1900. Despite French fears of an Islamic revival movement led by "Sanusi fanatics," Chadian adherents, limited to the Awlad Sulayman Arabs and the Toubou of eastern Tibesti, have never been numerous.

Chapelle writes that even though Chadian Islam adheres to the Maliki legal school (which, like the other three accepted schools of Islamic jurisprudence, is based on an extensive legal literature), most Islamic education relies solely on the Quran. Higher Islamic education in Chad is all but nonexistent; thus, serious Islamic students and scholars must go abroad. Popular destinations include Khartoum and Cairo, where numerous Chadians attend Al Azhar, the most renowned university in the Islamic world.

Chadian observance of the five pillars of the faith differs somewhat from the orthodox tradition. For example, public and communal prayer occurs more often than the prescribed one time each week but often does not take place in a mosque. Moreover, Chadian Muslims probably make the pilgrimage less often than, for example, their Hausa counterparts in northern Nigeria. As for the Ramadan fast, the most fervent Muslims in Chad refuse to swallow their saliva during the day, a particularly stern interpretation of the injunction against eating or drinking between sunrise and sunset.

Finally, Chadian Islam is not particularly militant. Even if young Muslims in urban areas are aware of happenings in other parts of the Islamic world, they have not responded to fundamentalist appeals.

Christianity

Christianity arrived in Chad in the twentieth century, shortly after the colonial conquest. Contrary to the dominant pattern in some other parts of Africa, however, where the colonial powers encouraged the spread of the faith, the earliest French officials in Chad advised against it. This recommendation, however, probably reflected European paternalism and favoritism toward Islam rather than a display of liberalism. In any case, the French military administration followed such counsel for the first two decades of the century, the time it took to conquer the new colony and establish control over its people. Following World War I, however, official opposition to Christianity softened, and the government tolerated but did not sponsor missionaries.

Since World War II, Chadian Christians have had a far greater influence on Chadian life than their limited numbers suggest. The missions spread the ideology of Westernization—the notion that progress depended on following European models of development. Even more specifically, Roman Catholic mission education spread the French language. Ironically, even though Islam spread more quickly and more widely than Christianity, Christians controlled the government that inherited power from the French. These leaders imparted a Western orientation that continued to dominate in the 1980s.

Protestantism in Chad

The Protestants came to southern Chad in the 1920s. American Baptists were the first, but missionaries of other denominations and nationalities soon followed. Many of the American missions were northern offshoots of missionary networks founded farther south in the Ubangi-Chari colony (now Central African Republic) of French Equatorial Africa (Afrique Equatoriale Française—AEF; ses Glossary). The organizational ties between the missions in southern Chad and Ubangi-Chari were strengthened by France's decision in 1925 to transfer Logone Occidental, Tandjilé, Logone Oriental, and Moyen-Chari prefectures to Ubangi-Chari, where they remained until another administrative shuffle restored them to Chad in 1932.

These early Protestant establishments looked to their own churches for material resources and to their own countries for diplomatic support. Such independence allowed them to maintain a distance from the French colonial administration. In addition, the missionaries arrived with their wives and children, and they often spent their entire lives in the region. This family-based expansion of the missionary networks was not peculiar to Chad in the 1920s. Some of the missionaries who arrived at that time had grown up with missionary parents in missions founded earlier in the French colonies to the south. Some missionary children from this era later founded missions of their own. Many remained after independence, leaving only in the early and or mid-1970s when Tombalbaye's *authenticité* movement forced their departure (see Fall of the Tombalbaye Government, ch. 1).

The puritanical message preached by many Protestant missionaries undermined the appeal of the faith. Rather than allowing a local Christian tradition to develop, the missionaries preached a fundamentalist doctrine native to parts of the United States. They inveighed against dancing, alcohol, and local customs, which they considered "superstitions." New converts found it almost impossible to observe Protestant teachings and remain within their communities. In the early years, Chadian Protestants often left their villages and settled around the missions. But abandoning village and family was a sacrifice that most people were reluctant to make.

Although language and doctrine probably discouraged conversion, the educational and medical projects of the Protestant missions probably attracted people. The missionaries set up schools, clinics, and hospitals long before the colonial administration did. In fact, the mission schools produced the first Western-educated Chadians in the 1940s and 1950s. In general, the Protestant missionary effort in southern Chad has enjoyed some success. In 1980, after a half-century of evangelization, Protestants in southern Chad numbered about 80,000.

From bases in the south, Protestants founded missions in other parts of Chad. For the most part, they avoided settling among Muslims, who were not responsive to their message. In the colonial capital of Fort-Lamy (present-day N'Djamena), the missions attracted followers among resident southerners. The missionaries also proselytized among the non-Muslim populations of Guéra, Ouaddaï, and Biltine prefectures. Although Christianity appealed to some in the capital (there were estimated to be 18,000 Christians in N'Djamena in 1980), efforts in other parts of the Sahel were relatively unsuccessful.

In the late 1980s, the future of the Protestant missions in Chad remained unclear. As noted, many Protestant missionaries were forced to leave the country during the cultural revolution in the early and mid-1970s. Outside the south, other missions have been caught in the cross fire of warring factions. Rebel forces have

*The Roman Catholic cathedral in N'Djamena, which was rebuilt in the
1980s following severe war damage
Courtesy Audrey Kizziar*

pillaged mission stations, and the government has accused the missionaries of complicity with the opposition.

Roman Catholicism in Chad

The Roman Catholic missions came to Chad later than their Protestant counterparts. Isolated efforts began as early as 1929 when The Holy Ghost Fathers from Bangui founded a mission at Kou, near Moundou in Logone Occidental Prefecture. In 1934, in the midst of the sleeping sickness epidemic, they abandoned Kou for Doba in Logone Oriental Prefecture. Other priests from Ubangi-Chari and Cameroon opened missions in Kélo and Sarh in 1935 and 1939, respectively.

In 1946 these autonomous missions gave way to an institutionalized Roman Catholic presence. This late date had more to do with European politics than with events in Chad. Earlier in the century, the Vatican had designated the Chad region to be part of the Italian vicarate of Khartoum. Rather than risk the implantation of Italian missionaries during the era of Italian dictator Benito Mussolini, the French administration discouraged all Roman Catholic missionary activity. For its part, the Vatican adopted the same tactic, not wishing to upset the Italian regime by transferring jurisdiction of the Chad region to the French. As a consequence of their defeat in World War II, however, the Italians lost their African colonies. This loss cleared the way for a French Roman Catholic presence in Chad, which a decree from Rome formalized on March 22, 1946.

This decree set up three religious jurisdictions that eventually became four bishoprics. The first, administered by the Jesuits, had its seat in N'Djamena. Although its jurisdiction included the eight prefectures in the northern and eastern parts of the country, almost all the Roman Catholics in *sahelian* and Saharan Chad lived in the capital. The diocese of N'Djamena also served as the archdiocese of all Chad. The second bishopric, at Sarh, also was delegated to the Jesuits. Its region included Salamat and Moyen-Chari prefectures. The third and fourth jurisdictions had their headquarters in Pala and Moundou and were delegated to the Oblats de Marie and Capuchin orders. The Pala bishopric served Mayo-Kebbi Prefecture, while the bishopric of Moundou was responsible for missions in Logone Occidental and Logone Oriental prefectures. By far the most important jurisdiction in 1970, Pala included 116,000 of Chad's 160,000 Catholics.

The relatively slow progress of the Roman Catholic Church in Chad has several causes. Although Roman Catholicism has been much more open to local cultures than Protestantism, the doctrine of celibacy probably has deterred candidates for the priesthood. Insistence on monogamy also has undoubtedly made the faith less attractive to some potential converts, particularly wealthy older men able to afford more than one wife.

The social works of the Roman Catholic Church have made it an important institution in Chad. Like their Protestant counterparts, the Roman Catholic missions have a history of social service. In the 1970s, along with priests, the staffs of most establishments included brothers and nuns who worked in the areas of health, education, and development. Many of the nuns were trained medical professionals who served on the staffs of government hospitals and clinics. It was estimated that 20,000 Chadians attended Roman Catholic schools in 1980. Adult literacy classes also reached beyond the traditional school-aged population. In the area of development, as early as the 1950s Roman Catholic missions in southern Chad set up rural development centers whose clientele included non-Christians as well as Christians.

Education

The establishment of Protestant mission schools in southern Chad in the 1920s, followed by Roman Catholic and colonial state establishments in later decades, marked the beginning of Western education in Chad. From the outset, the colonial administration required that all instruction be in French, with the exception of religion classes, which could be taught in local languages. As early as 1925, the state imposed a standard curriculum on all institutions wishing official recognition and government subsidies. The state thus extended its influence to education, even though the majority of Chadian students attended private mission schools before World War II.

Education in Chad has focused on primary instruction. Until 1942 students who desired a secular secondary education had to go to schools in Brazzaville, the capital of the AEF. This restriction obviously limited the number of secondary-school students. Between World War I and World War II, only a dozen Chadians studied in Brazzaville. Once in Brazzaville, students received technical instruction rather than a liberal arts education, entering three-year programs designed to produce medical aides, clerks, or low-level technicians. State secondary schools were opened in Chad in 1942, but recognized certificate programs did not begin until the mid-1950s.

At independence in 1960, the government established a goal of universal primary education, and school attendance was made compulsory until age twelve. Nevertheless, the development of standard curricula was hampered by the limited number of schools, the existence of two- and three-year establishments alongside the standard five- and seven-year *collèges* and lycées, and the Muslim preference for Quranic education. Even so, by the mid-1960s 17 percent of students between the ages of six and eight were in school. This number represented a substantial increase over the 8 percent attending school in the mid-1950s and the 1.4 percent immediately after World War II. Although the academic year in Chad parallels the French schedule, running from October to June, it is not particularly appropriate for a country where the hottest part of the April and May.

Quranic schools throughout the Saharan and *sahelian* zones teach students to read Arabic and recite Quranic verse. Although traditional Islamic education at the secondary level has existed since the nineteenth century, students seeking advanced learning generally have studied in northern Cameroon, Nigeria, Sudan, or the Middle East. In Chad, modern Islamic secondary schools have included the Ecole Mohamed Illech, founded in 1918 and modeled after Egyptian educational institutions. Other schools included the Lycée Franco-Arabe, founded by the colonial administration in Abéché in 1952. The lycée offered a blend of Arabic, Quranic, and secular French education. Numerous observers believed that although the creation of a French-Islamic program of study was commendable, the administration's major objective was to counter foreign Islamic influence rather than to offer a viable alternative curriculum.

Despite the government's efforts, overall educational levels remained low at the end of the first decade of independence. In 1971 about 88 percent of men and 99 percent of women older than age fifteen could not read, write, or speak French, at the time the only official national language; literacy in Arabic stood at 7.8 percent. In 1982 the overall literacy rate stood at about 15 percent.

Major problems have hindered the development of Chadian education since independence. Financing has been very limited. Public expenditures for education amounted to only 14 percent of the national budget in 1963. Expenditures increased over the next several years but declined at the end of the decade. In 1969 funding for education dropped to 11 percent of the budget; the next year it declined still further to 9 percent. In the late 1980s, the government allotted only about 7 percent of its budget to education, a figure lower than that for all but a few African countries.

Limited facilities and personnel also have made it difficult for the education system to provide adequate instruction. Overcrowding is a major problem; some classes have up to 100 students, many of whom are repeaters. In the years just after independence, many primary-school teachers had only marginal qualifications. On the secondary level, the situation was even worse; at the end of the 1960s, for example, the Lycée Ahmad Mangué in Sarh (formerly Fort-Archambault) had only a handful of Chadians among its several dozen faculty members. During these years, Chad lacked sufficient facilities for technical and vocational education to train needed intermediate-level technicians, and there was no university.

In the 1970s and 1980s, Chad made considerable progress in dealing with problems of facilities and personnel. To improve instruction, review sessions and refresher programs have been instituted for primary-school teachers. On the secondary level, increasing numbers of Chadians have taken their places in the ranks of the faculty. Furthermore, during the 1971-72 school year, the Université du Tchad opened its doors.

Another problem at independence was that the French curricula of Chadian schools limited their effectiveness. Primary instruction was in French, although most students did not speak that language when they entered school, and teaching methods and materials were often poorly suited to the rural settings of most schools. In addition, the academic program inherited from the French did not prepare students for employment options in Chad. Beginning in the late 1960s, the government attempted to address these problems. A number of model schools discarded the French style of a formal, classical education in favor of a new approach that taught children to reinterpret and modify their social and economic environment. Rather than teaching French as it was taught in French schools to French children, the model schools taught it more appropriately as a foreign language. These new schools also introduced basic skills courses in the fourth year of primary school. Students who would probably not go on to secondary school were given the chance to attend agricultural training centers.

Unfortunately, all of the preceding problems were complicated by a fourth difficulty: the Chadian Civil War. Little has been written specifically about how this conflict has disrupted education, but several effects can reasonably be surmised. Lack of security in vast parts of the country undoubtedly has made it difficult to send teachers to their posts and to maintain them there, which has been particularly problematic because as government employees, teachers often have been identified with government policies. In addition, the mobility occasioned by the war has played havoc with attempts to get children to attend classes regularly. The diversion of resources to the conflict has also prevented the government from maintaining the expenditure levels found at independence, much less augmenting available funds. Finally, the violence has taken its toll among teachers, students, and facilities. One of the more dramatic instances of this was the destruction and looting of primary schools, lycées, and even the national archives attached to the Université du Tchad during the battles of N'Djamena in 1979 and 1980.

To its credit, the government has made major efforts to overcome these problems. In 1983 the Ministry of Planning and Reconstruction reported that the opening of the 1982-83 school year was the most successful since the upheavals of 1979. In 1984 the Université du Tchad, the Ecole Nationale d'Administration, and the Ecole Nationale des Travaux Publics reopened their doors as well.

In the late 1980s, the Ministry of Education had administrative responsibility for all formal schooling. Because of years of civil strife, however, local communities had assumed many of the ministry's functions, including the construction and maintenance of schools, and payment of teachers' salaries.

Primary Education

In the late 1980s, primary education in Chad consisted of a six-year program leading to an elementary school certificate. In the south, most students began their studies at the age of six; in the north, they tended to be somewhat older. With the exception of schools that followed experimental programs, the curriculum adhered to the French model. Courses included reading, writing, spelling, grammar, mathematics, history, geography, science, and drawing.

Primary-school enrollment for the 1986-87 school year was more than 300,000 students. There were 6,203 instructors teaching in 1,650 schools, but 10 percent of the instructors were in nonteaching positions, yielding a pupil-to-teacher ratio of about sixty to one. Only about 40 percent of all primary-school-aged children attended class, and attendance was much greater in the south than in the Sahel or in the northern parts of the country (see table 2, Appendix A). Approximately 2.8 percent of primary-school children were enrolled in private schools, and most of these were in Roman Catholic mission schools concentrated in the south or near the capital.

Secondary Education

In 1983 secondary education in Chad continued to follow French models. Primary-school graduates competed for entrance into two types of liberal arts institutions, the *collège d'enseignement général* (called a *collège*, or CEG) or the lycée. The *collège* offered a four-year course of study, and the lycée offered a seven-year program. In both institutions, students took a general examination at the end of four years. *Collège* students who passed could be allowed to transfer to a lycée to complete their studies; successful lycée students continued at their institutions. At the end of seven years of secondary education, all students took comprehensive exams for the baccalaureate degree, called the *bac,* a requirement for admission to a university.

Students with primary-school certificates interested in teaching careers could enroll in a *collège* or lycée, or they could enter a teacher training school. The normal school program was six years long. The first four years were devoted to general education, much the same as at the *collège* or lycée, and the last two years concentrated on professional training. Students finishing this course were awarded an elementary-level teaching certificate. In 1986–87 Chad had sixty-one *collèges* and lycées. More than half of these schools were located in the N'Djamena area. There were 43,357 secondary students enrolled in the 1986–87 school year. In the 1983–84 school year, 5,002 *collège* students took the exam, with a success rate of 43.5 percent, or 2,174 students; 3,175 students took the *bac,* and 36.9 percent, or 1,173 students, passed. Although still low, the numbers of examination candidates suggested major improvements over 1960, when 2,000 students attended general secondary schools, and over 1968–69, when enrollment stood at 8,724. Finally, during the

A primary school in a bombed-out building in Kanem Prefecture
Courtesy UNICEF (Maggie Murray-Lee)

1986–87 school year, Chad had five institutions for training primary-school teachers, with a enrollment of 1,020 students.

Higher Education

When the country became independent in 1960, Chad had no university. For the first decade of the nation's life, students who wished to study beyond the secondary level had to go abroad. In the 1966–67 school year, eighty-three Chadians were studying outside the country; the following year, this number rose to 200. In the early years, almost all students seeking advanced education were male. The largest number went to France (30 percent in the academic year 1966–67, for example), but some Chadians studied in Belgium, Senegal, Côte d'Ivoire, and Congo. At that time, most students were pursuing degrees in education, liberal arts, agriculture, and medicine.

Pursuant to an agreement with France, the Université du Tchad opened in the 1971–72 academic year. Financed almost entirely through French assistance, the faculty of 25 welcomed 200 students the first year. By the 1974–75 academic year, enrollment had climbed to 500, and the university graduated its first class of 45. The imposition of compulsory *yondo* rites greatly disrupted the following school year, but after the overthrow of Tombalbaye and the end of the *authenticité* movement, the university continued to grow (see Classical African Religions, this ch.). Enrollment rose from 639 in 1976–77 to a high of 1,046 in 1977–78. Enrollment then dropped slightly to 974 in 1978–79. Unfortunately, the Chadian Civil War curtailed university activities in 1979 and 1980, when the first and second battles of N'Djamena threatened facilities and students alike. With the return of relative calm in the early 1980s, the university reopened. In 1983-84 the university had 141 teachers and 1,643 students.

In addition to the university, higher learning in Chad included one advanced teacher-training institution, the Ecole Normale Supérieure, which trained secondary-school instructors. Enrollment in the 1982–83 and 1983–84 school years came to about 200 students. Degree programs included history-geography, modern literature, English and French, Arabic and French, mathematics and physics, and biology-geology-chemistry.

Vocational Education

In 1983 vocational education was offered at three *lycées techniques industriels* (in Sarh, N'Djamena, and Moundou), and the Collège d'Enseignement Technique in Sarh. Enrollment figures for three of the four technical schools stood at 1,490 in 1983.

Primary-school graduates interested in technical or vocational training could follow two courses. They either could enter a first-level, three-year program (*premier cycle*) at a *collège* (after which they could transfer to one of the four technical schools) or they could enroll directly in one of the lycées for a six-year program. Students completing the three-year *premier cycle* received professional aptitude certificates; those finishing the entire six-year course were awarded diplomas.

Apart from the *lycées techniques,* several other institutions offered vocational training in Chad in the early 1980s. These included the Ecole Nationale d'Administration, which opened in 1963 in N'Djamena; a postal and telecommunications school in Sarh; a school for technical education related to public works; and the Ba-Illi agricultural school. Other Chadians studied at technical training centers abroad.

In the late 1980s, advanced medical education was not available in Chad. The only medical training institution was the National School of Public Health and Social Work (Ecole Nationale de Santé Publique et de Service Social—ENSPSS) in N'Djamena. Its enrollment, however, has been very limited; in 1982 there were only twenty-eight students in nursing, three in social work, and thirty-three in public health.

Health and Medical Services

A range of diseases afflicts the populace of Chad. In 1983 infectious and parasitic diseases were the most prevalent ailments, followed by respiratory afflictions and nervous disorders. In 1988 a severe epidemic of meningitis affected N'Djamena, in particular. By 1987 only one case of acquired immune deficiency syndrome (AIDS) had been reported to the World Health Organization; however, it was likely that incidence of the disease was many times higher, especially in the southern areas near Cameroon and Central African Republic.

By the early 1960s, the government made a substantial effort to extend the country's limited health infrastructure. Despite the ensuing civil conflict, the government has attempted to maintain and expand health services. Foreign assistance has allowed the construction of new buildings and the renovation of existing facilities, as well as the laying of groundwork for training health care professionals.

By the early 1980s, health facilities included five hospitals (at N'Djamena, Sarh, Moundou, Abéché, and a locality in Mayo-Kebbi Prefecture). Two polyclinics served the population of the capital region. Medical centers numbered 18, and there were 20 infirmaries and 127 dispensaries. Private medical facilities numbered seventy-five, and twenty social centers administered to the needs of Chadians in all prefectures except Biltine and Borkou-Ennedi-Tibesti.

Despite apparent progress in health care delivery, it is difficult to determine if growth in the number of facilities represented an increased capacity or merely a reorganization and reclassification of health establishments. The only data available in 1988, for example, showed that despite the increase in numbers of units, the hospitals, medical centers, and infirmaries increased the number of beds by only 238 more than the number recorded in 1971. Modern health care was also very unevenly distributed. Such facilities in Chad have long been concentrated in the south and remained so in 1983. For example, eleven of the eighteen medical centers were found there, along with three of the five hospitals, and private care followed the same pattern, with sixty-four of seventy-five centers in the southern prefectures. In theory, therefore, people in the less populated *sahelian* and Saharan regions had to travel very long distances for modern medical care. In fact, distance, lack of transportation, and civil conflict probably discouraged most people from making the effort.

A continuing shortage of trained medical personnel has compounded the difficulty of providing adequate, accessible health facilities. In 1983 Chad's medical system employed 42 Chadian doctors, 8 pharmacists, a biologist, 87 registered nurses, 583 practical nurses, 59 nurses specializing in childbirth, 22 midwives, 19 health inspectors, and 99 public health agents. Foreign assistance provided another 41 doctors, 103 nurses, and 2 midwives.

More detailed information concerning health care in Chad was unavailable in the late 1980s, largely because of the Chadian Civil War, which had disrupted government services for many years. As a result of this conflict, there were probably fewer health personnel in the late 1980s than earlier in the decade, particularly in the *sahelian* and Saharan zones, where nurses abandoned rural infirmaries. Mortality levels in Chad have been high for a long time, but the war may have reversed the limited progress made in the 1960s in dealing with the country's many health problems. Although the conflict was far from resolved in the late 1980s, the Habré government had been much more successful than its predecessors in consolidating control over the *sahelian* and Saharan regions of the country where modern health care has been the least available. Although resources remained scarce, greater international attention to Chad's plight produced more foreign assistance than in the past.

* * *

In the late 1980s, reliable studies on Chad in English remained scarce. For a useful general study of Chad, the reader should consult Jean Chapelle's *Le peuple tchadien: ses racines et sa vie quotidienne.* A slightly more recent study, *Tchad: la genèse d'un conflit* by Christian Bouquet, covers some of the same ground but focuses on the context of Chadian underdevelopment and civil conflict. The much drier volume, *Le Tchad* by Jean Cabot and Christian Bouquet, offers a more detailed survey of the physical environment. In English, Dennis D. Cordell's *Dar al-Kuti and the Last Years of the Trans-Saharan Slave Trade* analyzes Chad's role in Saharan commerce, the Muslim slave trade, and the expanding Islamic world of the nineteenth century. Finally, Samuel Decalo's *Historical Dictionary of Chad* is one of the very few general references to the country in English.

There are a number of good regional studies of Chadian society and religion. Basic literature on the Sara of the *soudanian* zone includes Robert Jaulin's controversial *La mort sara,* a study of the *yondo;* Jean-Pierre Magnant's important *La terre sara, terre tchadienne;* and Françoise Dumas-Champion's *Les Masa du Tchad.* Annie M.D. Lebeuf's *Les principautés Kotoko* remains the essential study of the Kotoko. Albert Le Rouvreur's *Sahéliens et sahariens du Tchad* surveys the northern two-thirds of the country. Within this region, basic reading should include Jean Chapelle's now-classic *Nomads noirs du Sahara,* a study of the Teda and Daza; Jean-Claude Zelt-ner's *Les Arabes dans la région du Lac Tchad;* and Dennis D. Cor-dell's "The Awlad Sulayman of Libya and Chad," in *Canadian Journal of African Studies.* In *Survivances pré-islamiques en pays zaghawa,* Marie-José Tubiana analyzes the retention of pre-Islamic beliefs and practices in eastern Chad. In *Pilgrims in a Strange Land,* John A. Works, Jr. has written a good study of Hausa communities in Chad and their role in the spread of Islam. (For further informa-tion and complete citations, see Bibliography.)

Chapter 3. The Economy

Typical Chadian village, with grass huts and large earthen pots for storing grain

WHEN FRANCE GRANTED INDEPENDENCE to Chad in 1960, it left the new government with an essentially traditional economy, having a small industrial sector, an agricultural sector dominated by cotton, and an inadequate transportation sector. Moreover, the country had few trained technicians or capable administrators. In spite of well-intentioned efforts by a series of civilian and military governments, throughout the 1970s and 1980s, the combination of prolonged civil strife, chronic drought, and political uncertainty aborted most progress.

By the late 1980s, even though there had been a lull in the fighting, better rains, and a modicum of political stability, Chad was still one of the poorest countries on earth and one of the least endowed with resources. The economy had not improved appreciably since independence and, by some measurements, was probably worse than in 1960. Reliant on foreign aid and vulnerable to the uncontrollable forces of the international cotton market, Chad could hope to make only incremental gains in its quest to achieve a viable, self-sustaining economy.

Growth and Structure of the Economy

Chad's remoteness, its inadequate infrastructure, its recent history of war, drought, and famine, and its dependency on a single cash crop—cotton—for export earnings made it one of the poorest nations of the world. In the mid-1980s, Chad's gross national product (GNP—see Glossary) per capita was only US$160, which clearly reflected the extent of the nation's impoverishment. In the mid-1980s, Chad ranked among the five poorest nations of the world according to World Bank (see Glossary) statistics.

Chad's economy was based almost entirely on agriculture and pastoralism. In 1986 the World Bank estimated that approximately 83 percent of the country's economically active population worked in agriculture, 5 percent worked in industry, and 12 percent were engaged in services, including government employment, trade, and other service activities. Cotton processing, which includes ginning raw cotton into fiber for export, some spinning and weaving, and producing edible oil from cotton seed for local consumption, dominated industry.

Figures for the gross domestic product (GDP—see Glossary) also reflected agriculture's importance. In 1986 the World Bank estimated that 46.3 percent of Chad's GDP came from agriculture and pastoralism. Industry and manufacturing accounted for only 17.9 percent of GDP, while services represented 35.7 percent of GDP.

Geography and climate played an influential role in Chad's economy. The country is divided into three major climatic zones— Saharan, *sahelian*, and *soudanian*—which are distinguished by the level of annual average rainfall. There are only two productive zones—the *soudanian* cotton-producing zone of the south, sometimes called Le Tchad Utile (Useful Chad), and the central *sahelian* cattle-herding region. The northern Saharan region produces little.

In 1987 Chad's economy was dependent on a single cash crop— cotton. Like most other single-crop economies in the Third World, when world commodity prices were high, conditions improved. When those prices fell, conditions worsened. Despite several important swings, during the 1970s and particularly in the early 1980s, cotton prices were good. Chad's cotton revenues peaked in 1983 and 1984, but in 1985 world cotton prices fell steeply, nearly crippling the cotton industry. This decline forced a major economic restructuring under the auspices of the World Bank and foreign donors. To revive the cotton industry, a 1986 restructuring program curtailed all cotton-derived revenues to the government until world prices rebounded. This program forced cutbacks on the production of raw cotton and limited the level of government support to producers for improved cropping methods, ginning, and other related industrial operations.

Cattle and beef exports followed cotton in economic importance. Estimates of the value of these exports varied greatly because large numbers of livestock left the country "on the hoof," totally outside the control of customs officials. Nevertheless, cattle and beef exports accounted for 30 to 60 percent of all exports from 1975 through 1985, depending on the value of the cotton crop in a given year. Approximately 29 percent of Chadians depended almost entirely on livestock for their livelihood in the early 1980s, and livestock and their by-products represented around 26 percent of GNP.

Chad's lack of resources limited the exploitation of mineral deposits. There were known deposits of bauxite in the southern regions, and reports indicated deposits of uranium and some other minerals in the Tibesti Mountains and Aozou Strip (see Glossary). Even in late 1987, however, no bauxite was being mined, and because of hostilities in the northern zones, claims of mineral deposits there had not been verified. Chad's only mining industry was the traditional exploitation of sodium carbonate (natron) in dried beds around Lake Chad.

Oil offered one of the few reasons for economic optimism. In 1974 a consortium of companies led by Conoco discovered oil near Rig Rig, north of Lake Chad. Plans to exploit these reserves, estimated at 438 million barrels, and to build a small refinery to serve Chad's domestic needs were delayed in the late 1970s and early 1980s because of the Chadian Civil War. In 1986 the government—with World Bank support—revived the idea, and plans called for operations to begin in the early 1990s. Nonetheless, these deposits would ensure only Chad's domestic needs, and no oil would be exported. In 1985 Exxon, which had become the leader of the exploratory consortium, discovered oil in southern Chad, near Doba. The size of the reserves was not known, although it was believed to be large. Exxon, however, suspended drilling in 1986 when world oil prices fell.

Remoteness and distance are prime features of economic life in Chad. Transportation and communications are difficult, both internally and externally. Douala, Cameroon, the nearest port from N'Djamena, is 1,700 kilometers away. By the mid-1980s, the only paved roads linking the capital to the interior, some 250 kilometers of hardtop, had disappeared because of insufficient maintenance. Of the estimated 31,000 kilometers of dirt roads and tracks, only 1,260 kilometers were all-weather roads. The remainder became impassable during the rainy season. There were no railroads in Chad.

Since independence, Chad has relied on outside donors and regional institutions for economic survival and development. Chad's principal sponsor has been France, which has subsidized the budget. Through the mechanisms of the Lomé Convention (see Glossary) between the members of the European Economic Community (EEC) and their former colonies in Africa, the Caribbean, and the Pacific (ACP), France has also subsidized Chad's cotton production and exports. French companies have dominated trade, and French banks have controlled Chad's finances.

Information on Chadian government finances was fragmentary and inconsistent. The political instability from 1976 to 1982 left large sections of the country beyond any form of central control, and during this period the state had very few finances. After 1982, however, fragmentary estimates indicated a growing importance of donor finances and a decline in internally generated revenues. In addition, during the 1980s military spending was high. Although the proportion of real government expenditures for defense was difficult to assess, it could have represented as much as 70 percent of government spending. Despite a measure of political stability after 1982, the situation worsened in 1985 with the collapse of cotton revenues. In 1986 the World Bank and the International Monetary Fund (IMF—see Glossary) joined in efforts by other donors, including France, the EEC, and the United States, to stabilize Chad's financial and budget difficulties.

Role of Government

Both before and after the Chadian Civil War, the government participated actively in the economy and fostered a liberal economic development policy. It encouraged foreign investment, both public and private, and in 1987 had under review the Investment Code of 1963. The objective was to minimize regulations for the private manufacturing sector and particularly for small- and medium-sized enterprises.

The government considered the public sector a complement to, and not a substitute for, the private sector. Even so, because of the country's narrow productive base and limited cash economy, the government was forced to play an active role in the economy. This participation primarily took the form of mixed public and private marketing enterprises, called parastatals. As a partner in these ventures, the government participated in the planning and controlling of the economy and became a key actor in the service sector through the parastatals, which employed thousands of individuals (see Manufacturing, Mining, and Utilities, this ch.; Government Finances, this ch.).

Agriculture

In 1986 approximately 83 percent of the active population were farmers or herders. This sector of the economy accounted for almost half of GDP. With the exception of cotton, some small-scale sugar production, and a portion of the peanut crop, Chad's agriculture consisted of subsistence food production. The types of crops that were grown and the locations of herds were determined by considerable variations in Chad's climate (see Physical Setting, ch. 2).

The *soudanian* zone comprises those areas with an average annual rainfall of 800 millimeters or more. This region, which accounts for about 10 percent of the total land area, contains the nation's most fertile croplands. Settled agricultural communities growing a wide variety of food crops are its main features. Fishing is important in the rivers, and families raise goats, chickens, and, in some cases, oxen for plowing. In 1983 about 72 percent of all land under cultivation in Chad was in the *soudanian* region.

The central zone, the *sahelian* region, comprises the area with average annual rainfall of between 350 and 800 millimeters. The minimum rainfall needed for the hardiest of Chad's varieties of

A livestock market in Massakoury
Courtesy Michael R. Saks

millet, called *berebere,* is 350 millimeters. The western area of the zone is dominated by the Chari and Logone rivers, which flow north from their sources in southern Chad and neighboring countries (see fig. 3). The courses of these rivers, joining at N'Djamena to flow on to Lake Chad, create an ecological subregion. Fishing is important for the peoples along the rivers and along the shores of Lake Chad. Flood recession cropping is practiced along the edges of the riverbeds and lakeshore, areas that have held the most promise for irrigation in the zone. International donor attention focused on this potential beginning in the mid-1960s. Particular attention has been paid to the traditional construction of polders (see Glossary) along the shores of Lake Chad. Land reclaimed by the use of such methods is extremely fertile. Chad's only wheat crop is cultivated in these polders.

In the rest of the *sahelian* region, the hardier varieties of millet, along with peanuts and dry beans, are grown. Crop yields are far lower than they are in the south or near rivers and lakes. Farmers take every advantage of seasonal flooding to grow recession crops before the waters dry away, a practice particularly popular around Lake Fitri. The *sahelian* region is ideal for pasturage. Herding includes large cattle herds for commercial sale, and goats, sheep, donkeys, and some horses are common in all villages.

The Saharan zone encompasses roughly the northern one-third of Chad. Except for some dates and legumes grown in the scattered

93

oases, the area is not productive. Annual rainfall averages less than 350 millimeters, and the land is sparsely populated by nomadic tribes. Many of Chad's camel herds are found in the region, but there are few cattle or horses.

Chad's subsistence farmers practice traditional slash-and-burn agriculture in tandem with crop rotation, which is typical throughout much of Africa. Sorghum is the most important food crop, followed by millet and *berebere*. Less prevalent grains are corn, rice, and wheat. Other secondary crops include peanuts, sesame, legumes, and tubers, as well as a variety of garden vegetables.

Crop rotation in the *soudanian* zone traditionally begins with sorghum or millet in the first year. Mixed crops of sorghum and/or millet, with peanuts, legumes, or tubers, are then cultivated for approximately three years. Farmers then return the land to fallow for periods up to fifteen years, turning to different fields for the next cycle. Preparation of a field begins with cutting heavy brush and unwanted low trees or branches that are then laid on the ground. Collectively owned lands are parceled out during the dry season, and the fields are burned just before the onset of the first rains, usually around March. Farmers work most intensively during the rains between May and October, planting, weeding and protecting the crops from birds and animals. Harvesting begins in September and October with the early varieties of sorghum. The main harvest occurs in November and December. Farmers harvest crops of rice and *berebere,* grown along receding water courses, as late as February.

The cropping cycle for most of the *sahelian* zone is similar, although the variety of crops planted is more limited because of dryness. In the polders of Lake Chad, farmers grow a wide range of crops; two harvests per year for corn, sorghum, and legumes are possible from February or March to September. Rice ripens in February, and wheat ripens in May.

As with most Third World countries, control of the land determines agricultural practices. There are three basic types of land tenure in Chad. The first is collective ownership by villages of croplands in their environs. In principle, such lands belong to a village collectively under the management of the village chief or the traditional *chef des terres* (chief of the lands). Individual farmers hold inalienable and transmittable use rights to village lands, so long as they, their heirs, or recognized representatives cultivate the land. Outsiders can farm village lands only with the authorization of the village chief or *chef des terres*. Renting village farmlands is possible in some local areas but is not traditional practice. Private ownership is the second type of tenure, applied traditionally to the small plots cultivated in wadis or oases. Wells belong to individuals or groups with rights to the land. Ownership of fruit trees and date palms in the oases is often separate from ownership of the land; those farmers who plant and care for trees own them. State ownership is the third type, primarily for large enterprises such as irrigation projects. Under the management of parastatal or government employees, farmers enter into contractual arrangements, including paying fees, for the use of state lands and the benefits of improved farming methods.

Detailed and reliable statistical information on Chad's agriculture was scarce in the late 1980s; most researchers viewed available statistics only as indicators of general trends. The one region for which figures were kept was the *soudanian* zone through survey coverage by officials of the National Office of Rural Development (Office National de Développement Rural—ONDR), who monitored cotton production. These officials also gathered information on food production, but this effort was not carried out systematically. Survey coverage of the *sahelian* zone was first hampered, then prevented, by civil conflict from the mid-1970s to the early 1980s.

Moreover, figures from international and regional organizations often conflicted or differed in formulation. For example, total area devoted to food production was difficult to estimate because sources combined the area of fields in production with those lying fallow to give a total for arable lands. The arable land figure has shown a gradual increase since 1961. Estimated then at 2.9 million hectares, it rose to almost 3.2 million hectares in 1984. In 1983 there were about 1.2 million hectares in food production and in 1984 slightly more than 900,000 hectares. Therefore, perhaps a third of Chad's farmlands were in production in a given year, with the balance lying fallow.

Cotton

Background of Cotton Cultivation

Cotton is an indigenous crop to southern Chad. In 1910 the French colonial administration organized market production on a limited scale under the direction of the military governor. By 1920 the colonial administration was promoting the large-scale production of cotton for export. The French saw cotton as the only exploitable resource for the colony and as an effective means of introducing a cash economy into the area. Indeed, the elaboration of colonial administration went hand in hand with the extension of cotton production throughout the region.

France's motives were clear: it sought to ensure a source of raw materials for its home industries and a protected market for its exports abroad. France also intended that taxes derived from commercial ventures within the colonies would offset the expenses of the colonial administration. Therefore, customs duties on cotton exports from Chad, then a part of French Equatorial Africa (Afrique Equatoriale Française—AEF; see Glossary), were paid to the governor general at Brazzaville (in contemporary Congo), as were duties on exports from other colonies under regional administration. Revenues from a head tax were paid in cash locally and went directly to the lieutenant governor of the colony. Not surprisingly, virtually the only means of earning the money to pay the tax was by the sale of cotton to the French.

In 1928 exploitation of cotton within the colony was placed in the hands of Cotonfran, a private company. Under the terms of the contract between the colonial administration and Cotonfran, the administration maintained a certain quantity of production by the villages, and Cotonfran bought at least 80 percent of that production. The cotton was ginned locally, but no further transformation was permitted; all the cotton fiber was then exported to France.

The colonial administration fixed the quantity of cotton produced and the price paid to the peasant producer on the basis of calculations furnished by Cotonfran of costs and expectations for the price of cotton on the world market. France reorganized village administration by replacing traditional chiefs with individuals more amenable to the colonial power, which assured the proper cultivation of the cotton crop and the collection of taxes. This system included forced labor and the subordination of growing food crops to cotton.

Production Factors

In 1988 the entirety of Chad's cotton was produced in the five *soudanian* prefectures of Mayo-Kebbi, Tandjilé, Logone Occidental, Logone Oriental, and Moyen-Chari, plus the Bousso region of Chari-Baguirmi Prefecture, which juts down into the *soudanian* zone (see fig. 1). Few regions outside these prefectures offered sufficient water and population to sustain cotton production. Moreover, in this land of difficult transport, areas producing a cash crop also needed to be able to grow enough food for their people. Typically, the cultivation of cotton and food crops was carried on side by side. Efforts to extend the cultivation of cotton to the neighboring *sahelian* prefectures of Salamat and Guéra have had little success. In 1983 and 1984, with production at its highest in a decade, these two prefectures represented only .5 percent of total production.

Cotton being unloaded from a truck in Pala, Mayo-Kebbi Prefecture
Courtesy Michael R. Saks

Suggestions also have been made from time to time to bring cotton production to the fertile borders of Lake Chad. Trials have shown the high yields possible there, estimated at 3,000 to 4,000 kilograms per hectare. As of 1987, however, farmers in the Lake Chad area had not taken voluntarily to cotton production. Traditionally, farmers have resisted government efforts to control local production of such crops as wheat, and the history of coercion and government intervention associated with cotton was no inducement.

The government has introduced methods to increase crop yield, which include the expanded use of fertilizers and insecticides. Even so, compared with crop yields of more than 1,000 kilograms per hectare for other francophone West African states (such as Cameroon, Mali, and Côte d'Ivoire), until 1982 Chad's crop yields did not significantly exceed 500 kilograms per hectare; from 1983 to 1987, yields averaged almost 750 kilograms per hectare.

Area under cotton cultivation reached a peak in 1963 of 338,900 hectares. From 1963 until the end of the 1970s, the area under cotton cultivation averaged 275,000 hectares. In the 1980s, however, the area has been consistently less than 200,000 hectares. By 1983 the area of land under cotton cultivation had dropped by 36 percent from the average during the 1960s and 1970s. Several sources estimated the area in southern Chad under cotton cultivation at 30 to 40 percent of all land in cultivation, and in some areas of

97

Mayo-Kebbi Prefecture, it may have been higher (see table 3, Appendix A).

Cotton production has exhibited wide swings. Factors such as climatic conditions, production prices, and civil strife have influenced production. The first crop to exceed 100,000 tons came in 1963, but the 1970s were the best years for production, which from 1971 to 1978 remained well above 100,000 tons per year. Chad reached its all-time record production in 1975. Production suffered from 1979 to 1982 because of the Chadian Civil War and hit a twenty-year low in 1981. In 1983, with the return of some political stability and higher market prices, production improved but then fell from 1984 to 1987, a reflection of declining world cotton prices.

Once the crop is harvested, the producers must sort the cotton to separate lower quality yellow cotton from higher quality white cotton. Since the late 1970s, the proportion of white cotton generally has been 90 percent or more of total production. Going back to the 1960s, the quality of Chadian cotton had been consistently high, except for 1972 and 1973, when the proportion of yellow cotton rose to 18 percent. Since 1980 the quality has remained high at initial sorting, with white cotton representing more than 95 percent of the crop and accounting for 98 percent of production in 1984.

Administrative Structure

In 1989 the official structure responsible for the production and marketing of cotton was composed of the ONDR under the Ministry of Agriculture and Rural Development, of Cotontchad, and of the Cotton Price Stabilization Board (Caisse de Stabilisation des Prix du Coton—CSPC). Founded in 1965, the ONDR was originally given responsibility to monitor, improve, and assist all agricultural production. By the mid-1980s, however, the government's emphasis on cotton production made the ONDR an important factor for the cotton industry only. Cotontchad, successor to Cotonfran, was founded as a parastatal company in 1971 to collect, buy, gin, transport, and export the cotton crop. The company also had responsibility for elements of the small national textile, soap, and edible oil industries. The CSPC's task was to stabilize prices paid to peasant producers by funding operating losses incurred by Cotontchad. Assuring a constant price to the producer not only helped maintain a certain level of production for Cotontchad but also limited costs to the company by holding down producer prices. The ONDR, the CSPC, Cotontchad, and the government itself were involved in determining producer prices. In addition, the CSPC supported the program to improve yields. Between 1971 and 1983,

Irrigation farming near Mao in Kanem Prefecture
Courtesy UNICEF (Maggie Murray-Lee)

an estimated 57 percent of all payments by the CSPC were made in conjunction with the program to improve cotton production.

Other major actors in the cotton industry were the private banks, the French Textile Development Company (Compagnie Française pour le Développement des Textiles—CFDT), and French and EEC institutions, as well as the World Bank. Private banks provided the credits necessary to Cotontchad and to the peasants to finance the opening of each planting season and especially to provide capital for the import and distribution of fertilizers and insecticides. The CFDT marketed Chad's cotton on the world market. The CFDT also contributed to the smooth operation of Cotontchad through technical agreements to maintain equipment and to provide expertise in improving cropping methods through the ONDR. In addition, the CFDT supported research carried out by the Cotton and Textile Research Institute (Institut de Recherche sur le Coton et les Textiles—IRCT), a small public research facility located near Doba. Subsidies to Chad's cotton production under the Lomé Convention were paid through the Stabex system (see Glossary) of the EEC. Those funds were channeled to the CSPC for price support to the producers. The CSPC also received portions of funds needed to assure payments to producers from Cotontchad as well as from the central government. Between 1971 and 1983, virtually all income to the CSPC derived from rebates paid by Cotontchad into the system.

After 1984 the system became far more dependent on external sources of funds (such as Stabex) because of sharply reduced income to Cotontchad. In addition to Stabex, the EC's European Development Fund (EDF) contributed directly to the program of improving yields. French assistance remained crucial to the system. The Central Fund for Economic Cooperation (Caisse Centrale de Coopération Economique—CCCE) was a shareholder in Cotontchad, and the other arm of French foreign aid, the Cooperation and Aid Fund (Fonds d'Aide et de la Coopération—FAC), directed assistance to the southern zone in support of the cotton complex. FAC also provided direct assistance to the government, which, among other things, helped pay the salaries of officials and functionaries, especially those in the ONDR.

Pricing Mechanisms

Prices paid to Chad's cotton producers, the peasants of the southern *soudanian* zone, have risen slowly over the years. The structure included separate prices for white cotton and for yellow cotton. From 1971, when the distinction arose, to 1978, the price for white cotton was CFA F50 per kilogram (for value of the CFA

F—see Glossary) and stayed at this level during much of the period of heavy civil conflict until 1982. From 1982 to 1985, the price increased steeply to CFA F100 per kilogram, at which point it had leveled by 1987, despite downward pressure because of the fall in world prices and a new program of cost reductions by Cotontchad under World Bank direction. The price paid for yellow cotton has not kept pace with this rise, reaching only CFA F40 per kilogram in 1983, where it remained through 1987.

The price paid to the producer traditionally has not covered actual production costs, either for the peasant or for Cotontchad. As much as 50 percent of the costs of production has been borne by outside donors, primarily from the EDF, through the Stabex system. Between 1981 and 1984, the EDF financed between 70 and 80 percent of the costs of the program to improve yields, largely through subsidies to the CSPC for price support and subsidies for Cotontchad in the initial purchase of insecticides and fertilizers. The costs of improvements have been reimbursed only partially from payments made by producers through the ONDR.

Restructuring the System

By 1987, because world prices were still insufficient to recoup costs, Cotontchad was rapidly going broke. In the mid-1980s, annual net losses were estimated at CFA F18 billion. Net losses per kilogram of ginned cotton were estimated at CFA F453 in 1985 and CFA F298 in 1987. These figures stood in contrast to 1984, when there was a net profit of CFA F193 per kilogram. Cotontchad's position was not expected to improve unless the world price of cotton reached the CFA F600-per-kilogram range.

With World Bank backing and support from France, the Netherlands, and the EC, restructuring of Cotontchad began in 1986 with government implementation of the Emergency Cotton Program. At the producer level, the program called for freezing the price paid producers at the CFA F100-per-kilogram level through 1988 and studying new methods of fixing producer prices to reflect world market conditions. Subsidies on improved inputs, such as fertilizer and insecticides, were eliminated as of 1987, with producers assuming the costs. Cotton production was to be limited to about 100,000 tons by restricting the area under production to 75,000 hectares during the program period. At the company level, Cotontchad sold nonessential assets to the private sector (including 2 aircraft and about 150 vehicles), closed its branch office in Bangui, Central African Republic, and laid off administrative staff. It also closed six ginneries and reduced the number of cotton collection centers in accordance with the production target of 100,000 tons.

For its part, the government exempted Cotontchad from taxes, particularly export duties, and suspended its contributions to the CSPC, the ONDR, and the Debt Amortization Fund (Caisse Autonome d'Amortissement—CAA). Staffs at the CSPC and the ONDR were reduced, and the roles of both organizations were reviewed.

Subsistence Farming

Since the 1950s, Chad's food production has declined (see table 4, Appendix A). Even so, despite pockets of malnutrition remaining in areas where rains failed or locusts damaged local crops, the overall picture for Chad's food production was good in the 1985–87 period. The rebound of food production in this period was the result of good rains, the return of political stability, and the absence of major conflict in the *sahelian* and *soudanian* zones. The downturn in cotton production and added restrictions on its cultivation also released lands and labor for farmers to put into food production. Production was so high in these years that, for the first time in a decade, it was estimated that Chad had returned to food sufficiency. This followed a cereal shortfall in the drought years of 1984 and 1985 of around 325,000 tons. Total cereal production rose thereafter to the 700,000-ton level, well above the estimated 615,000 tons of grains needed for food sufficiency.

Yet the overall food sufficiency registered by Chad in these years served to underscore the problem of regional imbalances in cereal production. The *sahelian* zone experienced a chronic shortfall in cereal production, whereas the *soudanian* zone traditionally had a cereal surplus. The *soudanian* zone was also the biggest producer of all subsistence food crops and of cash crops. It was estimated that the *soudanian* zone produced between 53 and 77 percent of Chad's total cereal production from 1976 to 1985, with the average falling in the 60- to 70-percent range. But because the populations of the two regions were approximately equal, the lack of a good transport system and marketing mechanisms to allow the rapid transfer of the southern surplus to the northern zones was a constant problem. This danger was especially threatening during times of drought affecting the *sahelian* zone.

Sorghum and Millet

Chad's most important subsistence crops were sorghum, millet, and *berebere.* Areas under production for these grains showed a downward trend after the mid-1950s, dropping from an average of 1.5 million hectares to around 1 million hectares in the 1960s and 1970s and falling to levels averaging 750,000 hectares between 1981 and 1986. Taking an average for all lands devoted to grain production during the years from 1981 to 1985, according to the Food and Agriculture Organization (FAO), sorghum and millet cultivation accounted for 85 percent of the total area. Between 1980 and 1985, these coarse grains accounted for 80 to 95 percent of all grain production.

Wheat

In 1987 wheat was Chad's least important cereal grain. Farmers planted the crop in polders around the shores of Lake Chad, and some small planting also was done in the oases and wadis of northern Chad. Replacing an earlier state operation, the Organization for the Development of the Lake (Société pour le Développement du Lac—SODELAC) was founded in 1967 to organize cultivation and provide wheat for the state-owned flour mill at N'Djamena, the Grands Moulins du Tchad. The flour mill began operations in 1964 but closed in 1980; as of 1987, operations had not resumed. In the late 1970s, plans to plant some 20,000 hectares of wheat in polders failed because warfare around Lake Chad affected the infrastructure of SODELAC and the construction of new polders and because farmers resisted SODELAC-controlled production.

Wheat production generally followed trends similar to the production of other cereals, remaining low in the 1960s and 1970s but reaching a high in 1983. In 1984, however, production fell sharply. The bulk of wheat was traded through traditional channels to those herders in the northern regions of Chad who preferred wheat to millet or sorghum.

Rice and Corn

At the time of the French conquest, rice was grown on a small scale. Before World War I, the Germans on the Cameroon side of the Logone River encouraged the spread of rice cultivation. By World War II, the French imposed cultivation in the areas of southern Chad near Laï and Kélo, along the Logone River. Although production was destined originally for colonial troops, the taste for rice spread in some localities. What was originally intended by the French as a commercial cash crop had become a local subsistence crop by the 1980s.

The Development Office for Sategui Deressia (Office de Mise en Valeur de Sategui-Deressia—OMVSD), founded in 1976, replaced Experimental Sectors for Agricultural Modernization (Secteurs Expérimentaux de Modernisation Agricole—SEMAA), originally responsible for the organization, improvement, transformation, and commercialization of rice. Efforts by these organizations to extend

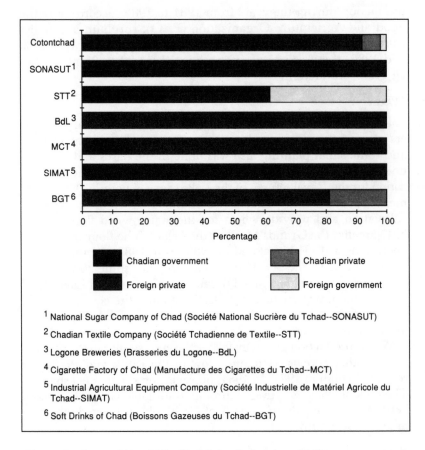

Figure 6. Ownership of Chad's Major Industries, 1987

commercial rice cultivation had mixed results. The area under rice cultivation has increased since the 1950s. Yet even in the 1980s, the greater part of this area was cultivated by traditional means. Schemes for controlled paddies at Bongor and Laï put only 3,500 hectares and 1,800 hectares, respectively, into cultivation before political events of the late 1970s and early 1980s disrupted efforts and international donor funding ceased. The bulk of rice production from traditional floodwater paddies was traded to the towns and cities or was consumed locally.

Corn was a crop of minor importance, grown in and around village gardens for local consumption. Production from the late 1960s through the mid-1980s remained in the 20,000- to 30,000-ton range. By 1987 no efforts at commercialization had been made, nor had the government tried to improve and extend corn production.

Peanuts

Peanuts have become an important food crop in Chad. Peanuts were eaten roasted or dry, and their oil was used in cooking. Peanuts were cultivated in both the *soudanian* and the *sahelian* zones. Production of peanuts was more stable than that of any other major crop, staying in the 90,000- to 100,000-ton range from the 1950s through 1987, with dips in drought years. The area under peanut production also remained stable, although kilograms-per-hectare yields declined slightly. The drought-resistant nature of peanuts made their production particularly important for the peoples of the *sahelian* zone, where peanuts were planted alone or in combination with millet in the first year of rotation; in the *soudanian* region, peanuts were traditionally planted in the third year of crop rotation.

Although considerable efforts were made to commercialize peanut production, most efforts failed. Through the 1960s and 1970s, about 97 percent of the annual crop went to local consumption. What remained was sold to various edible oil manufacturing concerns, none of which succeeded. For example, a Chinese-built peanut oil mill at Abéché, finished in 1969, never operated. Local farmers sold surplus peanuts through traditional channels, rather than to the state monopoly set up in 1965, the National Trading Company of Chad (Société Nationale de Commercialisation du Tchad— SONACOT). This parastatal bought local produce for sale abroad or domestically to state-run commercial operations. Unlike Cotontchad, SONACOT was never given the means to compel farmers to sell their crops, and it did not have the resources to compete with prices offered by traditional traders. With the collapse of central authority in 1979, SONACOT disappeared. The only commercial sales of peanuts were then limited to Cotontchad purchases in the south, but by 1987 these had been halted to reduce costs.

Tubers

The importance of tubers has grown dramatically over the years. Cassava and yams were the most important crops in this category, with much smaller production of potatoes, sweet potatoes, and coco yams (taro). Grown only in the *soudanian* zone, tubers were once neglected, although such cultivation is widespread in other parts of subtropical West Africa. Estimates in the 1950s put tuber production at 50,000 tons annually. Production rose and by 1961 it exceeded 200,000 tons. From 1961 to 1984, the proportion of roots and tubers in the national diet rose from 6 to 17 percent. The reason for this important shift in eating habits among people of the *soudanian* zone was the hedge these crops provided against famine in years when drought reduced millet and sorghum production.

Livestock

Livestock raising, and in particular cattle herding, is a major economic activity. Animal husbandry was the main source of livelihood for perhaps a third of Chad's people. The growing importance of cattle and meat exports underscored this point. In the 1960s and 1970s, these exports were estimated at between 25 and 30 percent of all merchandise exports. The proportion of these exports grew in the 1980s as the value of cotton exports declined. It was impossible, however, to know with certainty the actual values of cattle exports. For processed meat exports, less uncertainty existed because these exports were controlled from the slaughterhouse to the point of export; in 1985 processed meat exports represented less than 1 percent of all merchandise exports. The real value of Chad's cattle herds was in the export by traditional traders to markets in Cameroon and Nigeria. These "on the hoof" exports passed largely outside the control of customs services. Therefore, these exports were neither counted nor taxed. Perhaps one-fourth of cattle's estimated 30-percent share of total exports, was officially recorded.

The size of Chad's herds was also difficult to determine. Considered to have declined in the mid-1970s and again in the early 1980s because of drought and warfare across the *sahelian* zone, herds, estimated to be growing at a rate of 4 percent annually, reached some 4 million head of cattle, 4.5 million sheep and goats, 500,000 camels, and 420,000 horses and donkeys by the mid-1980s. Sheep and goats were found in all regions of Chad.

Before the drought of the 1980s, the *sahelian* zone held the largest herds, with about 80 percent of the total cattle herd. Smaller numbers of cattle were found in the *soudanian* zone, along with about 100,000 buffaloes used in plowing cotton fields. Camel herds were concentrated in the dry northern regions. Herders practiced transhumance—seasonal migrations along fairly well-set patterns.

With the 1984–85 drought, transhumance patterns changed. Camels were brought farther south into the *sahelian* zone in search of water. Cattle were herded even farther south, sometimes through Salamat Prefecture into Central African Republic.

The government and international donor community had contemplated considerable improvements for Chad's livestock management, but these plans were undermined by the Chadian Civil War, political instability, and an inadequate infrastructure. The most successful programs have been animal vaccination campaigns, such as an emergency project carried out in 1983 to halt the spread of rinderpest. The campaign reached some 4.7 million head of cattle across the nation and demonstrated the capabilities of Chad's animal health service when given external support. The Livestock and Veterinary Medicine Institute of Chad (Institut d'Elevage et de Médecine Vétérinaire du Tchad—IEMVT), which was financed by foreign aid, was capable of producing vaccines for Chad as well as for neighboring countries. Despite plant capacity, by 1984 a lack of a trained staff limited production to vaccines for anthrax and pasteurellosis.

Two institutional efforts to manage cattle marketing were attempted in the 1970s and 1980s. The Chadian Animal Resources Improvement Company (Société Tchadienne d'Exploitation des Ressources Animales—SOTERA), a mixed enterprise formed as a livestock company with participation by some traditional livestock traders, began operations in 1978. Its aim was to control live animal exports through a license system and to have a monopoly on exports of chilled meat and hides. It was hoped at the time that the association of traders to SOTERA would increase the effective collection of export taxes on livestock by 50 to 75 percent. By 1984, however, SOTERA handled only a small portion of the domestic market and less than 30 percent of the export trade. A second institution, the Center for the Modernization of Animal Production (Centre de Modernisation des Productions Animales—CMPA), was engaged in marketing dairy products, supplying chicks to farmers, and overseeing the sale of eggs and the processing of feed. But, among other problems, the CMPA was unable to compete with local traders for milk needed to produce cheese for sale. Although highly subsidized, this venture also was unsuccessful and demonstrated the resilience of the traditional private network for marketing produce.

Despite these institutional difficulties, the international community continued to support efforts to expand animal health services to Chad's herders. Some estimates suggest that the nation's herds could be increased by 35 percent if the distribution of water were improved, extension services were made more available, and animal health services were expanded.

Fishing

With its two major rivers, Lake Chad, and many runoff zones, in the 1970s Chad ranked high among Africa's producers of inland freshwater fish. With the drought and diversion of the waters of some rivers, however, production declined in the 1980s. Traditionally, fish has been an important source of protein for those living along the rivers and lakes, and fishing was also a means of earning cash. Because it was practiced in an entirely traditional manner and totally outside the control of government or modern commercial enterprises, there was no accurate statistical information on fishing.

In the 1960s, 1970s, and 1980s, total production of fish was estimated at between 60,000 and 120,000 tons per year. But because these figures represent production for the Logone River and Lake Chad, which are shared with Cameroon, Niger, and Nigeria, Chad's fish production amounted to an estimated 70 percent of the total. The largest part of the catch—perhaps two-thirds—was consumed locally. In areas adjacent to urban centers, some portion—usually the best of the catch, such as large Nile perch (called *capitaine* in Chad)—was marketed fresh. Along Lake Chad and the river borders with Cameroon, the surplus catch was dried, salted, or smoked before being sold. Between 1976 and 1985, production of dried, salted, or smoked fish was estimated at 20,000 tons annually, representing from 20 to 25 percent of Chad's total annual catch. A large share of the commerce in preserved fish was carried on with markets in Cameroon and Nigeria. Small dried or salted fish called *salanga* were most popular on the markets of Cameroon. Larger smoked fish called *banda* were generally exported to the major Nigerian market of Maiduguri.

Through the mid-1980s, Chad had taken few steps to control or modernize fishing or to promote fish conservation, although some plans had been made in the 1960s and 1970s. Perhaps the most significant innovation applied by Chadian fishermen has been their use of nylon netting, which began in the 1960s. During the periods of conflict, no government plans could be carried out to control fishing. Although considerable potential existed for the development of the Chadian fishing industry, because of insufficient government interest traditional production and marketing of freshwater fish was likely to remain unchanged for the near term.

Forestry

Like most states of the African Sahel (see Glossary), Chad has suffered desertification—the encroachment of the desert. Traditional herding practices and the need for firewood and wood for construction have exacerbated the problem. In the early 1980s, the country possessed between 13.5 million and 16 million hectares of forest and woodlands, representing a decline of almost 14 percent from the early 1960s. To what extent this decline was caused by climatic changes and to what extent by herding and cutting practices was unknown. Regulation was difficult because some people traditionally made their living selling wood and charcoal for fuel and wood for construction to people in the urban center. Although the government attempted to limit wood brought into the capital, the attempts have not been well managed, and unrestricted cutting of woodlands remained a problem.

Manufacturing, Mining, and Utilities

Manufacturing

The small industrial sector was dominated by agribusiness, and Cotontchad in particular. Next in importance were the National Sugar Company of Chad (Société Nationale Sucrière du Tchad—SONASUT), the Chadian Textile Company (Société Tchadienne de Textile—STT), the Logone Breweries (Brasseries du Logone—BdL), and the Cigarette Factory of Chad (Manufacture des Cigarettes du Tchad—MCT). Observers estimated that these five industries generated some 20 percent of GDP. Of lesser importance were the Farcha Slaughterhouse (Abattoir Frigorifique de Farcha), the Industrial Agricultural Equipment Company (Société Industrielle de Matériel Agricole du Tchad—SIMAT), and Soft Drinks of Chad (Boissons Gazeuses du Tchad—BGT).

During the Chadian Civil War, the facilities and equipment of many industries were badly damaged. Most industrial operations either ceased or were reduced greatly, and almost all foreign investors withdrew from the country. Those operations that did continue on a reduced scale were limited to the *soudanian* region, which was not involved directly in large-scale fighting. By 1983, with the reestablishment of political stability on a national scale, the five major industrial concerns resumed full operations, and the less significant ones, such as SIMAT and the BGT, were rebuilt.

With the exception of the two bottling companies (the BGT and the BdL), which were privately owned, all the other important industries were either parastatals with majority government ownership or mixed companies with important government participation (see fig. 6). For the most part, private participation was limited to French investors; investment by private Chadian interests was extremely rare. French companies were also important shareholders in the larger Chadian companies, such as Cotontchad. Except for Cotontchad, whose top management was Chadian, all the other major industries were run by expatriate directors, accountants, and mid-level managers who, for the most part, were French.

Industrial output grew rapidly in 1983 and 1984, as industries resumed operations that had been interrupted by war. By 1984 and 1985, prewar levels of output had been either reached or exceeded.

Growth slowed for all industries after 1985, however, because of the dramatic downturn of world cotton prices, and output in 1986 began to decline.

Cotton fiber production by Cotontchad, which directly reflected production of raw cotton, fell sharply in 1985. This decline was stabilized in 1986–87 by emergency support from international donors. These donors prescribed retrenchment programs to prevent the total collapse of the cotton industry. The restrictions imposed on the production of ginned cotton fiber, however, reduced by half the number of ginning mills, with raw cotton production limited to about 100,000 tons. Production of edible oils by Cotontchad was also affected by the program of cost savings.

Other industries were affected directly by the fall of cotton prices. STT textile production slowed, as did the production of agricultural equipment by SIMAT, which made plowing equipment for use in cotton planting. Furthermore, the drop in revenues to farmers in the *soudanian* zone for their cotton and peanut production affected their ability to buy equipment. Lost revenues to farmers, along with the reduction in the numbers of workers needed in ginning operations, took a toll on cash earnings and therefore on buying power. By 1986 the ripple effect of these lost revenues in the cotton sector was widespread. The downturn in production in all industries left Chad with considerable unused capacity, ranging from 15 to 50 percent.

A number of other factors resulted in the slump in Chadian industry. Commercial sale of goods was low in a largely cash poor or nonmonetary economy. The decline in the cotton sector, which had provided the largest infusion of cash into the economy, further reduced consumer demand. Another impediment to industry was the high local cost of production compared with the cost of production in neighboring countries. Factors that raised local production costs included high transportation costs, overdependence on imports, and restricted economies of scale for small operations. Imported inputs were equivalent to about 30 percent of industrial turnover for Cotontchad, the BdL, and the STT and to about 60 percent for the MCT. Local substitutes for inputs were often more expensive than imported equivalents. Imports were often marketed to subsidize local production by a given industry. An example was SONASUT's importing refined sugar at less than local production costs, selling it locally, and using the proceeds to subsidize sugarcane production on SONASUT plantations. Interlocking relationships of production among companies also kept production costs high. For example, the BGT used SONASUT's refined sugar in its production of soft drinks, according to a convention with the government to use local inputs, even though imported refined sugar was cheaper.

Before the warfare of the 1979–82 period, Chad's industrial sector included between 80 and 100 small- to medium-sized enterprises, in addition to the major manufacturing industries. Most processed agricultural products or competed in the import-export trade. About half were local subsidiaries of foreign-owned firms or were Chadian firms with significant foreign capital. The foreign-owned distributorships sold agricultural equipment, construction materials, and petroleum products.

Since 1983 the return of foreign investment has been slow because of the high costs of rebuilding and a continuing perception of political uncertainty. Of the approximately twenty enterprises that had reopened by the late 1980s, most were import-export enterprises that lacked a formal relationship with the banking sector. Most Chadian-owned enterprises had managed to reestablish themselves. Yet by 1986, small enterprises that had assembled bicycles, motorcycles, and radios remained closed.

The lack of access to credit was another impediment to business expansion in Chad. Despite the reopening in 1983 of the Bank of Central African States (Banque des Etats d'Afrique Centrale— BEAC) and of two commercial banks, the International Bank for Africa in Chad (Banque Internationale pour l'Afrique au Tchad— BIAT) and the Chadian Credit and Deposit Bank (Banque Tchadienne de Crédit et de Dépôt—BTCD), the high proportion of available credit going to Chad's major industries limited credit available to smaller enterprises (see Banking and Finance, this ch.). Moreover, the banks invoked strict criteria for loan eligibility because of the high risk of lending in Chad. Few owners of small businesses knew sufficient accounting and technical skills to meet bank information requirements for loans.

Mining

The only mineral exploited in Chad was sodium carbonate, or natron. Also called sal soda or washing soda, natron was used as a salt for medicinal purposes, as a preservative for hides, and as an ingredient in the traditional manufacture of soap; herders also fed it to their animals. Natron deposits were located around the shore of Lake Chad and the wadis of Kanem Prefecture.

Natron occurs naturally in two forms: white and black. More valuable commercially, hard blocks of black natron were exported to Nigeria. White natron was sold on local markets, principally in N'Djamena and farther to the south. Although efforts were made in the late 1960s to control the commercialization of natron through

111

the creation of a parastatal, by 1970 those efforts had failed because of resistance by traditional chiefs and traders who controlled production through a system of perpetual indebtedness.

A number of other mineral deposits are known, but none had been commercially exploited by the mid-1980s. Bauxite is found in the *soudanian* zone, and gold-bearing quartz is reported in Biltine Prefecture. Uranium is reported in the Aozou Strip, as are tin and tungsten in other parts of the Tibesti Mountains, but exploration reports in 1971 for these three minerals did not indicate large or rich deposits. As of 1987, conflicts in the region prevented further exploration.

By far the potentially most important resource is oil. In 1970 a consortium of Conoco, Shell, Chevron, and Exxon started exploration and in 1974 discovered minor oil deposits at Sédigi, near Rig Rig, to the north of Lake Chad (see fig. 7). Total reserves at Sédigi were estimated at 60 million tons, or roughly 438 million barrels of oil. Exploration in 1985 by the Exxon-led consortium discovered potentially large deposits near Doba in the southern region of Chad. Further efforts were suspended in 1986 when world oil prices continued to drop, although the consortium maintained a liaison office in N'Djamena in 1988.

Plans existed in the late 1970s to exploit the deposits at Sédigi and to construct a small refinery at N'Djamena. Those plans lapsed during the conflicts of the late 1970s and early 1980s but were revived in 1986 by the government with the support of the World Bank. The reasons for proceeding with plans to exploit these deposits and build a refinery were clear. The cost of importing petroleum products exceeded the cost of extracting and refining domestic crude, even when international oil prices were low. The plans, which anticipated operations to begin in the early 1990s, included well development in the Sédigi field, a pipeline to N'Djamena, a refinery with a 2,000- to 5,000-barrels-per-day (bpd—see Glossary) capacity, and the transformation or acquisition of power-generating equipment in the capital to burn the refinery's residual fuel oil. The refinery's output would satisfy 80 percent of Chad's annual fuel needs, including all gasoline, diesel, butane, and kerosene; lubricants and jet fuel, however, would still have to be imported.

Water and Electricity

In the late 1980s, public utilities in Chad were extremely limited. The Chadian Water and Electricity Company (Société Tchadienne d'Eau et d'Electricité—STEE), was the major public utility company. The government held 82 percent of the shares and CCCE held 18 percent. STEE provided water and electricity to the four main urban areas, N'Djamena, Moundou, Sarh, and Abéché. The company supplied water, but not electricity, to six other towns. Despite old equipment and high maintenance costs, STEE was able to meet about half of peak demand, which increased significantly from 1983 to 1986. Production of electricity rose by 35 percent from 1983 to 1986, and the supply of water increased by 24 percent during the same period. In 1986 STEE produced 62.1 million kilowatt-hours of electricity and supplied 10.8 million cubic meters of water.

In N'Djamena the majority of households had access to water. There were, however, only about 3,000 officially connected customers, a good proportion of which were collective customers. There were also an estimated 1,500 illegal water connections. The rest of the people received water from standpipes. Some 5,000 customers were officially connected for electricity in the capital in 1986, with an unknown number of illegal connections. Because electricity was so expensive and because electrical appliances were beyond the means of most people, the consumption of power per household was low. The high cost of electricity also hindered the expansion of small- and medium-sized enterprises.

Transportation and Communications

As a landlocked state, Chad has no ports. The nearest ports were all located on the Atlantic Ocean. Douala, Cameroon, at 1,700 kilometers from N'Djamena was the closest port. Furthermore, there were no railroads in the country. Two ancient land routes connected Chad to the Mediterranean Sea and the Red Sea. The first, more than 3,000 kilometers across difficult desert tracks, led north to Benghazi, Libya. The second, to the Red Sea via Sudan to Port Sudan, was 2,600 kilometers from Abéché and 3,350 kilometers from N'Djamena. Neither route has been used for commercial traffic in modern times. There were only two Atlantic routes of commercial importance in the 1970s and 1980s. One was the Nigerian rail-connected routes to Port Harcourt or Lagos via Maiduguri; the other was the Cameroonian route to Douala via rail from Ngaoundéré. Because of Nigeria's internal political difficulties and its troubled relations with its neighbors, the Nigerian route was intermittently closed to Chadian traffic in the 1980s, leaving open only the Cameroonian route to surface traffic into and out of Chad.

Until 1985 there was no permanent bridge across the Chari River to N'Djamena. Access to N'Djamena from Kousséri, Cameroon, was by ferry. When water levels fell during the drought of 1984 and 1985, ferries sometimes were unable to make the crossing. To alleviate this problem, in 1985 a pontoon bridge was constructed

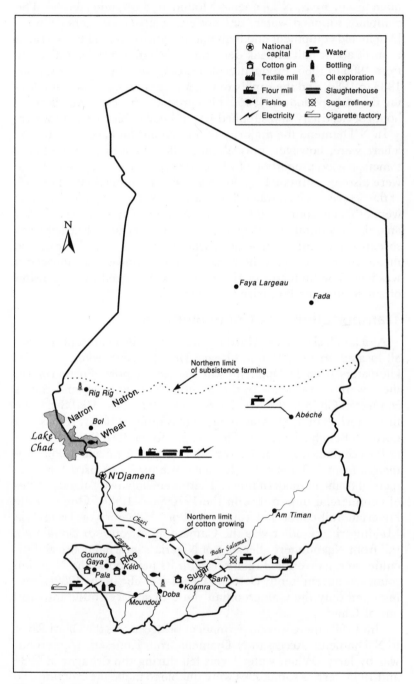

Figure 7. Economic Activity, 1987

over the Chari River. A similar situation existed farther south where, in 1986, a bridge was constructed at Léré, across the Mayo-Kebbi River. This bridge replaced ferry transport, formerly the only means of crossing, and linked southern Chad with Cameroon.

The closest rail links to Chad were the Nigerian rail system from Maiduguri to the ports of Lagos and Port Harcourt and the Cameroon system from Ngaoundéré to Douala. Both were connected to Kousséri in Cameroon, across the Chari River from N'Djamena, via all-weather roads, then on to Chad via the bridge over the Chari (see fig. 8).

The country's external traffic amounted to some 350,000 tons per year in the mid-1980s. For the most part, this traffic was carried on the road and rail route to Douala via Ngaoundéré. A great part of this traffic did not leave Chad via the capital. Chad's largest export, ginned cotton, took routes directly from the southern region to Cameroon via Léré (Chad) and Garoua (Cameroon) before reaching the rail at Ngaoundéré. Petroleum products were imported entirely by road, whether from Cameroon or from Nigeria.

As a member of the Customs Union of Central African States (Union Douanière des Etats d'Afrique Centrale—UDEAC), Chad exported and imported goods through a free storage area at Douala. The facility was completed in 1985 with funding from the EC and served both Chad and Central African Republic. The facility permitted long-term storage of goods exported from or imported into Chad. Agreements with Cameroon under UDEAC auspices allowed reductions of 50 percent on port taxes and of 25 percent on the total charged for handling costs. A quota for rail transport was also established whereby Chadian importers and exporters paid only 65 percent of rail charges to transport their goods and the remaining 35 percent was assumed by Cameroon.

Land Transport

In 1988 the road system in Chad remained deteriorated or underdeveloped. At one time, two paved roads linked the capital to the interior: one to Massaguet, 80 kilometers to the northeast, and the other to Gélendeng, 160 kilometers to the south. Both roads, however, had virtually disappeared by 1987 because of lack of maintenance. Of the 253 kilometers of paved roads reported in 1978, none were still paved in 1987. Chad had about 7,300 kilometers of dirt roads and tracks that were partly maintained; only 1,260 kilometers were all-weather roads. About 24,000 kilometers of rural marked tracks received no maintenance at all. Most of this road and track network was passable only during the dry season.

115

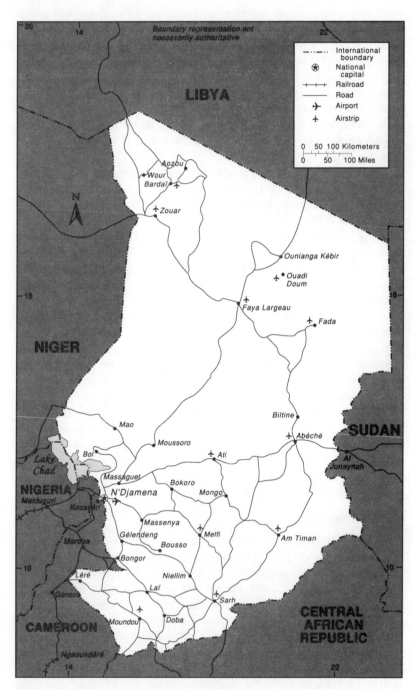

Figure 8. Transportation System, 1988

Considerable foreign donor attention was focused on land transportation problems. In addition to the externally financed bridges constructed to allow passage to Cameroon, the National Office of Roads (Office National des Routes—OFNAR) under the Ministry of Public Works, Housing, and Urban Development used technical assistance and training financed by the United States Agency for International Development (AID) and the United Nations International Development Agency (IDA). In 1987 three OFNAR subdivisions operated in N'Djamena, Sarh, and Moundou. Plans existed to open subdivisions in Abéché and Mongo as road rehabilitation advanced into these areas. The National Quarry Office (Office National des Carrières—OFNC) was created in 1986 under the Ministry of Public Works, Housing, and Urban Development to manage quarry operations at Dandi (north of N'Djamena near Lake Chad), using a large crusher financed by AID. The crushed stone was to be used for road improvements.

Government plans for the rehabilitation of the national road network called for the reconstruction of 3,800 kilometers of priority roads from 1987 to 1992. In 1987 about 2,000 kilometers were receiving spot repairs. The network of priority roads would reestablish the all-weather links between the capital and Sarh via Gélendeng and Niellim. It would also connect Sarh to Léré via Moundou in the south and N'Djamena to Am Timan via Bokoro and Mongo. The reconstruction and maintenance of the system would depend on the success of IDA- and AID-funded efforts to restore the capabilities of the OFNAR and to start the operation of the Dandi quarry.

Domestic freight traffic amounted to approximately 265,000 tons per year in the early 1980s. More than 100,000 tons of this traffic was in the southern regions, which included the transport of the cotton crop from collection points to ginning mills and then to points of export. The transport of food in normal nondrought years averaged around 50,000 tons annually. The internal transport of petroleum products represented some 25,000 tons annually of the total domestic freight, with the distribution of beer, sugar, and miscellaneous consumer goods making up the balance.

Transport during the rainy season was difficult, particularly between the capital and *sahelian* and *soudanian* zones. To avoid the swollen rivers and runoffs, Chadian traffic often was forced to pass by way of Cameroon, taking all-weather and paved roads via Maroua from Léré or Bongor and then on to Kousséri and N'Djamena. Travel in the rainy season via Maroua to Mayo-Kebbi Prefecture was a day or day-and-one-half journey; the internal route south from N'Djamena toward Mayo-Kebbi Prefecture could take two weeks or longer.

The main transport carriers in Chad in 1987 were the Cooperative of Chadian Transporters (Coopérative des Transporteurs Tchadiens—CTT), Cotontchad, and the United Nations Development Programme (UNDP) Emergency Food Programme transport fleet. The CTT was an association of private truck owners having a government-granted monopoly on all internal and external transport, except for the operations of Cotontchad and other parastatals with private trucking fleets. In 1985 the CTT had 382 members, who owned 580 trucks with a total capacity of 16,700 tons, as well as 108 tanker trucks for fuel transport with a capacity of 3,427 cubic meters. The CTT transported some 150,000 tons of dry cargo and an estimated 8,700 cubic meters of petroleum products in the same year. Not all transporters participated in the cooperative. Trucks with capacities of five tons or less carried unrecorded but significant amounts of goods over short distances.

Cotontchad, which was not a member of the CTT, was the single largest carrier in Chad. In 1985 it operated about 260 heavy trucks and another 100 light- to medium-weight vehicles that transported the cotton crop from collection points to ginning operations and on to export terminals. In 1986, as a part of the emergency restructuring program to reduce transport costs, the company sold about eighty of its large tractor trailer trucks to the CTT, which was expected to take responsibility for the long-distance import-export movement of the cotton crop.

The UNDP fleet in 1985 consisted of 240 trucks to transport emergency food during the drought. In 1987 the number of UNDP trucks fell to about 150, and these trucks were underused. In the late 1980s, the fleet brought supplies and food to remaining pockets of malnutrition, especially to those areas hit by locust infestations. The government was anxious to maintain this fleet for use during any renewed drought, despite the overcapacity and possible competition the fleet's operations might pose for the CTT.

By 1987 overall trucking capacity exceeded demand for domestic and import-export transport. Much of the fleet was also mismatched for domestic needs, being either oversized or suited more for the paved and all-weather roads leading into the country. Moreover, many trucks were in poor condition. To compound the problem, there were insufficient maintenance and support facilities available to keep vehicles in good repair. Studies were under way in 1987 to improve this situation, with particular attention to breaking up the CTT's monopoly.

Air Transport

Chad was regularly served by two international air carriers in

1987, Air Afrique and the French-owned Air Transport Union (Union des Transports Aériens—UTA). These carriers shared four flights weekly through Chad's only international airport, at N'Djamena, with connections to Paris twice weekly and also south to Bangui and Brazzaville twice weekly. N'Djamena's airport was capable of receiving the largest aircraft, including Boeing 747 and Airbus passenger airplanes used by the two carriers, and giant cargo aircraft such as the C–5A used in military supply. The airport was rehabilitated after armed hostilities in 1980 and 1981 destroyed all control and support facilities. Rehabilitation included widening and extending the runway. Other smaller regional carriers handled traffic to Khartoum (Air Sudan) and to Douala (Cameroon Airlines). Chad's own airline, Air Tchad, served internal routes to Abéché, Sarh, and Moundou and to other points on an occasional basis. In 1987 Air Tchad was equipped with a nineteen-seat Twin Otter and a forty-four-seat Fokker 27. Internal traffic also was served by several small four- to six-passenger aircraft owned privately or by international organizations. In addition to the airport at N'Djamena, smaller fields at Abéché, Sarh, and Moundou were capable of receiving small jet traffic and propeller aircraft. Small dirt strips were also located in several towns throughout the country.

Communications

Chad's telecommunications system was one of the least developed in Africa. International telecommunications were conducted by the parastatal International Telecommunications Company of Chad (Société de Télécommunications Internationales du Tchad—STIT) under the responsibility of the Ministry of Posts and Telecommunications. Telephone and telex service between Paris and N'Djamena assured communications with the international community. No direct links, however, existed in 1986 between Chad and its African neighbors; all telecommunications passed via Paris. Some internal telephone service connected Abéché, Moundou, Sarh, and N'Djamena. The only means of internal communications was by shortwave radio. Postal service via air between Paris and N'Djamena existed. However, postal service beyond the capital, except to Moundou and Sarh, was limited. In 1987 international mail had to be delivered to the central post office in the capital a day before the next scheduled flight to Paris to assure delivery. Mail arriving in N'Djamena was posted to boxes at the central post office for pickup by box owners. No delivery was available to residences or businesses, all official addresses in the capital being post office boxes.

Trade and Commerce

Historically, Chad has been a country of traders. The ancient kingdoms of Kanem, Borno, and Wadai built their power on trade with Libya, Egypt, and Sudan (see Era of Empires: A.D. 900–1900, ch. 1). During the colonial period, trade increased with francophone countries and Nigeria. In the 1970s, the structure and direction of external trade remained similar to the pattern of colonial times, the most important trading partners being France and Nigeria. Exports to France were principally cotton fiber, and imports were finished manufactured goods and equipment. Much of the trade with Nigeria, consisting of cattle, fish, natron, and other traditional products, was unrecorded and did not pass through official channels. Since the civil upheavals of the late 1970s and early 1980s, which restricted all external trade, unofficial trade with Nigeria has resumed. Official trade with France declined after 1982, primarily because many French-affiliated firms closed during the conflicts. As of late 1987, many of those concerns had not reopened.

Controlling smuggling and black market activity was very difficult. Chad and its neighbors had few resources that could be devoted to border control. Collusion among smugglers and border patrols and customs agents was common. Moreover, Chad's unofficial trade with Nigeria, Cameroon, and Central African Republic has historical and social roots. Tribal and extended family connections across borders encouraged traders to maintain long-range commercial and financial networks beyond colonial and, later, national government control and taxes. Traders unofficially exported the bulk of Chad's exports of cattle, fish, and other traditional products. Unofficial imports consisted of petroleum products and consumer goods, such as sugar, cooking oil, soap, and cigarettes, that competed with production by national industries. The permeability of Chad's borders and the informality of traditional trading networks denied the government revenues ordinarily derived from export-import duties. Locally produced goods and legal imports fared badly in this market, burdened as they were with high production costs, lack of economies of scale, and price distortions imposed by government controls.

Exports

The bulk of Chad's official exports were agricultural products, which have accounted for 80 to 95 percent of all exports since independence. Of these exports, cotton fiber was most important, followed by cattle and beef exports. The value of Chad's cotton fiber exports rose steadily in the 1970s (see Cotton, this ch.). During the early 1980s, as armed conflict took its toll on cotton production, the value of cotton fiber exports dropped. The return of political stability in 1983 and increased cotton production coincided with a rise in world cotton prices, resulting in dramatic increases in the value of Chad's cotton exports in 1983 and 1984. The value of these exports more than doubled from 1982 to 1983 and almost doubled again in 1984.

The downturn of world cotton prices in 1985 caused a collapse in cotton exports. The value of cotton fiber exports from Chad in 1985 was less than half that of the record 1984 level; the value fell even further in 1986. In 1984 cotton fiber had represented 73 percent of the value of all Chad's exports, but in 1986 it represented only 43 percent. The value of all exports also reflected the decline, falling from a high in 1984 of almost CFA F48 billion to around CFA F34 billion in 1986.

The estimated value of Chad's cattle exports remained more stable from 1983 to 1986. As the value of cotton fiber exports declined, the relative importance of cattle exports to the Chadian economy grew.

Imports

Since the late 1960s, the economic significance of imported manufactured and capital goods has grown considerably. From 1967 to 1970, manufactured goods of all types accounted for 46 to 50 percent of Chad's imports. By 1975 manufactured goods accounted for 65 percent of imports. The total value of all imports also grew, doubling between 1965 and 1970 to almost CFA F13 billion. Total imports continued to grow through 1978 to nearly CFA F36 billion before showing a serious decline from 1979 to 1981 because of the heavy fighting. Imports increased after 1982, reaching around CFA F37 billion in 1983 and then doubling by 1985. The leap in imports between these years reflected not only the increase in imported manufactured and capital goods needed to rebuild the shattered economic infrastructure but also an increase in food assistance in these years of drought. The downturn of imports between 1985 and 1986 indicated in part a decline in food imports with the return of good rains.

Direction of Trade

Throughout the 1960s—Chad's first decade of independence—France remained its most important official trading partner. In 1970 France absorbed 73 percent of Chad's exports and provided some 40 percent of Chad's imports. Between 1979 and 1985, Chad diversified its markets by trading more actively with Spain, the Federal

Republic of Germany (West Germany), and particularly Portugal, which absorbed the bulk of Chad's exports, mainly cotton fiber. By 1985 France ranked sixth behind Portugal, West Germany, Cameroon, Spain and the Benelux countries (Belgium, The Netherlands and Luxembourg; see table 5, Appendix A). Chad's exports of beef and other traditional products to its neighbors, and especially to Nigeria, did not appear in official trade figures.

Although losing significance as a customer, France remained Chad's most important supplier. In 1985 France supplied almost one-fourth of Chad's total imports. The United States ranked second, followed by Cameroon, Italy, and the Benelux countries; unspecified West European countries accounted for about 21 percent of Chad's imports in 1985. Chad had little trade with Middle Eastern and North African countries. Both official and black market oil imports came from either Cameroon or Nigeria. Chad had no declared trade with the Soviet Union or East European countries.

Balance of Payments and Finance

Balance of Payments

With the exception of the 1979–81 period, which were years of heavy conflict when collapsed imports were offset by some continued cotton exports, Chad has run deficits in its trade balance since the 1960s (see table 6, Appendix A). The size of these deficits depended on the world cotton market. In 1984, when Chad had high export earnings as a result of record cotton production and high world cotton prices, the trade deficit was modest. The following year, when world cotton prices fell, production declined. Export earnings from cotton were half those of 1984, and total export earnings on all goods dropped by one-third. Problems with the cotton sector continued in 1986 and 1987. World cotton prices remained low, and the fall in the value of the United States dollar aggravated the situation because world cotton prices were quoted in dollars. At the same time that export earnings dropped, Chad's imports rose. The value of imports increased by almost 40 percent in 1985. A large part of this rise resulted from oil exploration, which was only partially offset by direct investments in Chad by the oil drilling companies. Increased imports of fertilizers and insecticides for Cotontchad's expanded program to improve production in those years also contributed to the trade deficit. The net result of these events was that the modest trade deficits of 1983 and 1984 grew into large deficits in 1985 and 1986.

A ferry over the Chari River
Courtesy Audrey Kizziar
Trucks carrying medical supplies over dirt tracks in the sahelian zone
Courtesy UNICEF (Maggie Murray-Lee)

123

Banking and Finance

Chad has been a member of the BEAC since independence. The BEAC, with the backing of the French treasury, served as the central bank of its member states: Cameroon, Central African Republic, Chad, Congo, Equatorial Guinea, and Gabon. Consequently, Chad has adhered to the Franc Zone, using as currency the African Financial Community franc, (Communauté Financière Africaine—CFA; for value of the CFA franc—see Glossary). Use of the CFA franc, which was tied to the value of the French franc (FF) at CFA F50 to FF1, gave Chad a stable, convertible currency. This factor spurred trader confidence in the value of the currency and in the ability to convert to hard currency acceptable as payment for imports. It was particularly helpful to the economy to have a stable currency backed by regional and international cooperation and not subject to political whim as governments and coalitions fought for power in Chad. Reconstruction after 1982 would have been far slower and more difficult had currency value suffered the volatility, inflation, and distrust of traders so often encountered in other Third World nations.

All banking offices closed in 1979 and 1980 when N'Djamena was the scene of heavy fighting. The BEAC reopened in 1981 along with the BIAT, the BTCD, and the Development Bank of Chad (Banque de Développement du Tchad—BDT). Only the International Bank for Commerce and Industry in Chad (Banque Internationale pour le Commerce et l'Industrie du Tchad—BICIT) had failed to reopen by late 1987, leaving Chad with only three banks plus the central bank. Of the three banks, only the BIAT—the local subsidiary of the French-owned International Bank for West Africa (Banque Internationale pour l'Afrique Occidentale—BIAO) was totally under private ownership. The government and the French bank Crédit Lyonnais shared joint ownership of the BTCD, along with some other smaller investors. The BDT was the principal government-controlled bank for development purposes; it received considerable support from the CCCE, a key arm of French foreign assistance programs.

In Chad the flow of credit and cash traditionally followed the rhythm of the cotton-growing season. Cotontchad, by law required to buy all cotton produced at preset prices, made short-term loans from the banks before planting each year to import materials for its cultivation improvement programs and to pay the producers for their crops at harvest. The credit portfolios of Chad's banks reflected this situation. In 1986 almost 90 percent of the claims on banks were short-term loans, more than 70 percent of which were consigned to Cotontchad. Overall, Cotontchad claimed 64 percent of all credit available to the economy. In 1984, with rising cotton production and good world prices, credit extended by the BEAC expanded quickly. This credit permitted an adequate level of industrial and consumer imports but drained the BEAC's exchange reserves. With the collapse of world cotton prices in 1985, Cotontchad's revenues dropped, and foreign exchange flowing into Chad declined. As a result, the BEAC's exchange reserves dropped precipitously in 1986. Operations in the banking sector ground to a halt as Cotontchad fell into arrears on repayments of its short-term debt. In late 1986, the BEAC negotiated a rescheduling of about three-fourths of the short-term debt, allowing a ten-year maturity, including a five-year grace period with an interest rate of 6 percent. The solution neither reduced the exposure of the private banks for loans to Cotontchad nor directly improved the general credit situation for other potential borrowers, especially the small- and medium-sized enterprises that often were squeezed out of the market. It did, however, save Chad's banking structure and Cotontchad from immediate collapse by buying time for longer-term solutions to be formulated with the aid of foreign donors.

No mechanisms existed for extending credit directly to farmers beyond assistance for cotton production. Before the Chadian Civil War, the BDT and the ONDR extended credit on a limited basis, as did the government's Rural Action and Development Fund (Fonds de Développement et d'Action Rurale—FDAR). But these credits for marketing agricultural products were not repaid, and the FDAR ceased operations in 1981. In 1985 the government created the Fund for Rural Intervention (Fonds d'Intervention Rurale—FIR) to replace the FDAR. Through 1987 the government was unable to fund the FIR, and the international donor community did not provide agricultural credit on a sectoral level other than for cotton, which impeded Chad's intention to diversify its agricultural economy. In 1986 the World Bank financed a study and a long-term technical assistance program to determine credit needs and options for the design of an appropriate system of rural credits. These actions were taken in cooperation with other institutions, such as the ONDR (extension services) and SIMAT under the authority of the Ministry of Agriculture and Rural Development.

In 1983 the government imposed a five-year moratorium that froze all deposits and outstanding credits before 1980. The moratorium's purpose was to prevent a run on banks and to staunch capital flight when banks restored operations in early 1983 under the new government. The impact of the moratorium was twofold. On the one hand, it served to reduce credit available to the economy because entrepreneurs were unable to withdraw assets for investment or operations. On the other hand, the amount of frozen credits was more than double that of frozen deposits, so the action protected other businesses from service on debts during the hard times of recovery.

The longer-term financial situation was bleak. The problem of interest payments to the BEAC for rediscounted credits, which made up the majority of frozen credits, compounded by Cotontchad's difficulties in meeting its debt obligations to the banks, seriously strained Chad's banking system.

Government Finances

In 1983 the Ministry of Finance produced its first central government budget in four years. By 1986 the government had adopted a standardized nomenclature that resulted in more effective management of revenues and expenditures throughout government ministries. The government also initiated measures to improve tax administration, including the reorganization of customs inspections in the capital, the creation of tax enforcement teams and tax offices in secondary cities, and greater control over records for the largest tax-paying enterprises. The State Control (Contrôle d'Etat), an autonomous auditing unit directly attached to the presidency, performed audits and investigations throughout public agencies and enterprises to deter fraud and misuse of public funds.

Chad's public sector was small compared with the size of the economy. In 1977 total government revenues amounted to about 9 percent of GDP. The deficit of 2.6 percent of GDP, although low when compared with such figures for other nations, was nevertheless significant because the figure represented one-third of total government revenues in that year. In absolute terms, revenues and expenditures were small but increasing from 1983 through 1985. The small size of government was a consequence of its reestablishment after the conflicts ended in 1982 and the limited resources of administration. The government's preference for a liberal economy, with the public sector a complement to, and not a substitute for, the private sector, also helped to hold down the size of the central administration. The sharp increases in expenditures and revenues from 1983 to 1985 reflect the reinstitution of government operations after 1982 and the increases in cotton-generated revenues during these years of good crops and high world cotton prices. The equally sharp decline in revenues in 1986 reflected the drop in world cotton prices and the halt in Cotontchad's contributions to the central treasury through duties on cotton exports. In the mid-1980s, expenditures, elevated by defense spending and the needs of a stable administration, first stagnated and then dropped somewhat. The reduction, however, did not keep pace with declining revenues, resulting in a 90 percent increase in the deficit in 1986.

During the same year, under terms of the Emergency Cotton Program, Cotontchad ceased all fiscal contributions to the government. The government's challenge was to control the fiscal deficit in the absence of cotton revenues either by cutting expenditures or by generating additional revenues. There was little room for movement on the expenditure side. Military outlays and salaries of government employees were the largest budget items. Defense spending was highly unpredictable and unlikely to be reduced quickly in the face of continued insurgency in the north. The officially declared defense expenditures were between 34.5 and 37.6 percent of government spending from 1984 to 1986 (see Defense Expenditures, ch. 5). Clearly, however, such figures represented only a part of total military spending, which may have been as high as 70 percent of government expenditures.

Government salaries were also difficult to reduce. The reinstitution of administrative government activities in 1982 brought the number of civil servants to between 20,000 and 23,000 by 1985. This increase reflected not only the government's renewal of operations but also its policy of national reconciliation. In part, that policy guaranteed positions to the most important former civil servants—largely those from the southern regions—who wanted to reenter government service. In the 1985–86 period, the government paid civil servants only 60 percent of their salaries, based on salary scales set in 1967. Although salaries for civil servants were low, the government was often unable to finance the whole wage bill without external budget support, and it often delayed payments until disbursements were covered by international donors.

Expenditures on government goods and services were low, as evidenced by the general scarcity of basic equipment and supplies in government offices. Civil servants often functioned without desks, chairs, paper, and such office equipment as typewriters and copying machines. Moreover, cutting expenditures for parastatals achieved no savings because the government did not subsidize their operations directly. The parastatals relied on their own sources of local revenues or foreign donor support. Donors also financed public investment and a large part of recurrent costs associated with development projects.

The government's financial resources consisted of fiscal revenues, special funds, and exceptional taxes. The small size of Chad's modern, monetary sector limited the tax base. With the fall of world cotton prices and reduced production and income both to Cotontchad and to peasant producers, the tax base shrank even more in 1985. In the mid-1980s, relatively few economic agents bore the tax load. Taxes were derived particularly from the five major industries—Cotontchad (exempted in 1986), the STT, the BdL, SONASUT, and the MCT. Their burden included (in order of importance) import-export duties, excise taxes, corporate taxes, and turnover taxes. In 1986 fiscal revenues amounted to 5 percent of GDP, compared with 9 percent in 1977 and 15 percent in the peak year of 1971. This percentage compared unfavorably with those in some other African states, such as Central African Republic (12 percent), Mauritania (22 percent), and Senegal (19.5 percent).

In 1984 the government first imposed exceptional taxes to finance national reconstruction. All salaried employees, whether in government or in the private sector, were taxed one month's salary. In 1985 the government repeated the effort to combat the effects of drought and in 1987 introduced a variable tax to support the war effort. Although these taxes placed a burden on taxpayers, the government did not account for these taxes in the official budget.

Several special funds either collected taxes on behalf of the government or derived revenues from their own activities. The two most important funds were the CSPC, and the Petroleum Products Fund (Fonds d'Intervention des Produits Pétroliers—FIPP). The CSPC's mandate included stabilizing producer prices for cotton furnished to Cotontchad, financing the deficit of Cotontchad, and playing a part in industrial and commercial operations of the cotton sector. The plan called for 80 percent of any Cotontchad surplus to go to the CSPC, with Cotontchad retaining the remainder. Any Cotontchad deficit was to be financed by the CSPC. From 1972 through 1984, Cotontchad transferred about CFA F21 billion to the CSPC. The CSPC, however, did not finance Cotontchad's deficits, which were particularly acute after 1985. Rather, the CSPC used its resources to subsidize the ONDR and the IRCT to invest in other public enterprises and to finance its own administrative costs. Since 1986, under the Emergency Cotton Program, Cotontchad ceased contributions to the CSPC, which no longer played its mandated role. FIPP was set up to equalize petroleum import prices from Nigerian and Cameroonian sources, so that Chad would not become overly dependent on either source for its fuel supplies. FIPP was to tax cheaper Nigerian imports, thereby subsidizing Cameroonian imports, breaking even in the process. But the system never worked properly and ultimately led to considerable fraud, with cheaper Nigerian imports often receiving subsidies after leaving

Cameroon. Poor border control also contributed to FIPP's inability to stabilize and equalize imports and prices on petroleum. In 1987 the government, along with the donor community, were reviewing the roles of these two institutions.

The National Debt and Foreign Assistance
National Debt

The CAA was responsible for servicing Chad's external public debt. The CAA collected revenues not included in the government budget to service the debt. Those revenues consisted mostly of unit taxes on manufactured goods and taxes on the profits of industry, banks, and the surpluses of other special funds. In 1985 and 1986, losses of revenues from the cotton sector also affected the CAA's revenues. In 1986 the CAA compensated by imposing new taxes on other industries, and it also strengthened its administration and collection abilities.

From 1980 to 1985, Chad's annual external debt averaged US$169 million (see table 7, Appendix A). In 1987 Chad's public and publicly guaranteed debt (outstanding and disbursed) stood at about US$206 million, amounting to 25 percent of GDP. Three-fourths of the debt was given on concessional terms; two-thirds of this amount was owed to multilateral creditors, and one-third was owed to bilateral donors. One-fourth of the debt represented non-concessional loans that predated the 1979–82 conflict and were owed to suppliers, private financial institutions, and certain bilateral creditors, such as Kuwait. Even before hostilities escalated in 1979, Chad's credit-worthiness was low and through 1987 was insufficient to tap private financial markets. Only official creditors lent to Chad. The volume of lending was low in the 1983–85 period, but in 1986 the World Bank resumed lending, and France increased its lending. In 1987 lending on concessional terms to Chad reached pre-1977 levels of about US$40 million a year. Chad's actual debt service ratio—as a proportion of export earnings on goods and services—was low in 1986, standing at 1.5 percent. When payments on arrears and the BEAC payments to the IMF (which were to be transferred to the CAA in 1988) were added, Chad's total debt service ratio stood at between 5 and 7 percent. Although considered low by most standards, this situation created a heavy burden for the CAA and the Chadian government. For the 1987–89 period, Chad faced scheduled debt service on existing loans of between US$10 and US$13 million per year, more than double the amount the government was able to pay in the 1985–87 period. Debt service of US$10 million represented about 15 percent of expected government revenues in 1987, not including unsettled existing arrears. The CAA's efforts to increase revenues by instituting new taxes and by improving administration were encouraging throughout 1987. In late 1987, observers were unable to predict how Chad would cope with its long-term debt problems, especially in the face of a shrinking tax base, which was exacerbated by difficulties in the cotton industry.

Foreign Assistance

Since independence, all of Chad's several governments have relied on foreign assistance to meet current expenses, to finance government and trade deficits, to combat drought and famine, to wage war, and to rebuild from the ravages of war. France provided the most aid, with some also from multinational organizations, such as the EEC, the United Nations (UN), and the World Bank, and from bilateral donors, such as the United States, Italy, and West Germany. Donor assistance has fluctuated. It fell during the conflicts of the late 1970s and early 1980s, particularly from 1979 through 1982. Some donors, such as the United States, halted all aid between 1980 and 1982, when Goukouni Oueddei, who was supported by Libya, held power (see Transition to Northern Rule, ch. 4). France, however, continued to provide some form of nonmilitary aid to Chad throughout the period, but it was channeled to the south and not to the central government. As other donors pulled out, the share of French aid relative to all official aid to Chad rose from 23.6 percent in 1978 to 42.2 percent in 1980. In 1982, as other donors returned, the proportion of French aid to all official aid to Chad began to decline, amounting to only 18 percent by 1985. Despite this relative decline and the increased aid from other donors, especially UN organizations and the United States, France remained Chad's most important donor, both in absolute terms and as a percentage of total official aid, for all years except 1985. In that year, the World Food Programme (WFP) was Chad's single largest donor because of drought; that aid, therefore, consisted of food aid and not development assistance.

Because of drought between 1983 and 1985 and because of the needs of recovery from the dislocations of war, foreign aid in these years focused on emergency assistance. Famine relief, health, and sanitation formed the base of this assistance, with funds also directed to correcting the most basic logistics problems of food delivery to the country. As the rains improved in 1985, resulting in good harvests, a shift away from emergency operations toward longer-range development planning began. Budget support also increased after 1985 in response to lost government operating revenues because

A tailor plies his trade on a street in N'Djamena
Courtesy Joseph Krull

of the cotton crisis. By 1987 about 85 percent of estimated aid flows provided for development assistance, and 12 percent supported the budget. Disbursements of food aid fell from the high of 176,000 tons in 1985, when the international community responded to drought across Africa, to an estimated 1987 shipment of 30,000 tons, used as food security reserves to relieve chronic pockets of malnutrition. The shift in emphasis accompanied a rise in overall disbursements, which were expected to reach US$250 million in 1987.

Almost all of Chad's external assistance during the ten years before 1986 was on concessional terms. After 1986, however, the proportion of loans compared with grants increased significantly. In the 1983–85 period, with emphasis on emergency aid in health and nutrition, loans represented only 9 percent of aid disbursements. In 1986, with the shift to project development assistance, renewed World Bank lending, and the need to target money to the cotton sector, loans increased to 14 percent of total aid disbursements. In 1987 donors were expected to increase the proportion of loans in overall aid to as much as 33 percent, all on a concessional basis.

In the mid-1980s, foreign donors financed all public investment in Chad. Recurrent costs also were financed by donors, in large part for programs and projects to rehabilitate the economy and to provide basic social services in health care and education. Roughly half of the projected aid disbursements in 1987 supported public investment to rebuild and expand the nation's socioeconomic infrastructure; about 19 percent supported recurrent costs of the government, and about 21 percent supported operating costs of the parastatals.

A sectoral analysis of projected aid in 1987 showed about 32 percent of donor assistance targeted to infrastructure, 26 percent to rural development, 22 percent to industry and energy, and 16 percent to social services, including health and education. Regional distribution of aid for the same year proposed about 16 percent of project assistance to the capital and its environs, 21 percent to the *sahelian* zone, 26 percent to the *soudanian* zone, and 37 percent to projects cutting across regions. For ethnic and humanitarian reasons, several large donors concentrated their efforts in particular regions of the nation. Italy focused its aid in the Kanem and Lac prefectures, the EDF on Chari-Baguirmi Prefecture, and West Germany on Mayo-Kebbi and Ouaddaï prefectures.

The terms of aid disbursements projected for 1987 were consistent with past trends and took into consideration the financial constraints on the Chadian government and economy. Approximately two-thirds of donor aid consisted of grants. The remaining one-third of loans came almost entirely from multilateral organizations on concessional terms. Overall, 40 percent of the disbursements in 1987 came from bilateral donors, with France the largest (24 percent), followed by Italy (11 percent), the United States (6 percent), and West Germany (4 percent). The multilateral organizations accounted for 55 percent of disbursements, of which the IDA was the largest contributor, providing 15 percent. Other UN organizations provided 11 percent, and EC agencies gave 12 percent.

By 1986 the international donor community, led by the World Bank and the IMF, recognized the need for concerted action in Chad. Once the drought ended and essential reconstruction from war damage had begun, the widespread economic dislocation caused by Cotontchad's difficulties forced the government and its donors to consider long-term structural adjustments for the whole economy. The adoption of the Emergency Cotton Program in 1986 could only stave off short-term collapse and enable Cotontchad to position itself better until world prices improved. Diversification away from dependence on the cotton complex in agriculture, industry, and finance was essential. For the long term, incentives had to be found to stimulate other sectors of the economy.

In 1987 the government agreed to medium-term adjustment targets through 1990. As a result, the IMF began providing budget support to Chad, and the World Bank provided project assistance, as a part of a comprehensive package that included support from other donors. These coordinated efforts at adjustment focused on defining and implementing sectoral strategies for cotton, noncotton agriculture, livestock production and marketing, rural credit, reforestation, transportation, and human resources and training. Studies to implement comprehensive programs to rehabilitate government fiscal policies and management, to develop priorities for government investment programs, and to address questions relative to the operations of parastatals and public institutions, along with the management of public domestic and foreign debt, were all part of the package. On the one hand, fiscal and management practices would be tightened. On the other hand, the private sector would be encouraged by the loosening of monopoly operations by public institutions.

*　*　*

As of late 1987, there were few sources that addressed Chad's economy, and no single book dealt comprehensively with the topic. Economic information, however, could be found in general sources, the focus of which was most often political. The best books were in French and included Jean Cabot and Christian Bouquet's *Le Tchad: Que sais-je?*, Christian Bouquet's *Tchad: La genèse d'un conflit*, as well as Gali Ngothé Gatta's *Tchad: Guerre civile and désagrégation de l'état*. Among the few English-language sources was Michael P. Kelley's *A State in Disarray*, which contains a good section on the impact of foreign assistance on economic development.

Several periodicals provided valuable data on the Chadian economy in the 1980s. These periodicals include *Marchés tropicaux et méditerranéens; Bulletin de l'Afrique noire, Africa Economic Digest,* and the Economist Intelligence Unit's quarterly reports. Occasional articles in *Revue tiers-monde* and *Courier* were also helpful.

Publications of international organizations and government agencies provided much of the detail lacking in general narratives; however, figures often conflicted because of differing methods of compilation. These publications were produced by the United Nations, World Bank, International Monetary Fund, United States Agency for International Development, and a number of French government agencies. (For further information and complete citations, see Bibliography.)

Chapter 4. Government and Politics

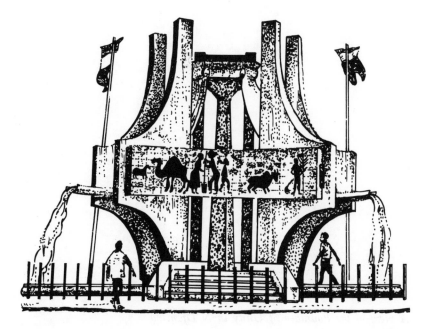

A view of the Fountain of Unity in N'Djamena

SEVERAL THREADS OF CONTINUITY ran through Chad's political development during its first twenty-eight years of independence that began in 1960. Dominated by a series of authoritarian regimes, most under military rule, Chad had no representative national institutions in 1988. Its ruling party, the National Union for Independence and Revolution (Union Nationale pour l'Indépendance et la Révolution—UNIR) was organized by the government in 1984; UNIR leaders were appointed by the president from among government officials, and the party served primarily to reinforce government policy. By late 1988, UNIR had not opened the political process to democratic participation.

Political fragmentation also characterized Chad's political development since independence. The Islamic northern and central regions and the colonially exploited south were divided by regional stereotypes rooted in their past, which included centuries of slave raids from the north. Subregional, religious, cultural, and individual differences complicated major regional divisions.

Chad's diverse population was drawn into power struggles in the drive for independence following World War II. Numerous political parties and coalitions sought foreign assistance to bolster weak popular support. The nation's first independent regime grew increasingly repressive during its fifteen years in power as its leader, François Tombalbaye, attempted to pacify this fractious population and transform southern economic domination into political control. Several dissident groups, most from the northern and central regions, united under the National Liberation Front of Chad (Front de Libération Nationale du Tchad—FROLINAT), but this coalition, too, was plagued by factional strife.

In the early 1970s, Tombalbaye contributed to his own eventual downfall by implementing the *authenticité* movement, an ill-conceived campaign that sought to impose southern-based ritual traditions on the nation's civil service. The resulting cycle of public protest and government repression culminated in a 1975 coup, in which Tombalbaye was killed. His successor, Félix Malloum, continued the pattern of concentrating political power in the executive branch of government but was persuaded to bring rebel leaders Goukouni Oueddei and Hissein Habré into his government. Their rebel forces eventually proved stronger than Malloum's army, and he was forced out of office in 1979. His successor, Goukouni, was the first of Chad's insurgent leaders to become president of Chad.

A series of unsuccessful coalition governments oversaw Chad's descent into a state of civil war. The major coalition, the Transitional Government of National Unity (Gouvernement d'Union Nationale de Transition—GUNT), was led by Goukouni, whose relatively conciliatory style of governing contrasted with the previous pattern of authoritarian regimes. His critics considered him weak and indecisive, and he was strongly influenced by Libyan leader Muammar al Qadhafi, whose primary aims were to install a sympathetic Muslim leader in Chad, expand Libya's influence in the region, and reduce Western influence across the continent.

A salient feature of Chad's foreign policy since independence has been foreign intervention—especially by Libya, Chad's aggressive neighbor to the north, and France, the former colonial power. Libya took advantage of Chad's instability in the early 1970s to press its claim to the Aozou Strip (see Glossary) in northern Chad, based on centuries of close ties among border populations and an unratified 1935 Franco-Italian agreement, which had been ignored by intervening governments. French ties with Chad, based on historical, commercial, political, and strategic interests, rivaled those of Libya, and the Aozou Strip provided an arena in which this rivalry could be pursued. In addition, neighboring countries, especially Sudan and Nigeria, also took an active role in events in Chad, hoping to achieve a favorable balance of power in the region. Other Central African and West African states sought to contain Chad's violence and avoid being caught up in the spreading instability.

Chad's political shifts in the early 1980s resulted from international fears of Libyan intervention through influence in Goukouni's regime, France's revised African policy following the Socialist Party's election victory in 1981, and military gains by Habré. Habré had served in governments led by Tombalbaye, Malloum, and Goukouni, and he had led insurgencies against all. Finally in 1982, with loyal northern forces and French and United States support, Habré ousted Goukouni and proclaimed himself president of Chad.

Habré's patrimonial state was another authoritarian regime. A written constitution empowered him to appoint almost all high officials and reduced the legislative branch to a token assembly. He determined the pace and direction of activity in all branches of government. At the same time, Habré gained popular support by stabilizing Chad and working to establish peace. He also began to reintroduce social services to a population for whom warfare had been the most noticeable sign of government activity.

In 1988 factional dynamics in Chad still resembled precolonial politics. Habré was a master strategist in this arena, and he succeeded in winning over numerous former opponents through combined military and political means. Nevertheless, the threats of new rifts among allies and of future alliances among enemies still existed, in keeping with the model of the segmentary political systems that had dominated the region for centuries.

To strengthen existing ties among former opponents and to mobilize grass-roots support for his government, Habré proclaimed his intention in 1988 to transform the ruling party, UNIR, into a people's vanguard party. Many people in outlying areas were still skeptical of the need for an increased governmental presence, however, and many southerners still considered national government a northern imposition. Both problems underlined the political challenge that faced Chad as the 1990s approached.

Political Background

Preindependence Factions

Chad became part of French Equatorial Africa (Afrique Equatoriale Française—AEF; see Glossary) in 1905 and became a separate colony within the AEF in 1920 (see Arrival of the French and Colonial Administration, ch. 1). Colonial policy exploited the agricultural potential of the south, exacerbated regional animosities that were the result of centuries of slave raids from the north, and failed to prepare Chadian citizens for self-rule. During World War II, the colonial governor general, Félix Eboué, brought Chad to international attention by leading the AEF in support of Charles de Gaulle's Free French movement.

After the war, Gabriel Lisette and other political activists, including François Tombalbaye, established the Chadian Progressive Party (Parti Progressiste Tchadien—PPT). The PPT protected southern interests in competition with the more influential Chadian Democratic Union (Union Démocratique Tchadienne—UDT). The UDT was dominated by expatriates, who treated Chad's political arena as a forum for debate over events in Paris (see Decolonization Politics, ch. 1).

More than two dozen political parties and coalitions arose to oppose this Eurocentric view of local politics and to compete with the UDT and the PPT. These groups were generally aligned as southerners, northerners who sought to share in the nation's economic development, other northerners who opposed modernization, and socialist groups who hoped to replace the European-dominated economy with one oriented more toward local needs. Further fragmentation occurred along subregional and religious lines and over the question of the future role of expatriates in Chad.

Chad's 1946 constitution declared it an overseas territory of France. As French citizens, its people elected representatives to a territorial assembly, which in turn elected delegates to a French General Council for the AEF and to several governing bodies in France. Chadians demanded further political rights, however, including training in administrative and technical areas that would lead to self-government and the right to set their own political agenda independent of other francophone states. The PPT won a plurality in the Territorial Assembly, and Lisette became head of the first government established under the *loi cadre* of 1956, an enabling act that made Chad an autonomous republic within the French Community, instituted universal suffrage, and established a single electoral roll.

Demands for greater local control of politics led to dramatic political shifts in the late 1950s. The UDT, attempting to shed its expatriate emphasis, was reorganized and renamed Chadian Social Action (Action Sociale Tchadienne—AST). The AEF was dissolved in 1958 amid rising African demands for autonomy. A series of unstable provisional governments followed the ouster of Lisette as the PPT's leader in 1958. His successor, Tombalbaye, became head of the Territorial Assembly in 1959 and head of the nation's first independent government in August 1960.

Southern Dominance, 1960-78

Tombalbaye banished Lisette and many of his supporters from Chad and eliminated Lisette's power base by dividing the Logone region of the south into three prefectures. Tombalbaye openly discriminated against the north, ignored the growing national political awareness that was evident during the postwar years, and established a repressive regime that contributed to Chad's fragmentation during his fifteen-year tenure as president.

Major regional rifts were complicated by intraregional divisions, especially in the north, where numerous warlords, each with an ethnic-based following or cadre of supporters, attempted to overthrow Tombalbaye's regime. In 1966 northern rebels united as the FROLINAT. They established bases in Sudan and received assistance from Algeria and Libya, but FROLINAT, too, was divided over military and political issues, attitudes toward Libya, interpretations of Islam, and individual leadership style (see The FROLINAT Rebellion, 1965-79, ch. 5). An important split occurred in 1969 between northern factions and those from Chad's eastern and central regions, which had dominated the group for three years. Northern factions went on to form FROLINAT's Second Liberation Army (see Appendix B).

The headquarters of the PPT, with President François Tombalbaye's picture on the sign
Courtesy Michael R. Saks

Tombalbaye expelled French troops from Chad but otherwise perpetuated the dependence established under colonial rule. He employed French advisers in many government posts and allowed France to control most of the nation's financial operations. Tombalbaye also strengthened presidential authority and resisted recommendations of his expatriate advisers, who urged him to decentralize authority to provincial officials and traditional leaders. Rather than assuage northern grievances or pacify the increasingly numerous rebel armies, Tombalbaye responded with repression. He dissolved the National Assembly in 1963 and eliminated rival political parties. He also jailed outspoken critics and closed down most public media. His repressive style and rebel violence were mutually reinforcing, leading Tombalbaye to recall French troops.

Amid increasing destabilization in the early 1970s, Tombalbaye sought first to protect southern interests. He implemented the *authenticité* movement, an ill-conceived campaign (modeled on that of Zairian president Mobutu Sese Seko) that deemed southern cultural characteristics more authentic than those of the north. Opponents successfully exploited public outrage when Tombalbaye required civil servants to undergo *yondo*—traditional initiation rites indigenous only to his ethnic constituency among the Sara population of the south (see Classical African Religions, ch. 2). Weak

141

efforts to pacify the north by granting limited autonomy to traditional leaders and releasing prominent political prisoners served only to recruit new dissidents.

After Muammar al Qadhafi seized power in Libya in 1969, he exploited Chad's instability by stationing troops in northern Chad and by channeling support to Chadian insurgents. Although Tombalbaye expelled Libyan diplomats in 1971, blaming them for inciting a coup attempt and inspiring unrest, in general he sought a balance between concessions and resistance to Qadhafi's regional designs, hoping to persuade Qadhafi to reduce his support for Chadian insurgents. Tombalbaye voiced a willingness to cede the Aozou Strip and did not object to Libyan troops' being stationed there after 1973. Chad erupted in renewed protests against Tombalbaye's unpopular and weakened regime, culminating in a successful coup against him in 1975.

General Félix Malloum, a former government critic imprisoned by Tombalbaye, proclaimed himself head of the Supreme Military Council (Conseil Supérieur Militaire—CSM), which seized power in 1975. As a southerner with strong kinship ties to the north, Malloum believed that he could reconcile Chad's divided regions and establish representative institutions. He set a high priority on freeing Chad from French economic and political control, but in this effort he was unsuccessful. He sent French combat forces home, but he retained several hundred French advisers and renegotiated a series of military accords to ensure emergency aid.

Malloum was unable to convert dissatisfaction with Tombalbaye's regime into acceptance of his own. His opponents exploited popular displeasure with the remaining French presence by recruiting new dissidents. In response to this threat, Malloum seized control of all branches of government and, in the increasingly repressive manner that characterized his presidency, banned almost all political activity. His opposition coalesced around FROLINAT, which established alternative administrations in outlying areas to compete with N'Djamena. In 1978, in the face of mounting violence, Malloum reluctantly called for the return of French forces (see Civil Conflict and Libyan Intervention, ch. 5).

Transition to Northern Rule

In 1978 officials in Chad and neighboring countries attempted to craft a coalition that could control the country through military force and still claim to have some popular support. Urged by African heads of state and French advisers, Malloum attempted to bring FROLINAT faction leaders Hissein Habré and Goukouni Oueddei into the government, but these two northerners soon clashed with

Troops being reviewed in 1970 at Fada
Courtesy Michael R. Saks

Malloum and each other. While Habré's troops engaged government forces, Goukouni seized the opportunity to occupy government buildings and claim control of N'Djamena. Talks were held first in Sudan and then in Nigeria, but by late 1979 neighboring states were working primarily to contain Chad's spreading violence and limit Libyan interference in regional affairs (see Relations with Other African States, this ch.).

As N'Djamena became a war zone, with fighting among FROLINAT factions and southerners going on between 1979 and early 1982, outsiders proclaimed the disintegration of the state. Although major disruptions occurred, the government struggled to maintain basic official functions. Executive functions were allocated according to ministerial portfolios and were given limited attention. Many buildings in the capital city were destroyed, but a small civil service continued to operate. Public services were erratic but not absent. Still, the government fought for its survival rather than to protect its citizens, and thousands of people sought refuge in rural areas or neighboring countries.

Talks in Lagos and Kano in 1979 culminated in the formation of GUNT, led by Goukouni, which incorporated several rival northern commanders. Malloum left the country, and the locus of governmental power shifted from south to north, largely because of northern military successes, popular discontent throughout the

143

country, and pressure from neighboring states for an end to Chadian violence. National unity became increasingly ephemeral, however, as members of this coalition were polarized between Habré and Goukouni. Goukouni was the son of the *derde,* a respected traditional leader among the Teda population of the north, one of the Toubou groups that had generally been receptive to the Libyan-based Sanusiyya brotherhood before independence (see Languages and Ethnic Groups; Islam, ch. 2). In his view, Libyan interests in Chad were valid. Goukouni requested Qadhafi's assistance against Habré in 1980, bringing Libyan troops into the country as far south as N'Djamena.

As head of state, Goukouni did not implement promised democratic reforms, but neither did he tolerate unlimited reprisals against the south. Instead, he was relatively tolerant of minor expressions of dissent, warned security forces against harsh retaliation in the south, and gave local administrators limited autonomy.

Both allies and opponents perceived this relatively conciliatory attitude as a presidential weakness and a hesitant style of leadership. Indeed, this hesitancy was apparent in 1981 when Qadhafi proclaimed a merger between Libya and Chad. Following international and domestic protests, Goukouni reversed his position and balked at Qadhafi's regional demands.

French political shifts in 1981 also had an important impact on events in Chad. The election of François Mitterrand as French president heralded a reorientation in African policy. Socialist leaders vowed to reduce the overall French presence in Africa and to avoid an open confrontation with Libya, a major source of French oil imports. French support shifted cautiously to Habré, who appeared willing to resist Libyan domination with outside support and whose decisive leadership had been demonstrated against French troops for over a decade. France's Socialist Party pursued its goal of reducing its interventionist profile in Africa by persuading francophone states, through the Organization of African Unity (OAU), to send peacekeeping troops to Chad. Goukouni called for the removal of Libya's forces, but when Habré's Armed Forces of the North (Forces Armées du Nord—FAN) moved on the capital, they encountered almost no resistance from the OAU-sponsored Inter-African Force (IAF). As a result, in June 1982 FAN seized N'Djamena and proclaimed Habré head of state.

Habré's decisiveness and his preference for French rather than Libyan patronage shifted the focus of government once again. He took limited steps to assuage regional dissent, relying on northerners in most military commands and top political offices but appointing southerners to several executive and administrative positions. Habré also reduced the aim of independence from French domination to the status of a long-term goal. France maintained vital economic, financial, military, and security assistance; underwrote the budget; effectively operated the banking system; and provided a variety of commercial and technical advisers. Furthermore, Habré used French and United States military assistance to repel Libyan troops, Libyan-supported insurgents, and local rebel forces (see Habré's Return to Power and Second Libyan Intervention, 1982–84, ch. 5). French funds also helped Habré co-opt former opponents.

As president, Habré brought more peace to Chad than that country had known in a decade. Habré vowed to remove Libyan forces from the north, reconcile north and south, and establish a democratic state. In his first six years in office, he took steps to accomplish some of these goals.

Structure of Government

Constitutional System

Between 1959 and 1988, Chad's constitution was revised six times and altered by several major amendments. The preindependence constitution adopted by the Territorial Assembly in March 1959 was modified at independence in 1960. The new document established a parliamentary system of government with an executive prime minister. Further revisions in 1962 strengthened the executive, and the 1965 constitution eliminated all rivals to the ruling party, the PPT. In 1973 President Tombalbaye codified in the constitution his version of the *authenticité* movement to reaffirm indigenous values. This movement required civil servants to undergo initiation rites common to some ethnic constituencies of the south. Following a military coup in 1975, in which Tombalbaye was killed, and the general deterioration of state institutions, lengthy negotiations in 1978 led to a new constitution that established an unsuccessful coalition among Chad's warring factions.

In June 1982, when Habré seized control of N'Djamena, he dissolved the existing government and in October promulgated the Fundamental Law, a document that served as an interim constitution through 1988. In July 1988, Habré appointed a constitutional committee to draft a new document to be presented to the government in 1989.

The Fundamental Law of 1982 declared Chad a secular, indivisible republic, with ultimate power deriving from the people. Both French and Arabic were adopted as official languages, and ''Unity-Work-Progress'' was adopted as the nation's motto. The constitution authorized the office of president, Council of Ministers (cabinet), National Advisory Council (Conseil National Consultatif—CNC, an interim legislature), and national army. It placed overriding authority for controlling all of these in the office of the president.

President

Article 2 of the Fundamental Law designated the president as head of state and government. He was chairman of the Council of Ministers, with a mandate to define the fundamental policy choices of the nation. The president was the commander in chief of the armed forces and head of an ostensibly civilian government. The Fundamental Law allowed the Command Council of the Armed Forces of the North (Conseil de Commandement des Forces Armées du Nord—CCFAN) to select the president. Habré dissolved the CCFAN when he established the ruling party, UNIR, in 1984. No succession procedures were in place after 1984, and most observers expected Habré to remain in office after the new constitution was presented to the government in 1989.

The Fundamental Law authorized the president to legislate by decree, and he often did so. He also appointed and dismissed ministers, legislators, and high-level civil and military officials. Only the president could initiate constitutional amendments; this procedure required, however, consultation with both ministers and legislators.

The president's international authority included negotiating and ratifying treaties and accords and guaranteeing Chad's observance of them. He was technically required to consult with ministers and legislators, but more often he simply notified them of his foreign policy decisions.

Council of Ministers

The president and twenty-three appointed ministers formed the Council of Ministers in 1988. The council's portfolios included agriculture and rural development; civil service; commerce and industry; culture, youth, and sports; national defense, veterans, and war victims; education; finance; food security and afflicted groups; foreign affairs; information and civic orientation; interior; justice; labor; livestock and rural water; mines and energy; planning and reconstruction; posts and telecommunications; public health; public works, housing, and urban development; social affairs and the promotion of women; state; tourism and the environment; and transportation and civil aviation. The president held the portfolio for defense. Only one woman served on the Council of Ministers. Executive appointments were divided among most regions of the

*A woman sells bottles of gasoline on a war-damaged street
in the capital
Courtesy United Nations (John Isaac)*

country, although northerners dominated most organs of government.

The general responsibility of the Council of Ministers was to carry out the wishes of the president, although constitutional language defined its task as overseeing national reconstruction, establishing a democratic way of life, guaranteeing fundamental rights of individuals and associations, and guaranteeing the effective participation of all social classes in the managing of public affairs. The council was also responsible for maintaining a national army, reorganizing the national police, reorganizing public enterprises and parastatals, developing an effective health care system, assisting victims of war, relaunching the economy, reforming the school system, devising an investment code to encourage domestic and foreign capital formation, reconstructing the communication system, and regaining Chad's self-sufficiency in food.

Article 18 summarized ministerial responsibilities in foreign policy. These responsibilities were to maintain friendship and cooperation with all peaceful countries, to uphold the principles of the United Nations (UN) and OAU, to support legitimate struggles by people under racial and colonial domination, to combat all forms of expansionism, and to practice nonalignment in foreign policy-making. Article 19 restricted ministers from holding a second

147

office in government, although many government officials in 1988 also held office in UNIR.

National Advisory Council

The Fundamental Law formalized the institution of a weak legislative branch of government. Thirty advisers, who served at the discretion of the president, made up the CNC in 1988. Although they were authorized to elect their own council president and two vice presidents, their mandate was only to advise the president regarding states of emergency and war and to consult with him regarding fundamental policy choices, international agreements, budgetary allocations, and general plans for political, social, and economic development. In practice, the CNC supported presidential policy.

As of 1988, the people of Chad had no elected representatives at the national level. The appointed CNC provided a formal structure for representative government and policy deliberation, but it was entirely subordinate to the executive branch. Legislators effected policy changes only if the president agreed with them.

Regional Government

Throughout the 1980s, Chad was divided into fourteen prefectures (see fig. 1). Each was further subdivided into subprefectures, administrative posts, and cantons. Most prefectures were divided into two to five subprefectures; the total number of subprefectures was fifty-four. Administrative posts and cantons were often organized around traditional social units, especially in areas where an existing bureaucratic structure could represent the state. In general, the national government relied on traditional leaders to represent its authority in rural areas. In many of these areas, civil servants could not maintain order, collect taxes, or enforce government edicts without the cooperation of respected local leaders.

Administrators at each of these levels (prefects, subprefects, administrators, and canton chiefs) were appointed by the president or the minister of interior and remained in office until the president dismissed them. Each prefect was assisted by a consultative council composed of ten or more members nominated by the prefect and approved by the minister of interior. Traditional leaders were often included, and council protocol was sometimes based on local rank and status distinctions.

During the 1960s, the government granted municipal status to nine towns, based on their ability to finance their own budgets. These municipalities generated most of their revenues through administrative fees, fines, and taxes, and they organized communal

*The residence of a subprefect, often the only symbol of government
in rural areas
Courtesy Michael R. Saks*

work projects for many city improvements. Their governing bodies were relatively autonomous municipal councils, chosen by popular consensus or informal elections. Each council, in turn, elected a mayor from its own ranks. The official policy of autonomy for municipal councils was generally overridden by the requirement that almost all council decisions be ratified by the prefect or the minister of interior.

Judicial System

Chad's legal system was based on French civil law, modified according to a variety of traditional and Islamic legal interpretations. In the late 1980s, the civilian and military court systems overlapped at several levels, an effect of Chad's years of warfare (see The Criminal Justice System, ch. 5). Civilian justice often deferred to the military system, and in some areas, military courts—many of which were established by rebel armies during the late 1970s—were the only operating courts. In the 1980s, the government was working to reassert civilian jurisdiction over these areas.

Chad's Supreme Court was abolished following the coup in 1975 and had not been reestablished by 1988. The highest court in the land was the Court of State Security, comprising eight justices, including both civilians and military officers, all appointed by the president. In addition, a court of appeals in N'Djamena reviewed decisions of lower courts, and a special court of justice established in 1984 heard cases involving the misappropriation of public funds.

Criminal courts convened in N'Djamena, Sarh, Moundou, and Abéché, and criminal judges traveled to other towns when necessary. In addition, each of the fourteen prefectures had a magistrate's court, in which civil cases and minor criminal cases were tried. In 1988 forty-three justices of the peace served as courts of first resort in some areas.

Chad also had an unofficial but widely accepted system of Islamic sharia courts in the north and east, which had operated for a century or more. Most cases involved family obligations and religious teachings. In other areas, traditional custom required family elders to mediate disputes involving members of their descent group, i.e., men and women related to them through sons and brothers. Civil courts often considered traditional law and community sentiment in decisions, and the courts sometimes sought the advice of local leaders in considering evidence and rendering verdicts.

Political Dynamics

Factionalism

Chad's political environment in the 1980s was a fluid, changing network, bearing the imprint of centuries of factional dynamics. Traditional authority has generally been diffuse, rather than concentrated in a single individual for an entire society. Clusters of descent groups defined the society in many areas. Factions arose when descent groups clashed, and strong leaders sought kin-group support in confronting one another. Social norms focused on preventing conflict through family law, religion, and authority relations, and a key feature of factional strife was the reunion that eventually followed many violent clashes.

As a result of these traditional beliefs and practices, many Chadians viewed politics according to a segmentary model of descent group fragmentation. They scorned the idea that national leaders, in fixed terms of office, could demand loyalties, regardless of the issues involved. From their perspective, centralizing power and authority served to deny, rather than to implement, democratic principles. In Chad, as in other faction-ridden political systems, opposition and alliance were constantly recalculated, as costs and benefits to the individual or kin-group were weighed. Politics were often blurred and not defined in terms of distinct bipolar rivalries.

Factional fragmentation in Chad occurred in response to predictable issues, such as France's postcolonial role, relations with Libya, the value of negotiation versus armed confrontation, and ethnic and regional balances of power. Rifts also resulted from basic disagreements over policy decisions, forms of retaliation against rivals, and personality clashes. Reconciliation often brought former rivals together in the face of a more threatening opponent.

Factions assumed particular importance after independence because of Chad's diverse ethnic groups, the traditional scorn for centralized authority, the weak impact of central government policies in the north, and the generally inadequate infrastructure that impeded communication among regions. Most important, northern resentment found its expression in numerous strong leaders—in effect, warlords—but instead of organizing under a strong warlord to secede, factional armies in the north sought to wrest control from the government and from each other.

Hissein Habré is an example of a leader whose career has demonstrated skill as a factional strategist. He entered politics after returning from graduate study in France in 1971, but he abandoned his original post in the Tombalbaye government to join the opposition FROLINAT. In this organization, he had personality clashes with a number of leaders, including FROLINAT's ideologue, Abba Siddick. In 1972 Habré formed an army of his own, allied with fellow northerner Goukouni Oueddei, in opposition to Siddick. Habré and Goukouni managed a fragile alliance for more than three years, despite differences in style and ability. Habré negotiated a large ransom payment from Paris for French hostages he and Goukouni kidnapped in 1974, but by the time the hostages were released in 1977, Habré and Goukouni had ended their alliance.

This arrangement did not last because Habré clashed with Malloum over regional and policy issues. Their confrontation allowed Goukouni to seize the capital and declare himself head of state. As minister of national defense, veterans, and war victims in Goukouni's regime, Habré continued to clash with his northern rival over policy, style, and, increasingly, over Libyan involvement in Chad. Habré fled N'Djamena and, with French and United States support, returned to oust Goukouni as head of state in June 1982.

Habré decided he would form alliances only from a position of strength, and he proceeded to defeat, intimidate, or co-opt a number of rebel leaders. He then moved to end factional strife, curb the nation's continuing violence, and extend the reach of government into the countryside. As of 1988, he had been fairly successful in his dual pursuit of national reunification and reconciliation. He had consolidated his control of Chad's fractious population through both military and political tactics, and, following the example of

151

his predecessors, he had strengthened the executive branch of government and postponed democratic reforms. Habré's authoritarian rule outweighed the nation's strong centrifugal tendencies, but just barely. He defeated numerous rebel armies between 1983 and 1987, and as a result of these clashes, the disarray among his opponents, and French financial assistance, he won over most former opponents.

Among those groups that rallied to Habré's government was the Action Committee of the Democratic Revolutionary Council (Comité d'Action et de Concertation du Conseil Démocratique Révolutionnaire—CAC–CDR), founded in 1984 as the intellectual wing of the opposition CDR. Under the leadership of Mahamat Senoussi Khatir, it declared support for Habré in 1985. The People's Armed Forces (Forces Armées Populaires—FAP), a former FROLINAT faction led by Goukouni, also declared support for Habré in October 1986, although Goukouni remained outside the country, attempting to negotiate a dignified return. Goukouni's one-time vice president and leader of the Chadian Armed Forces (Forces Armées Tchadiennes—FAT), Wadel Abdelkader Kamougué, was Habré's minister of agriculture and rural development in 1988. The Democratic Front of Chad (Front Démocratique du Tchad—FDT) was also won over by Habré. The FDT was a coalition of groups formed in Paris in 1985 in opposition to both Goukouni and Habré. Led by General Negué Djogo, the FDT shifted its support to Habré later that year. Djogo became Habré's minister of justice in early 1986 and was shifted to minister of transportation and civil aviation in mid-1988. Two other former FDT leaders also joined the government, one as minister of finance and the other as minister of culture, youth, and sports.

Several factions of *codos,* or commandos, were also convinced to rally to the government. *Codos* were southern rebel formations nominally united under the leadership of Colonel Alphonse Kotiga. Many of them declared their support for Habré during 1985 and 1986. Other small groups also rallied to Habré's government in 1986 and 1987, including the Democratic and Popular National Assembly (Rassemblement National Démocratique et Populaire—RNDP) and the Assembly for Unity and Chadian Democracy (Rassemblement pour l'Unité et la Démocratie Tchadienne—RUDT).

A number of groups remained actively opposed to the government in 1988. Several of these formed a coalition, the Supreme Council of the Revolution (Conseil Suprême de la Révolution—CSR) in 1985. The CSR included nominally united remnants of GUNT, which had controlled the national government under Goukouni's leadership from 1979 to 1982 (see Civil War and

A building showing the destructiveness of the Chadian Civil War
Courtesy United Nations (John Isaac)

Multilateral Mediation, 1979–82, ch. 1). Goukouni disappeared from the GUNT command while he negotiated unsuccessfully to return to Chad on his own terms in 1987. In 1988 he proclaimed his allegiance to Habré but soon thereafter announced the reorganization of the GUNT alliance under his command.

Another group in the CSR, the CDR, was founded in 1979 by Acyl Ahmat but in 1988 led by Acheikh ibn Oumar. The CDR formed the core of Habré's opposition in 1988, following military and political losses by GUNT. Also opposed to the government in 1988 were the Popular Movement for the Liberation of Chad (Mouvement Populaire pour la Libération du Tchad—MPLT), which had broken away from FAP under Aboubakar Abdel Rahmane's leadership, and its splinter group, the Western Armed Forces (Forces Armées Occidentales—FAO); several factions of FROLINAT, including those led by Hadjero Senoussi and Abdelkader Yacine; and the Movement for the National Salvation of Chad (Mouvement pour le Salut National du Tchad—MOSANAT), led by Boda Maldoun. MOSANAT, a Hajerai-based organization, maintained its antigovernment stance through several administrations. No remaining rebel army, by itself, posed an immediate threat to Habré's regime (see Internal Security Conditions, ch. 5).

National Union for Independence and Revolution

Habré's political support came primarily from northerners, the army that brought him to power, and civilians who admired his tough stand on such issues as opposition to Libyan interference in Chadian affairs. To broaden his support, in 1984 he undertook a program to extend the reach of government into rural areas, first by seeking the advice of the nation's prefects. Southern prefects advised that in addition to lingering animosity based on the early association of FAN with FROLINAT, which had worked to oust the southern-based government of Tombalbaye, a major concern in that region was the conduct of the army. The army had become, in effect, an obstacle to security.

In 1984 Habré dissolved the CCFAN and established a political party, UNIR. Habré retained broad power to control the party agenda, and he appointed military officers to nine of the fourteen positions on the party's Executive Bureau, which served as the primary liaison between the party and the government. To placate the south, six posts were allocated to southerners.

UNIR was designed primarily to mobilize and inspire popular participation in government and to enable the president to control that participation. Other important goals were to increase the civilian emphasis in government and, finally, to achieve peace between north and south. The party invoked national values such as brotherhood and solidarity, individual respect, confidence, and "healthy criticism and self-criticism." It also developed a repertoire of songs, chants, and sayings intended to bolster these aims.

The eighty-member UNIR Central Committee was important in extending the reach of the party throughout the nation. For this purpose, it employed groups of about sixty agents (*animateurs*) and ten organizers (*encadreurs*) in each prefecture to convert apathetic and war-weary citizens into party activists. Militant UNIR recruiters delivered public speeches on the need for unity, peace, and progress through the party organization and for reduced Libyan influence in Chad. They also helped recruit members to party affiliates, such as youth groups, women's organizations, and trade associations.

The main political impact of UNIR by 1988 was to maintain a cadre of elites on the periphery of the government. The party was successful at orchestrating political displays but had not inspired widespread loyalty. People generally remained skeptical of the ability of government to improve their lives. Rural citizens in particular had seen few benefits of national development and feared that the government's inevitable urban bias would make life even harsher for them.

The party's effectiveness as a democratic forum was hampered by the fact that the president controlled its agenda. UNIR provided very limited opportunities for debating government policy and had little patronage to dispense, except its own offices. It served primarily to convey to the president a sense of popular opinion and to reassure him that his government was not entirely out of touch with its constituency. In this role, UNIR usurped much of the limited power of the interim legislature, the CNC, and left the appointed legislators to act primarily as bureaucratic housekeepers. Habré reportedly intended to allow for greater democratic participation at some time in the future, but before doing so, he hoped to provide sufficient political indoctrination to guarantee support for party aims.

In 1988 Habré proclaimed his intention to convert UNIR into a people's party, a "revolutionary vanguard," for the purpose of grass-roots political mobilization. To begin this task, he created the People's Revolutionary Militia (Milice Populaire de la Révolution—MPR), but the MPR was not yet operational in mid-1988. As head of the UNIR Executive Bureau, the president was to appoint the leader of the MPR and control its agenda.

The MPR mandate was to reach people through the local party organization in each of the nation's administrative divisions. This structure—subdivided into groups, subgroups, sectors, and subsectors corresponding to the nation's prefectures, subprefectures, administrative posts, and cantons—was intended to provide UNIR with an apparatus for enforcing its decisions and a forum for promoting its programs. It would also augment the government's internal security apparatus.

Political Style

During his first six years as president, Habré's style of governing was essentially to juxtapose spheres of influence, including the Council of Ministers, a few close advisers, and personal friends and relatives, all of whom sought to influence presidential decision making. Habré was at the center of these spheres, each of which coalesced around his agenda. His political strategy was based on a segmentary model that exploited Chad's traditionally fluid, factional political dynamics.

Habré understood factional dynamics on several levels, first as one of the Toubou herdsmen among whom he was born and whose livelihood had for centuries depended on manipulation of the social system to their advantage, and as a Western-educated member of a small elite, whose political longevity depended on his ability to broker alliances. Habré used this traditional and modern background in his efforts to craft a stable nation out of a divided state torn by factional strife.

That people were tired of war also contributed to Habré's political successes in his first six years as president. A combination of resignation and opportunism brought former opponents into alliance with the president, who often was simply more tenacious than they were. To most of these former opponents, Habré's authoritarian regime was preferable to a return to civil war. Factional disputes were not always resolved; sometimes they were submerged and could be expected to recur.

Habré's military style was characterized as smart, tough, and decisive. Observers described him as a pragmatic military leader, undeterred by bureaucratic and political niceties and undistracted by sentiment, ideology, or foreign entanglements. Although he had a sizable following among civilians, as of 1988 he still governed largely as a military officer. He had not made the shift in style from supervising a military bureaucracy, in which orders were given and obeyed, to overseeing a civilian government that required broad consensus formation. Political communication was generally one directional, from the president down.

Habré established a reputation for ignoring seniority in making assignments, and, as a result, officers sometimes reported to their juniors when working on specific projects. One military commander, Hassane Djamouss, whose 1987 successes led to the rout of Libyan forces from much of the north, became a well-known example of this feature of Habré's style (see Repelling Libya's Occupying Force, 1985–87, ch. 5). Djamouss was a former minister of the civil service, trained as a livestock technician, but correctly judged by Habré to be a master strategist.

Habré also developed the reputation as a manager who set overall goals for his subordinates and left the mechanics of accomplishing those goals to lower-level managers. This decentralized responsibility and decision-making authority accorded well with traditional values of individualism held by many Chadian ethnic groups, and it had worked well in many military settings. A by-product of this feature of Habré's style was that officials with delegated responsibility commonly bypassed bureaucratic regulations in order to accomplish their goal. Adhering to the chain of command was not the measure of success in Chad's government of the 1980s.

Habré made several cautious attempts to bring peripheral ethnic groups into the political process. Most high civilian and military appointments were from his own or a closely related ethnic

President Hissein Habré (in white) at a 1985 meeting of the
United Nations Development Programme
Courtesy United Nations

group, but he appointed southerners and other non-Toubou civilians to several executive and administrative positions, despite occasional bureaucratic snarls that resulted from these attempts at national reconciliation.

Faced with internal threats to his regime, Habré's reaction was essentially repressive. Political opponents were often imprisoned or had their travel restricted. He broadened intelligence-gathering networks within the military (in 1986, for example, in response to growing opposition within the army) and expanded the power of the Presidential Guard (see The Chadian National Armed Forces, ch. 5). At the same time, he believed in his own power to "rehabilitate" and co-opt former opponents and was sometimes successful in gaining a measure of their trust.

During its first nearly three decades of independence, Chad had a strong president and weak state institutions, but it also enjoyed some benefits of the weakness of the state. It had been spared much of the flamboyant political posturing that was evident in a few more peaceful and prosperous nations. Habré had not squandered public resources on grandiose monuments to himself, nor had he encouraged a sycophantic cult of personality. Public office was not yet synonymous with extraordinary wealth, and, as a result, public cynicism toward government in the 1980s was surprisingly low.

Mass Media

Communication across Chad's troubled regional boundaries was difficult in the late 1980s. Even telephone service was erratic and subject to frequent interruption (see Communications, ch. 3). Media development had been slowed by security problems, infrastructural weakness, and general economic disarray. During the 1980s, some UN assistance was earmarked for improving print and broadcast media, but in a few cases, damaged equipment was destroyed as soon as it was repaired, and in general progress was slow.

In 1988 Chad's only radio network, Radiodiffusion Nationale Tchadienne (RNT), was able to reach the entire country through transmitters located at N'Djamena, Sarh, Moundou, and Abéché. RNT's *Voix de l'unité et du progrès* (Voice of Unity and Progress) broadcast news in French three times a day, as well as a variety of programs in Chadian Arabic and several local languages. Estimates of the number of radio receivers operating in Chad in the late 1980s ranged from 100,000 to 1 million. No television service was available, but in September 1988 France agreed to provide CFA F185 million to install a television station at N'Djamena to reach the surrounding area.

Print media, too, were limited by their lack of capital and equipment and by travel and communications difficulties. In 1988 the government-owned Chadian Press Agency (Agence Tchadienne de Presse) published a daily bulletin, *Info-Tchad,* in French, but its circulation was only 1,500. The UNIR information office also published a weekly newsletter, *Al Watan,* in French and Arabic. French newspapers such as *Le Monde* were also available, and government communiqués were circulated in most cities.

All media were owned and controlled by the government. Even the underground publication of antigovernment views was relatively rare, although Radio Bardaï broadcast antigovernment views on behalf of opposition groups, usually in Chadian Arabic. Chad's small journalistic community looked forward to the improvement of nationwide media as a means of educating and unifying the population.

Foreign Relations

Chad lacked established channels for foreign policy debate in the late 1980s. Few people were accustomed to formulating or expressing foreign policy concerns beyond the desire for peace and an end to foreign intervention. As a result, Chad's foreign policy reflected its colonial past, economic and military needs, and the quest for national sovereignty. Habré's overall plan for reinforcing national sovereignty was to eliminate Libyan intervention in the north, to reduce the nation's dependence on France, and, eventually, to proclaim a democratic state of Chad. Consistent with its liberal economy and relatively small public sector, Chad's foreign policy was pro-Western in the 1980s, but the basis for this orientation was rooted in its dependence on Western military assistance and foreign aid and investment, rather than on popular concern about superpower rivalries. Habré maintained in 1988 that the spread of communism posed a threat to Africa, but he intended, nonetheless, to assert Chad's nonalignment and autonomy from the West once peace with its neighbors was established.

After independence, Chad's importance in Africa increased, although its new stature derived more from its weaknesses than its strengths. It struggled to establish and maintain sovereignty within its boundaries, as Libya claimed a portion of northern Chad. Numerous dissidents within Chad considered Libyan domination preferable to Habré's administration of the 1980s or continued dependence on France. Some neighboring states hoped Chad would solve its internal problems and serve as a buffer against Libyan advances into the Sahel (see Glossary), pacify its warring rebel armies, and avoid destabilizing their regimes. Other neighboring states, especially Libya and Nigeria, hoped to exploit Chad's mineral wealth, and most of Chad's Arab neighbors saw it as a potential ally in the effort to weaken Western influence on the continent.

Libya and France were the key power brokers in Chad. Chad's relations with these two nations were interrelated throughout the 1980s, complementing one another in many instances. France's ties with its former colony were rooted in historical, economic, political, and security issues. Libya's long-standing ties with Chad, conversely, had cultural, ethnic, and religious bases—less important to governments but more so to many people in northern Chad. France and Libya also formulated policies toward Chad in the context of their own ambivalent relationship. France imported Libyan oil at favorable prices and assisted Libya's burgeoning military institutions yet faced the dilemma of arming both sides in the dispute over the Aozou Strip.

Within this foreign relations triangle, Chad's national leaders confronted many of the foreign policy issues that plagued the entire continent in the 1980s—the legacy of arbitrary colonial boundaries, the perceived need for strong armies to defend them, continuing postcolonial dependence, questions regarding the role of Islam in a secular state, and the problem of establishing African forms of democracy under these conditions. Viewed in this light, Chad's political environment was a microcosm of Africa's international concerns.

Relations with France

France was Chad's most important foreign donor and patron for the first three decades following independence in 1960. At the end of the 1980s, economic ties were still strong, and France provided development assistance in the form of loans and grants. It was no longer Chad's leading customer for agricultural exports, but it continued to provide substantial military support.

Chad remained a member of the African Financial Community (Communauté Financière Africaine—CFA; for value of the CFA franc—see Glossary), which linked the value of its currency, the CFA franc, to the French franc. French private and government investors owned a substantial portion of Chad's industrial and financial institutions, and the French treasury backed the Bank of Central African States (Banque des Etats de l'Afrique Centrale—BEAC), which served as the central bank for Chad and six other member nations (see Banking and Finance, ch. 3). Chad's dependence on France declined slightly during Habré's tenure as president, in part because other foreign donors and investors returned as the war subsided and also because increased rainfall after 1985 improved food production. French official attitudes toward Chad had changed from the 1970s policies under the leadership of Giscard d'Estaing to those of the Mitterrand era of the 1980s. Economic, political, and strategic goals, which had emphasized maintaining French influence in Africa, exploiting Chad's natural resources, and bolstering francophone Africa's status as a bulwark against the spread of Soviet influence, had been replaced by nominally anticolonialist attitudes. The election in France of the Socialist government in 1981 had coincided with conditions of near-anarchy in Chad, leading France's Socialist Party to reaffirm its ideological stance against high-profile intervention in Africa. Hoping to avoid a confrontation with Libya, another important client state in the region, President Mitterrand limited French military involvement to a defense of the region surrounding N'Djamena in 1983 and 1984. Then, gradually increasing its commitment to reinforce Habré's presidency, France once again increased its military activity in Chad (see The French Military Role in Chad, ch. 5).

Relations with Libya

Chad's relations with Libya, arising out of centuries of ethnic, religious, and commercial ties, were more complex than those with

France. Under French and Italian colonial domination, respectively, Chad and Libya had diverged in orientation and development. But even after Chad's independence in 1960, many northerners still identified more closely with people in Libya than with the southern-dominated government in N'Djamena. After seizing power in 1969, Libyan head of state Qadhafi reasserted Libya's claim to the Aozou Strip, a 100,000-square-kilometer portion of northern Chad that included the small town of Aozou. Libya based its claim on one of several preindependence agreements regarding colonial bound-aries, and it bolstered these claims by stationing troops in the Aozou Strip beginning in 1972. (Maps printed in Libya after 1975 included the Aozou Strip within Libya.)

Qadhafi's desire to annex the Aozou Strip grew out of an array of concerns, including the region's reported mineral wealth. He also hoped to establish a friendly government in Chad and to extend Islamic influence into the Sahel through Chad and Sudan, with the eventual aim of a Central African Islamic empire.

A complex set of symbolic interests also underlay Libya's pur-suit of territory and influence in the Sahel. Qadhafi's anticolonial and anti-imperialist rhetoric vacillated between attacks on the United States and a campaign focused on the postcolonial Euro-pean presence in Africa. He hoped to weaken Chad's ties with the West and thereby reduce Africa's incorporation into the Western-dominated nation-state system. Forcing the revision of one of the colonially devised boundaries affirmed by the OAU in 1963 was a step in this direction—one that seemed possible in the context of the troubled nation of Chad, which OAU members dubbed the continent's "weakest link."

Qadhafi attempted alliances with a number of antigovernment rebel leaders in Chad during the 1970s, including Goukouni, Siddick, Acyl Ahmat (a Chadian of Arab descent), and Kamougué, a southerner. Goukouni and Acyl were most sympathetic to Qadhafi's regional ambitions, but these two men clashed in 1979, leading Acyl to form the CDR. After Acyl's death in 1982, Libyan support swung strongly to Goukouni's GUNT (see Civil Conflict and Libyan Intervention, ch. 5).

By mid-1988 Qadhafi appeared more willing to come to an agree-ment with Habré than to continue to support Qadhafi's fractious allies, who had suffered losses at Habré's hands. Chadian and Libyan foreign ministers met in August 1988, and the two govern-ments agreed to further talks. At the same time, Libyan troops remained in the Aozou Strip, and its future status was uncertain (see Repelling Libya's Occupying Force, 1985–87, ch. 5).

Relations with Nigeria and Sudan

Within the complex and changing foreign relations triangle comprising Chad, France, and Libya, the large nations of Nigeria and Sudan were also important actors. Nigeria considered France its primary rival in its attempt to chart the course of West Africa's political development. Its generally paternalistic relations with Chad intensified after the coup that ousted President Tombalbaye in 1975. After that, limiting Libyan expansion while avoiding direct clashes with Libyan troops also became important goals. Nigeria sponsored talks among Chad's rival factions in 1979 and promoted a little-known civil servant, Mahmat Shawa Lol, as a compromise head of a coalition government. Lol's perceived status as a Nigerian puppet contributed to mounting opposition during his short term as president in 1979.

The two nations forged stronger ties during the 1980s. Hoping to benefit commercially and diplomatically by expanding regional trade relations, Nigeria replaced France as Chad's major source of export revenues. Bilateral trade agreements involved Chadian exports of livestock, dried fish, and chemicals and imports of Nigerian foodstuffs and manufactured goods. Both governments also recognized the potential value of the large informal trade sector across their borders, which neither country regulated. In addition, Nigerian industry and commerce employed several thousand Chadian workers.

Chad's relationship with Nigeria was not without its strains, however. Beginning in the late 1970s, clashes occurred around Lake Chad, where both countries hoped to exploit oil reserves. Both also sought to defuse these confrontations, first by establishing joint patrols and a commission to demarcate the boundary across the lake more clearly. Then in the early 1980s, the low level of Lake Chad brought a series of tiny islands into view, leading to further disputes and disrupting long-standing informal trade networks.

This relationship was also complicated by Nigeria's own instability in the north, generated by rising Islamic fundamentalism. Thousands of casualties occurred as the result of violent clashes in Nigeria throughout the 1980s. Most religious violence was domestic in origin, but Nigerian police arrested a few Libyans, and Nigerian apprehension of Libyan infiltration through Chad intensified.

Nigeria's 1983 economic austerity campaign also produced strains with neighboring states, including Chad. Nigeria expelled several hundred thousand foreign workers, mostly from its oil industry, which faced drastic cuts as a result of declining world oil prices.

At least 30,000 of those expelled were Chadians. Despite these strains, however, Nigerians had assisted in the halting process of achieving stability in Chad, and both nations reaffirmed their intention to maintain close ties.

Sudan, Chad's neighbor to the east, responded to Chad's conflict with Libya based on its own regional, ethnic, and cultural tensions. In Sudan, the Islamic northern region had generally dominated the non-Muslim south. Sudan's ties with Libya, although cautious during the 1970s, warmed during the 1980s, strengthening N'Djamena's fears of insurgency from the east.

The populations of eastern Chad and western Sudan established social and religious ties long before either nation's independence, and these remained strong despite disputes between governments. Herdsmen in both countries freely crossed the 950-kilometer border, seeking pastureland and water sources as they had for centuries. Muslims in eastern Chad often traveled through Sudan on the hajj, or annual pilgrimage to Mecca, and many young people from eastern Chad studied at Islamic schools in Sudan. In addition, Sudan's cotton plantations employed an estimated 500,000 Chadian workers in 1978.

At the same time, the basis for political enmity between these two nations was set in the early 1960s, when Chad's southern bias in government offended many Sudanese Muslims. Sudan allowed FROLINAT rebels to organize, train, and establish bases in western Sudan and to conduct raids into Chad from Sudan's Darfur Province. Refugees from both countries fled across their mutual border.

Following the coup that ousted Tombalbaye in 1975, relations between presidents Jaafar an Numayri and Malloum were surprisingly cordial, in part because both nations feared Libyan destabilization. Sudan sponsored talks among Chad's rebel army leaders in the late 1970s and urged Malloum to incorporate them into his government. (Numayri promoted the talents and intelligence of Habré, in particular, and persuaded Malloum to appoint Habré to political office in 1978.) These ties were strained in part because of Numayri's warming relations with Libyan leader Qadhafi.

As violence in Chad increased between 1979 and 1982, Sudan faced its own internal rebellion, and relations deteriorated after Numayri was ousted in 1983. In 1988 Habré assailed Sudan for allowing Libyan troops to be stationed along Chad's border and for continuing to allow assaults on Chadian territory from Sudan.

Relations with Other African States

Chad maintained generally close ties with its other African neighbors, but the primary base of these ties were Chad's economic and

163

security needs, together with other governments' concerns for regional stability. Overall, African states sought to protect their own interests—to isolate or contain Chad's continuing violence without becoming involved militarily. As France was attempting to transfer more responsibility to former colonies and subregional powers, francophone African leaders urged each other and the former colonial power to increase assistance to Chad. Each side partially succeeded.

African states had other reasons for ambivalence toward Chad in addition to their own security concerns. Chad's long-standing unrest, border conflicts, overall instability, and poverty contributed to its image as a relatively unimportant ally. It underwent frequent shifts in government; from 1979 to 1982, it was not always clear who was in charge. In 1982 Chad's new president, Habré, appeared to some African heads of state to be a Paris-educated northerner with aristocratic pretensions, who had not done enough to win their support.

Because of Chad's landlocked status and limited air transport service, Cameroon was an important neighbor and ally throughout most of the 1970s and 1980s. Imports and exports were shipped between Yaoundé and N'Djamena by rail and road, as were military and food assistance shipments. Cameroon became an increasingly important trading partner during the 1980s, following unsuccessful attempts in the 1970s to conclude multilateral trade agreements with Congo and Central African Republic. In 1987 Cameroon was Chad's third largest source of imports after France and the United States, and Cameroon purchased Chadian cotton and agricultural products.

The Cameroonian town of Kousséri had been an important supply center and refuge for Chadians during the worst violence of the late 1970s (see fig. 8). The population of the town increased from 10,000 to 100,000 in 1979 and 1980. Cameroon's government urged France to increase assistance to stem Libyan advances because officials feared direct confrontation with Libyan troops and the influx of weapons and refugees from Chad.

Zaire's President Mobutu Sese Seko was one of President Habré's most consistent allies in Central Africa. Even before Habré seized power in 1982, Mobutu's desire to lead Africa's pro-Western, anti-Qadhafi efforts and to compete with Nigeria as a subregional power had led him to provide military training and troops for the IAF in Chad.

Chad's relations with Central African Republic were not cordial, but the two nations were generally on good terms. Central African Republic controlled another important access route, and the two

An American C-5A delivers weapons at N'Djamena Airport
Courtesy Joseph Krull

nations had concluded a number of agreements regarding trade, transportation, and communication. Chad's President Tombalbaye had clashed with the former president of Central African Republic, Jean-Bedel Bokassa, over the establishment of a central African customs union in the late 1960s, however, leading Tombalbaye to close their common border. After this occurrence, Central African Republic remained fairly aloof from Chad's economic and security problems. Some Chadian refugees crossed into Central African Republic during the 1980s, but Bangui's major concern was preventing Chad's ongoing turmoil from spreading across its southern border.

Niger and Chad shared a number of common features of post-independence political development, but these two landlocked, poor nations were unable to contribute noticeably to each other's progress. The inhabitants of their northern provinces—primarily Tuareg in Niger and Toubou groups in Chad—were both referred to by Libyan leader Qadhafi as his ethnic constituents, and both nations complained of Libyan insurgence in these mineral-rich areas. At the same time, important segments of both societies supported Qadhafi's goal of establishing a Central African Islamic empire. Both nations also shared the dual heritage of Muslim and Christian influences and regional economic inequities, and both found themselves overshadowed by Nigeria's wealth and large population.

165

Chad had become one of Africa's intractable dilemmas in the 1970s, confounding leaders who sought peace and prosperity for the continent as a whole. Chad's conflict with Libya became symbolic of the OAU's frustrated attempts to impose a coherent framework on Africa, and it defied the OAU resolution to uphold colonially imposed boundaries and settle inter-African disputes peacefully. The OAU formed a series of ad hoc committees to mediate the Chad-Libya dispute, and in 1988 the six committee members—Algeria, Cameroon, Gabon, Mozambique, Nigeria, and Senegal—succeeded in bringing together foreign ministers from Chad and Libya to pursue diplomatic recognition and peace talks. The committee also requested written documentation of each side's claims to the Aozou Strip in the hope of finding a legal channel for curbing violence there.

Relations with the United States

United States interest in Chad increased steadily during the 1980s, as United States opposition to Libyan leader Qadhafi intensified and Chadian instability threatened to contribute to regional destabilization. During the 1960s and 1970s, the United States and Chad had maintained fairly low-level economic ties, including investment guarantees and project aid, such as Peace Corps involvement. Drought in the early 1970s brought United States food and agricultural aid to remote areas, including grain supplies, animal health services, and technical assistance. Other economic agreements included road building in the Lake Chad area and rural community development.

Although the United States considered Chad part of France's sphere of influence, it also provided a low level of military assistance until 1977. President Malloum's 1978 request for increased military aid to fight the FROLINAT insurgency coincided with a marked increase in Soviet activity in Africa, especially in Ethiopia, and increased Soviet arms shipments to Libya. United States relations with African states were redefined in accordance with the new strategic value assigned to African allies, and United States foreign policy shifted accordingly. Thus, in the 1980s United States interest and involvement in Chad increased.

For a time in the early 1980s, the United States commitment to military support for Habré was more enthusiastic than that of France, which hoped to preserve its relationship with Libya. Although military and financial aid to Habré increased, by 1988 United States advisers had begun to stress the need to reconcile warring factions and pacify rebel groups within Chad. United States support to Chad included several economic and military aid agreements, including training programs to improve the effectiveness of Habré's administration and to bolster public confidence in the government and intelligence-sharing to assist in countering Libyan forces in 1987.

Relations with Arab States

Despite centuries-old cultural ties to Arab North Africa, Chad maintained few significant ties to North African or Middle Eastern states in the 1980s. (Ties with Israel had been severed in 1972.) President Habré hoped to pursue greater solidarity with Arab nations in the future, however, viewing closer relations with Arab states as a potential opportunity to break out of his nation's postcolonial dependence and assert Chad's unwillingness to serve as an arena for superpower rivalries. In addition, as a northern Muslim, Habré represented a constituency that favored Afro-Arab solidarity, and he hoped Islam would provide a basis for national unity in the long term. For these reasons, he was expected to seize opportunities during the 1990s to pursue closer ties with Arab nations.

During the 1980s, several Arab states had supported Libyan claims to the Aozou Strip. Algeria was among the most outspoken of these states and provided training for anti-Habré forces, although most recruits for its training programs were from Nigeria or Cameroon, recruited and flown to Algeria by Libya. By the end of 1987, Algiers and N'Djamena were negotiating to improve relations. Lebanon's Progressive Socialist Party also sent troops to support Qadhafi's efforts against Chad in 1987, but other Arab states and the League of Arab States (Arab League) limited their involvement to expressions of hope that the dispute over the Aozou Strip could be settled peacefully.

*   *   *

Several scholars have analyzed Chad's political development during the 1980s. Robert Buijtenhuijs, in *Le Frolinat et les révoltes populaires du Tchad, 1965–1976* provides background on the role of the opposition coalition in shaping the political environment. Bernard Lanne's *Tchad-Libye: La querelle des frontières* analyzes the development of the dispute over the Aozou Strip. Virginia M. Thompson and Richard Adloff's *Conflict in Chad* provides valuable perspectives on attempts to bolster the faltering state in recent decades. Lanne's "Chad—Recent History" in *Africa South of the Sahara, 1988* synthesizes Chad's complex political dynamics in a brief, coherent narrative. William J. Foltz's *Chad's Third Republic* assesses President Habré's political success and prospects for the future. Several of René Lemarchand's publications—in particular, "Chad: The Road to Partition" and "Chad: The Misadventures of the North-South Dialectic"—provide insight into factional politics in segmentary lineage-based societies.

Other valuable works include Samuel Decalo's *Historical Dictionary of Chad* (1987 edition), which presents concise political entries and a comprehensive bibliography. Gali Ngothé Gatta's *Tchad: Guerre civile et désagrégation de l'état* and Michael P. Kelley's *A State in Disarray* assess internal and external factors contributing to Chad's political turmoil. Pearl T. Robinson's "Playing the Arab Card" describes Libya's evolving role, and Kola Olufemi's "Chad: From Civil Strife to Big Power Rivalry" traces the rising external involvement in Chad's political drama. Finally, several interviews with President Habré illuminate his political views. Selections from these are found in *Courier* (March–April 1987), Jean-Jacques Lafaye's "Consolider la victoire," and Guy Jérémie Ngansop's *Tchad: Vingt ans de crise.*

A variety of periodicals provide coverage of events in Chad, including *Africa Economic Digest, Africa Report, Africa Research Bulletin, Africa Today, Daily Report: Near East and South Asia* published by Foreign Broadcast Information Service, *Marchés tropicaux et méditerranéens, Le Monde, Politique africaine, Politique internationale, Washington Post* and *West Africa. Africa Contemporary Record* provides annual updates on political and economic developments and valuable chapters on France in Africa and the Organization for African Unity. (For further information and complete citations, see Bibliography.)

Chapter 5. National Security

An elderly hunter from southern Chad

AFTER CHAD GAINED its independence in 1960, its national army consisted of only about 400 men, mostly members of the Sara ethnic group who had distinguished themselves in French army service during World War II and later in Algeria and Indochina. By the mid-1960s, however, rebellion in northern and eastern Chad necessitated the enlargement of this army. The rebellion also caused French forces stationed in nearby countries to intervene repeatedly to assist the Chadian government.

By 1979 conditions had become chaotic. As many as eleven separate factional armies were contending for control, generating alliances and schisms at a bewildering rate. In the capital of N'Djamena, after the national army had been pushed aside, the two main northern rivals, Goukouni Oueddei and Hissein Habré, struggled for domination. Libya's intervention in 1980 on behalf of Goukouni resulted in the defeat of Habré's army. With only a few hundred of his hardiest followers remaining, Habré was forced to seek a haven in western Sudan. But after Libya withdrew under international pressure, Habré's revitalized army fought its way back to the capital, and he assumed power in 1982.

The confused pattern of civil warfare continued, but Habré gradually consolidated his political position and brought the resistance in the south under control. With the help of a French expedition, he repelled a new offensive from the north in 1983 that had been mounted by a coalition of opponents under Goukouni's leadership and backed by Libya's armor and air power. In 1986 a split developed among the insurgents in the north when the major part of Goukouni's army turned against the Libyans. Joined by these rebel forces, Habré's army was strong enough in early 1987 to wage a successful campaign to clear the Libyan invaders from most of Chad's vast northern territories and to threaten the Aozou Strip (see Glossary), which Libya had occupied since 1972.

In 1983 the military arm of Habré's movement became the nucleus of a new national army, the Chadian National Armed Forces (Forces Armées Nationales Tchadiennes—FANT). By 1987 FANT had evolved into a potent, mobile, and battle-tested military organization. It had acquired modern arms adapted to the rigorous conditions of the far-flung arena of conflict in the north. In addition to receiving arms deliveries from France and the United States, FANT had captured a large stock of Libyan armored vehicles, missiles, artillery, and matériel. In its stricken financial state, the country continued to be dependent on its Western backers for munitions and fuel, as well as maintenance and training support for its newly acquired weaponry. Its air arm was insignificant, but French transport and combat aircraft remained in the country. Moreover, the army's antiaircraft missile defenses had effectively blunted Libyan air assaults.

Habré had been remarkably successful in enlisting previously bitter adversaries in a common undertaking to regain the nation's territory. As part of the reconciliation with his former armed opponents, Habré had absorbed into FANT the remnants of the postindependence national army, dissident guerrilla fighters from the south, and most of the rebel coalition forces of his northern rival, Goukouni. Only the Presidential Guard, a select force mostly drawn from Habré's own ethnic group, retained its separate identity.

This large assemblage of manpower, however, could not be militarily justified as a permanent force once the Libyan danger was removed. For the future, a major problem for the military leadership would be the welding of FANT into an integrated force of sufficient loyalty to be entrusted with a primarily internal security mission and at strengths and equipment levels compatible with the country's financial means and defense requirements.

External and Domestic Security Concerns

At independence Chad's economic and strategic importance was limited. Isolated and landlocked, it boasted no developed natural resources, and most of its inhabitants lived at the subsistence level. There were few enduring disputes or traditional animosities likely to precipitate discord with its African neighbors. Because of Chad's good relations with its neighbors, it was a very unlikely candidate for international attention.

In spite of these factors, Chad's vast territories have been a demographic and cultural crossroads where outside forces have often competed for influence. The most significant of these forces has been Libya, whose efforts to assert itself in Chad have historical roots (see Civil Conflict and Libyan Intervention, this ch.). In modern times, however, these efforts have been ascribed to the ambition of Libyan leader Muammar al Qadhafi, who hoped to impose his concept of Islamic unity on African states bordering the Sahel (see Glossary). Asserting a legal claim to the Aozou Strip in northern Chad, Libya occupied the territory in 1972. To further his claim to the region, Qadhafi used troops from Libya's Islamic Legion—a unit whose members were recruited from among Muslims of Central Africa and West Africa. With no demonstrated economic value,

A former French Foreign Legion fort in Fada
Courtesy Michael R. Saks

the area was useful primarily as a forward base to facilitate Libya's interference in Chadian military and political affairs. In response to Libya's claims, Chadian forces, supplied by France and the United States, inflicted a series of defeats on Libya in 1987. These strokes alleviated the threat from Qadhafi, although continued Libyan occupation of the Aozou Strip left the ultimate resolution of the conflict undecided.

No other adjacent state has sought to stake out areas of influence or to assert territorial claims in Chad. In 1987 three of Chad's neighbors—Niger, Cameroon, and Central African Republic—had only nominal military establishments, which posed no threat to the relatively large and well-equipped Chadian army. Their mutual relations, moreover, were amicable, based on their shared experiences as members of the French colonial empire and continued military collaboration with France. Several regional states, including Cameroon, Gabon, and Zaire, have directly or indirectly supported Chad in its conflict with Libya.

Bordering Lake Chad, Nigeria, the most powerful of Chad's sub-Saharan neighbors, has been involved at various times with Chad in a peacekeeping role. One purpose of Nigeria's involvement was to reduce Chad's need for a French military presence; Nigeria has historically viewed French interests in Africa with suspicion. But a more important purpose was to prevent Qadhafi from gaining

173

a foothold in sub-Saharan Africa, from which he could further his vision of radical Arab socialism under an Islamic banner.

Chad's other large neighbor, Sudan, had given refuge to Habré and had helped reequip his army after its defeat in 1980 by the combined forces of Goukouni and Libya. Subsequently, fearful of offending Qadhafi and inciting him to aid the rebellion in its own southern region, Sudan adopted a neutral posture. Chad's border with Sudan remained volatile in 1988. Rebellious tribal groups, dispersed remnants of Goukouni's defeated northern forces, Libyan troops, and members of the Islamic Legion were all involved in cross-border fighting. In this environment, banditry could not easily be distinguished from civil conflict.

Since Chad's independence in 1960, the absence of cohesive social and economic forces has produced conditions of almost constant domestic turmoil and violence. Competing groups have tried to protect their own interests by supporting local ''armies''—often armed bands of no more than a few hundred ill-trained recruits. Badly equipped and lacking a stable source of funds, these factions turned to foreign patrons to keep their movements viable.

Concurrent with the success of his military campaigns, Habré pursued a policy of reconciliation with dissident groups. As a result, by 1987 he had either won over or defeated all his major rivals. Several former factional leaders who had contested Habré on the battlefield had been granted senior positions in the central government, and their forces either had been integrated into the national army or had peacefully demobilized. As of 1988, only two rivals of any stature remained—Goukouni and Acheikh ibn Oumar. Goukouni no longer commanded significant military forces, and his reconciliation with Habré remained a possibility. Oumar's Democratic Revolutionary Council (Conseil Démocratique Révolutionnaire—CDR) had been decimated in the 1987 fighting, and the smaller Arab groups that constituted his following were of little significance. Nonetheless, revival of these movements with the aid of Libyan patronage could not be ruled out. It was feared that Libya might use support for them as a pretext for renewed intervention.

Few observers believed that ethnic rivalries had been permanently suppressed or that new factional disputes would not arise to threaten domestic stability. In 1987 reports revealed that one small resistance force, recruited among the Hajerai ethnic group, had become active in the mountains of Guéra Prefecture (see fig. 1; Languages and Ethnic Groups, ch. 2). Known as the Movement for the National Salvation of Chad (Mouvement pour le Salut National du Tchad—MOSANAT), it claimed to have been formed in protest against heavy taxes and exactions by the government, which northerners dominated. In late 1987, however, MOSANAT rebels had fled across the nearby Sudanese border (see Internal Security Conditions, this ch.).

The Armed Forces

From independence through the period of the presidency of Félix Malloum (1975–79), the official national army was known as the Chadian Armed Forces (Forces Armées Tchadiennes—FAT; see Appendix B). Composed mainly of soldiers from southern Chad, FAT had its roots in the army recruited by France and had military traditions dating back to World War I. FAT lost its status as the legal state army when Malloum's civil and military administration disintegrated in 1979. Although it remained a distinct military body for several years, FAT was eventually reduced to the status of a regional army representing the south.

After Habré consolidated his authority and assumed the presidency in 1982, his victorious army, the Armed Forces of the North (Forces Armées du Nord—FAN), became the nucleus of a new national army. The force was officially constituted in January 1983, when the various pro-Habré contingents were merged and renamed FANT.

Origins and Early Development

When Chad became independent in 1960, it had no armed forces under its own flag. Since World War I, however, southern Chad, particularly the Sara ethnic group, had provided a large share of the Africans in the French army. Chadian troops also had contributed significantly to the success of the Free French forces in World War II. In December 1940, two African battalions began the Free French military campaign against Italian forces in Libya from a base in Chad, and at the end of 1941 a force under Colonel Jacques Leclerc participated in a spectacular campaign that seized the entire Fezzan region of southern Libya. Colonel Leclerc's 3,200-man force included 2,700 Africans, the great majority of them southerners from Chad. These troops went on to contribute to the Allied victory in Tunisia. Chadians, in general, were proud of their soldiers' role in the efforts to liberate France and in the international conflict.

The military involvement also provided the country's first taste of relative prosperity. In addition to the wages paid its forces, Chad received economic benefits from three years of use as a major route for Allied supply convoys and flights to North Africa and Egypt. By 1948 about 15,000 men in French Equatorial Africa (Afrique Equatoriale Française—AEF; see Glossary) were receiving military pensions. Many Chadian southerners, finding military life attractive, had remained in the French army, often becoming noncommissioned officers (NCOs); a few had earned commissions as well. The French wars in Indochina (1946–53) and Algeria (1954–62) also drew on Chadians in great numbers, enlarging the veteran population still further. Those men receiving pensions tended to form the economic elite in their villages. As southerners they did not become involved in later insurgent movements that developed in central and northern Chad.

Prior to independence, the French forces had been reorganized to redeploy some of the Chadian troops assigned to other African territories back into Chad. Following independence Chad's army was created from southern troops that had served with the French army. Initially, the army was limited to 400 men, some Chadian officers and many French commissioned officers and NCOs. Other soldiers were transferred into a larger paramilitary security force, the National Gendarmerie (see Police Services, this ch.). Equipped with light arms and other supplies, the army used facilities inherited from the French units that it had replaced.

Because the French army units in Chad provided security, a large indigenous force was unnecessary. Accordingly, the Chadian army was deliberately restricted in size. By 1966, however, the departure of the French administration from sparsely populated Borkou-Ennedi-Tibesti Prefecture in the north encouraged dissident forces in the central prefectures to rebel. In response the government expanded its armed strength to a 700-man infantry battalion with supporting light artillery and also activated an air unit (see The Air Force, this ch.).

The continued insurgency necessitated further enlargement of the army, to a total of 3,800 men by 1971. The army formed a paratroop company from 350 Chadians trained by Israeli instructors at a base in Zaire. In addition to strengthening the regular army, the government increased mobile security companies of the National Gendarmerie, equipped as light infantry, to a strength of more than 1,600 men. A third force, the National Guard (later known as the National and Nomad Guard), which had at least 3,500 members, provided security for officials, government buildings, and regional government posts.

Except for the small number of nomad guards, the army and other security components continued to be composed primarily of members from southern ethnic groups, especially the Sara. Little effort was made to enlist northerners, who, in spite of their reputation as fierce warriors, were not attracted to the professional army. Consequently, southern troops stationed in Borkou-Ennedi-Tibesti

Chadian military vehicles on parade, around 1970
Courtesy Michael R. Saks

Prefecture were looked upon as an army of occupation. They imposed humiliating restrictions in the northern settlements, and their abusive behavior was a source of bitterness.

The growing unpopularity of the country's first president, François Tombalbaye, impelled him to strengthen further the internal security forces and to employ a unit of Moroccan troops as his personal bodyguard. During the early 1970s, Tombalbaye doubled the size of the National and Nomad Guard and augmented the National Gendarmerie considerably. At the same time, he neglected and downgraded FAT, which the force interpreted as a lack of trust. These actions ultimately contributed to the decision by a small group of officers to carry out a coup in 1975 that resulted in Tombalbaye's death and a new government under Malloum's presidency.

Malloum's military regime insisted on the departure of the French troops. FAT, however, found itself increasingly unable to cope with the insurgency in the north, and, as a consequence, Malloum was obliged to invite the French back in 1978. As part of an effort at conciliation with one of the rebel factions, Habré was brought into the government. Habré rejected, however, the plan to integrate his FAN troops into the army, and his force soon demonstrated its superior resolution and strength by expelling Malloum's army from N'Djamena (see The FROLINAT Rebellion, 1965–79, this ch.).

Organization of the National Security Establishment

By the late 1980s, Chad's national security establishment was a conglomeration of former rebel armies under the command of Habré, whose troops were mostly from the north. The evolution of the national security establishment from an army of mostly southerners was rapid. This change occurred between April 1975, when Malloum assumed power, and early 1979, when the combined northern forces of Habré and Goukouni drove the southern-dominated FAT from N'Djamena.

Internecine conflict in the late 1970s and early 1980s, however, prevented Chad from achieving political or military unity. Erstwhile comrades Habré and Goukouni became bitter adversaries, and, with Libyan backing, Goukouni evicted Habré from the capital in 1980. Although forced to flee, Habré had fought his way back to N'Djamena by mid-1982. His occupation of the city was followed by victories in the south against his divided opponents (see Habré's Return to Power and Second Libyan Intervention, 1982–84, this ch.). With most regions of the country now under his authority, Habré assumed the presidency, promulgated a provisional constitution, the Fundamental Law of 1982, and introduced a cabinet and other institutions broadly representative of the existing political forces (see Constitutional System, ch. 4).

The Fundamental Law, which remained in effect as of 1988, declares that the president is the supreme commander of the army and is authorized to appoint high-ranking military officers, such appointments to be subject to implementing decrees approved by the Council of Ministers (cabinet). Article 21 of the Fundamental Law states that "under the authority of the President of the Republic, the Chief of State, and the government, the national army has the task of defending the national independence and unity, sovereignty, territorial integrity, the security of the country, and its preservation from subversion and any aggression. The army participates in the work of national reconstruction."

Habré, who had personally commanded the major element of the northern forces during most of the Chadian Civil War, retained the title of supreme commander and a large measure of control over the military establishment. In addition to his positions as president and supreme commander, Habré had assumed the ministerial portfolio of national defense, veterans, and war victims. In a practical sense, however, in 1988 the Ministry of National Defense, Veterans, and War Victims was not a fully staffed government department independent of the military command structure.

At the head of the military chain of command in 1988 was Hassane Djamouss, the commander in chief of FANT and the battlefield commander during the succession of military victories over Libya. His senior deputy with responsibility for administration and logistics was Zamtato Ganebang. The second deputy, Adoum Yacoub, formerly commander of the People's Armed Forces (Forces Armées Populaires—FAP), a rebel army in the north, was responsible for tactics and operations. Another former rebel leader, Oki Dagache Yaya, was the senior representative of the FAP units that had been integrated into FANT.

The creation of a five-member military cabinet attached to the presidency, on which several of the ethnic groups composing FANT were represented, was one of the measures adopted by Habré to provide a governmental role for his former opponents. The extent to which Habré relied on its advice on matters of military policy was not certain; some observers believe that Habré's former adversaries had been given symbolic positions having no real influence. The headquarters staff of FANT totaled about twenty officers and was composed of a number of bureaus patterned after those of the French military. Included were personnel (B-1), intelligence (B-2), operations (B-3), logistics (B-4), and communications (B-5). Others bureaus were tactics and recruitment. French advisers were detailed to all but the intelligence bureau (see fig. 9).

The Presidential Guard (Sécurité Présidentielle—SP) was responsible for the personal security of the president and performed other internal security duties as well. Although the Presidential Guard participated in combat missions, it functioned as an independent wing of the armed forces. The Presidential Guard depended on FANT headquarters for administration and was officially part of FANT's structure, but it operated as a separate army, often in semisecrecy. Dominated by soldiers of Habré's ethnic group, the Daza, it enjoyed many privileges and was assigned the most modern transportation equipment and weaponry. In 1987 the 3,600-man force was commanded by Ahmed Gorou.

Except for the north, which had been organized into a separate military region, the country was divided into twelve military zones, each with headquarters in a major town. The senior officer, generally a major of the Presidential Guard, held command responsibility for any military units within his designated zone. Subzones were located in smaller communities, usually under a lieutenant.

The Chadian National Armed Forces

As of mid-1987, FANT had a manpower strength of 28,000, exclusive of the Presidential Guard. At the time of its official

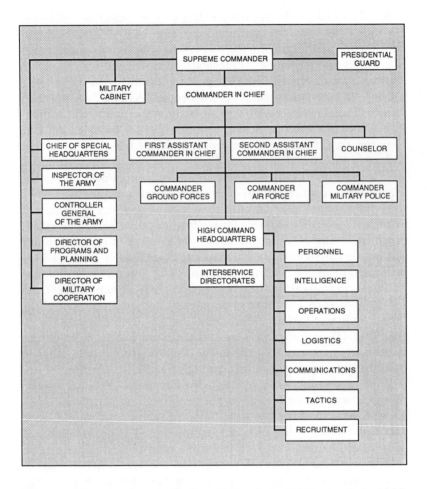

Figure 9. Organization of Chadian National Armed Forces, Late 1985

establishment in 1983, FANT consisted primarily of FAN troops, the well-disciplined and hardened combat veterans who had been the original followers of Habré. FANT gradually expanded, recruiting members of the former national army, FAT, who were predominantly southerners of the Sara ethnic group. Later, additional southerners, the commandos or *codos* who had opened a guerrilla campaign against the government in 1983, were won over after two and one-half years of negotiations. Assigned to rehabilitation camps for retraining, the physically fit among them were also inducted into FANT. Finally, in the latter half of 1986, after FAP, the largest component of Goukouni's northern rebel army, had revolted against its Libyan ally, FAP soldiers were merged into FANT to join the campaign against the Libyan bases in Chad (see Appendix B).

Under Chadian law, both men and women reaching the age of twenty-one were obligated for one year of military or civic service. There was no systematic conscription system; young men were simply rounded up periodically in their communities and required to serve in the army for longer or shorter periods as military needs dictated. According to one source, very few members of FANT were conscripts in 1987. Women served in the military, but their exact duties were unknown.

The Chadian army has never been organized at higher than battalion level. As of 1987, four battalions had been established within FANT. Sometimes known as "commando battalions," they were far smaller than standard battalions, with no more than 400 soldiers in each. Two of the battalions had completed training in Zaire, and the training of a third was under way. The fourth battalion existed mainly on paper; the companies assigned to it were still operating independently.

The bulk of the remainder of FANT consisted of 127 infantry companies. Each company had a nominal strength of about 150 men but in many cases as few as 100 because of casualties and other forms of attrition. The organizational pattern was flexible; a new company could be formed as needed by detaching troops from existing units and then might be dismantled after the operational need had ended. Moreover, a force of wheeled armored vehicles was organized separately into armored squadrons, each ordinarily supplied with ten or eleven vehicles along with truck-mounted recoilless rifles and antitank missiles, and subdivided in up to four armored sections. The armored squadrons could be detailed as needed to operate in conjunction with infantry companies.

FANT had no separate elements dedicated to airborne operations. Soldiers trained as paratroopers, however, were scattered throughout FANT and the Presidential Guard after they had received instruction from the French teams that visited Chad and other French-speaking African states annually for this purpose.

Because of the chaotic conditions and the severe financial constraints on the government, systematic promotions in the officer corps had been suspended in the 1970s. As a result, many officers with senior responsibilities were lieutenants or captains, or they held no formal military rank at all. Officers of Habré's original FAN were known simply as *camarade* (comrade), and many, like the commander in chief, Djamouss, continued to be addressed in this way. Trusted associates of Habré were sometimes detached from civilian posts and given temporary military commands.

Those officers of the former national army, FAT, who rallied to FANT were guaranteed retention of their former ranks, but not positions of equivalent responsibility. Accordingly, a major or colonel sometimes served under a lieutenant or captain. On occasion, an officer selected for training abroad might be granted the rank appropriate for the program to which he had been nominated, in effect resulting in his promotion. Thus, Idris Deby, the former commander in chief of FANT, was promoted to lieutenant colonel in conjunction with his attendance at the French war college. With the exception of two generals no longer holding active commands in 1988, the highest rank in FANT was that of colonel.

The main fighting units of FANT, a group that had performed superbly against the Libyans during the 1987 offensive, were young but toughened by several years of harsh desert warfare. Their tactics of rapid movement and sudden sweeps upon an unsuspecting enemy were reminiscent of their nomadic warrior forebears. Decentralized decision making reportedly permitted field commanders to mount major attacks on their own initiative. Limited by poor communications, these commanders, in turn, sometimes described only general objectives in advance of an attack and depended on individual unit leaders to coordinate blows of devastating surprise and firepower.

Foreign military observers were impressed by FANT's fighting style and rated it highly for esprit and combativeness. Nevertheless, the discipline and orderliness of a traditional army were not greatly in evidence. Except for members of the Presidential Guard, who favored the desert camouflage uniform of the United States Army if it were available, the troops did not wear a standard uniform. Personal gear sometimes consisted merely of a prayer rug—which also served as a sleeping pad—and a sheepskin for warmth. Shower clogs were considered adequate footgear, nor were the rations what one might expect in a regular army. Individual combat rations were often no more than green tea, dried dates, and hard biscuits. Occasionally, meat from a slaughtered sheep or camel would be available. A FANT veteran could survive desert heat on as little as one liter of water a day.

Unreliable payment of wages was a persistent problem for FANT troops. The bitterness in the south against the central government, which had resulted in outbreaks of violence between 1983 and 1985, was caused in part by confiscations of food and personal property by unpaid FANT troops. As of 1983, it was reported that FANT soldiers were paid the equivalent of US$140 for each major battle, although those qualified to fire large-caliber weapons and missiles could earn much more. By 1986 a system of monthly payments was in effect, but, owing to the government's financial distress, both soldiers and civil servants were on half pay. In practice, only the Presidential Guard received its wages in full and on a timely basis. The salary of an NCO in the Presidential Guard was about US$70 a month; officers could earn up to US$150. In FANT, the officer's basic salary of about US$70 a month was likely to be augmented by supplemental allowances based on the position being filled. Djamouss, the highest paid officer in FANT, earned about US$1,000 a month, plus the use of an automobile and a house and other privileges.

Although the military victories of 1987 had imparted a sense of national pride and unity to FANT that had not existed previously, the dependability of the troops newly recruited from other armed factions had not yet been fully demonstrated. In early 1988, long-standing animosities and ethnic rivalries remained, and morale among ordinary soldiers was believed to be no better than fair. Rates of desertion and absence without leave were high, although not yet serious enough to affect the army's performance. Nevertheless, in spite of its austerity, military life provided food, clothing, and minimal cash compensation. For many recruits, these modest benefits compared favorably with the impoverished conditions they faced when they returned to civilian existence.

Training

France has played a paramount role in the training of the Chadian armed forces since independence. In 1980, during the worst fighting of the Chadian Civil War, the French withdrew their training mission and other forms of military cooperation. French involvement resumed in 1983 when Habré appealed for help against renewed Libyan intervention in northern Chad (see Foreign Military Cooperation, this ch.). As of late 1987, the French training mission consisted of about 250 officers and enlisted men. Of the 10,000 soldiers composing FANT at its inception in 1983, about 8,000 had been rotated through French training by 1987. The principal training sites were at N'Djamena, Koundoul, and Moussoro. At an instructional center at Mongo, thousands of former *codos* (commandos) had been "recycled" by French trainers, assisted by a large cadre of Chadian military. A small number of *codos* had been integrated into FANT, but most had been organized into work brigades for service as agricultural or road laborers.

The French-supervised training was complicated by the extreme variation in educational and experience levels of the soldiers. In some cases, combat veterans had to be combined with new recruits. Most enlisted men were illiterate and did not understand French; when an interpreter was unavailable, instruction was done by demonstration and imitation. The wide range of equipment and weapons in the growing Chadian inventory presented a further challenge for the French instructional teams.

An interservice officers' school staffed by the French was located at N'Djamena. In 1986 the school graduated its first class; an earlier school on the same site had suspended operations in 1979. The annual intake of thirty-five cadets was selected from those civilian and military candidates who had a junior high school level education. The two-year program combined general and military subjects; graduates were commissioned as infantry platoon leaders with the rank of second lieutenant.

A number of officers were also selected for advanced training abroad, principally in France and in other francophone countries of Africa. According to Chadian government data, in 1987 it was expected that forty officers would be assigned to schools in France, thirty-one to Senegal, and about forty to Congo, Côte d'Ivoire, and Zaire combined. A total of forty officers and NCOs had received training in the United States in infantry and engineering skills and in equipment repair and maintenance. In addition, United States mobile training teams visited Chad in the late 1980s for periods of one week to two months to offer instruction in the use of new weapons.

Equipment

FANT's unique combat requirements have dictated equipment policies. These requirements include the capability to shift troops and equipment across vast distances over rough desert tracks, along with the need for cross-country movement to avoid mines and to achieve surprise. In 1987 superior maneuverability and swiftly applied firepower enabled FANT to offset Libya's heavier armor and to reduce the danger of counterattacks from the air. To achieve mobility, FANT favored light armored vehicles and four-wheel drive pickup trucks. The main armored vehicles were French-manufacture Panhards mounted with 90mm guns and supplemented by several V–150 Cadillac Gage Commandos manufactured in the United States. The principal antitank weapons were 106mm and 112mm recoilless rifles and the French Milan missile mounted on trucks especially designed for desert operations. The FANT arms inventory was greatly augmented in late 1986 and early 1987 by military aid from France and the United States. The aid included additional Panhard armored vehicles, two-and-one-half

Chadian troops receiving instruction on the use of antitank weapons
Courtesy Joseph Krull

ton all-terrain trucks, fresh stocks of French and American anti-tank missiles, and American-built jeeps. Toyota pickup trucks were purchased separately (see table 8, Appendix A).

Surface-to-air missile defense consisted primarily of the United States-supplied shoulder-launched Redeye and Soviet SA–7s captured from Libya. In late 1987, it was reported that the United States planned to supply the more advanced Stinger as well. In the late 1980s, France had provided equipment and training for an air defense platoon of Panhard armored vehicles mounted with radar and 20mm cannons.

Small arms carried by individual soldiers had been obtained from a variety of sources. The weapons included Soviet-origin Kalashnikov rifles, the American M–14, the Belgian FAL, the Swiss SIG-Manurhin, the French MAT–49, and some Israeli Uzis, as well as many rifles of World War II vintage.

The series of victories over Libyan forces in 1987 resulted in a vast accumulation of armor, weapons, and aircraft, much of it in good operating condition. The captured matériel included tracked and wheeled armored vehicles, rocket launchers, antiaircraft radar systems, light aircraft, helicopters, and pickup trucks (see table 9, Appendix A). It was uncertain to what extent this arsenal could be effectively introduced into FANT in view of the operating expense and maintenance burden, not to mention the need for training personnel in the use of a variety of complex weapons systems. Some Chadian army commanders were opposed to employing heavy armored equipment because of its unsuitability to combat conditions in Chad and to the tactics that had proved so successful for FANT. Others were said to be intrigued with the idea of developing an armored element based on tanks.

The Air Force

The small Chadian air force, which in 1987 had fewer than 200 men assigned to it, was a branch of the army. When activated in the early 1960s, its inventory consisted of one C–47 transport aircraft, together with five observation aircraft and helicopters, all flown by French pilots. By the mid-1960s, the air force had a number of Chadian pilots. Within a decade, an additional thirteen C–47s were acquired, as well as several French-built utility aircraft and helicopters. The capabilities of the air force remained limited to transport, communications, and liaison, however. The air force was used extensively in support of French and Chadian units operating against rebel activity in the north. French fighter aircraft were regularly rotated into the country from neighboring bases for rapid deployment exercises. After the withdrawal of French forces from Chad in 1975, the government reached an agreement with France, which provided for continued French logistical support and training of pilots and mechanics.

In 1976 the air force began to acquire a modest combat capability in the form of seven propeller-driven Douglas AD–4 Skyraiders obtained from France. Flown primarily by French and other contract pilots, these aircraft were used for several years in support of antiguerrilla campaigns in the north. As of 1987, the surviving Skyraiders were no longer operable. In 1985 Chad acquired from France two Swiss-built Pilatus PC–7 turboprop trainers, armed with 20mm guns. These aircraft were suitable for counterinsurgency operations, but as of late 1987 they had been used only for reconnaissance or liaison duties.

The United States had supplied Chad with four C–130 Hercules transport and cargo aircraft in the mid-1980s, of which two remained in operation in 1987. Three of the C–47s and one DC–4 were also still in use. Seven L–39 Albatros jet fighter-trainers of Czechoslovak manufacture captured from Libya were not in operating condition; in any event, the air force did not have jet-qualified pilots. Several of the Italian SF–260 Marchetti turboprop trainer aircraft captured at Ouadi Doum and Fada were reportedly being flown on reconnaissance missions. Armed with 20mm cannons, these light aircraft brought new ground support and counterinsurgency potential to the air force. None of the helicopters previously supplied by France remained in the inventory as of 1987 (see table 10, Appendix A).

As of late 1987, Lieutenant Mornadji Mbaissanabe was serving as acting commander of the air force. Pilots and crews were of Chadian, French, and Zairian nationalities. France had undertaken responsibility for repair and maintenance of the aircraft, although the actual maintenance teams were of diverse origins. Spare parts and major overhauls for the C–130s were being provided by the United States; France provided service depot visits, crew training, and fuel.

Defense Expenditures

An accurate picture of the actual economic burden of defense costs in 1987 could not be obtained because of the limited statistical data available from Chadian government sources. Officially, defense expenditures came to about CFA F9.0 billion in 1984, CFA F9.4 billion in 1985, and CFA F8.4 billion in 1986 (for value of the CFA F—see Glossary). These expenditures constituted slightly in excess of 37 percent of the total budget in 1984 and 1985 and slightly less than 35 percent in 1986.

It was believed, however, that actual defense expenditures were considerably higher than those given in official figures. Moreover, the available data did not reflect most of the assistance received from France, which was used to meet personnel and operating needs. The expansion of FANT and the heavy financial burden imposed by the fighting in 1987 undoubtedly necessitated a further upsurge in defense outlays. In view of the small proportion of the government budget that could be met through taxation and other domestic revenues, continuation of a high level of French subsidy was indispensable to cover such ongoing military costs as fuel, supplies, munitions, and wages (see Government Finances, ch. 3).

In addition to official budget expenditures, it was reported that a further CFA F2 billion had been raised annually since 1984 on behalf of FANT in the form of ''voluntary'' donations collected from private citizens and businesses by officials of the only recognized political party, the National Union for Independence and Revolution (Union Nationale pour l'Indépendance et la Révolution—UNIR; see National Union for Independence and Revolution, ch. 4). In spite of the fund-raising, FANT troops received only five months' pay during 1986.

Civil Conflict and Libyan Intervention

By the close of 1987, Chad had experienced conditions of chronic warfare for twenty-two years. During the first fourteen years of this period (1965–79), Muslims of the north and central regions had pursued a guerrilla campaign against the central government, which was dominated by non-Muslim, French-speaking southerners. The military occupation of N'Djamena by northern insurgents in 1979 was an important turning point. Although the struggle continued with increasing severity, its shape now changed. Differences between north and south persisted but had become secondary to the developing conflict between the two northern rivals—Habré and Goukouni. Habré's skills as a military commander repeatedly enabled him to prevail against domestic military opponents. He could not withstand, however, the combined onslaught of the forces of Goukouni and his Libyan collaborators when Qadhafi interceded in strength in 1980 and again in 1983.

French troops returned to Chad in 1983 to block the southward advance of the Libyans, imposing a de facto cease-fire and partition of the country. The south and central regions were controlled by Habré, protected by a French line of defense, and the north was occupied by the armies of Goukouni shielded by Libyan ground and air power.

In the late summer of 1986, the balance of military power shifted when most of the troops of Goukouni's coalition rebelled against their Libyan allies. Isolated and demoralized, the Libyans were driven from their Chadian bases in a series of stunning blows by Habré's army in the early months of 1987. The conflict had been transformed from a civil war, in which Libya was backing one of the claimants to authority in Chad, into a national crusade by a virtually united Chad to drive Libyan forces from its territory.

The FROLINAT Rebellion, 1965–79

The prolonged civil warfare in Chad had its origins in a spontaneous peasant uprising in Guéra Prefecture in 1965 against new taxes imposed by President Tombalbaye. The rebellion represented a rekindling of traditional animosities between the Muslim northern and central regions and the predominantly non-Muslim people of the south who had dominated the government and civil service since independence. After unrest broke out in other areas, the various dissident groups were merged into the National Liberation Front of Chad (Front de Libération Nationale du Tchad—FROLINAT) at a meeting in Sudan in 1966, although FROLINAT leaders at first had little contact with the fighting men in the field. From its starting point in Guéra, the rebellion spread to other east-central prefectures. The struggle broke out in the north in early 1968, when the always-restive and warlike Toubou nomads destroyed the army garrison at Aozou.

The government asked the French to intervene when rebel activity threatened some of the administrative posts in the east and north. A French expeditionary force succeeded in recapturing most of the FROLINAT-held regions, but, after the withdrawal of the French in 1971, FROLINAT was again able to operate relatively freely. Internal divisions, however, prevented FROLINAT from capitalizing immediately on the weaknesses of the Tombalbaye regime. Early on, the movement's ideologue, Abba Siddick, lost control to more militant factions. Goukouni broke with the First Liberation Army, which Siddick commanded, and formed the Second Liberation Army, later known as FAN. As of 1973, northern Borkou and Tibesti subprefectures were occupied by the Second Liberation Army, leaving the First Liberation Army in control in Ennedi Subprefecture (see Appendix B).

In the meantime, Goukouni had been joined by the young and dynamic Habré, who had been named commander in chief of the Command Council of the Armed Forces of the North (Conseil de Commandement des Forces Armées du Nord—CCFAN). Habré, however, was ousted in 1976, when he objected to Goukouni's willingness to cooperate with Libya to further the struggle against the central government. The two leaders also differed over Habré's kidnapping of French citizens and holding them for ransom as a means of raising funds.

Most of FROLINAT's First Liberation Army was reunified under Goukouni's overall command as FAP during 1977. (Habré reclaimed the name FAN for his followers.) Equipped with freshly supplied Libyan weapons, FAP carried on a broad offensive against government troops until a cease-fire was laboriously negotiated in March 1978. The truce was soon broken by Goukouni, whose troops soundly defeated the government army and threatened N'Djamena. French forces were again airlifted into the country and were decisive in routing FAP in a series of sharp engagements during the spring of 1978. During the course of the fighting, much of the new equipment FAP had received from Libya was abandoned.

In spite of the French rescue effort, the Malloum government was weakened both politically and militarily by the defeats administered to FAT, the national army. To shore up his position, Malloum offered Habré the post of prime minister in a government of national unity under the former's presidency. The new government, however, failed to function because it was paralyzed by factional differences. Clashes between FAT and Habré's FAN were frequent in the capital. General fighting broke out between the two forces in February 1979. The poorly led, less aggressive FAT troops were soon driven out of N'Djamena by FAN. When the fighting ended, the looting and summary executions that followed precipitated a mass exodus of southern civilians. Mutual reprisals followed. Massacres of Muslims in southern towns were countered by executions of southern officials in eastern areas controlled by FAN.

French troops present in the N'Djamena area did not intervene; French neutrality in effect favored Habré, although the French attitude toward him was divided. Goukouni's FAP, meanwhile, had descended from the north to fight alongside FAN. By March 1979, the struggle had resulted in a de facto partition of Chad: the Muslim armies of FROLINAT controlled the capital, together with the northern and central prefectures, and Malloum controlled the five southernmost prefectures.

First Libyan Intervention, 1980–81

Efforts by the Organization of African Unity (OAU) through most of 1979 brought temporary reconciliation among the warring factions. Nigeria acted as host to four conferences—the first two in Kano and the second two in Lagos—that gave rise to the Transitional Government of National Unity (Gouvernement d'Union Nationale de Transition—GUNT). Goukouni served as president, Wadel Abdelkader Kamougué of FAT as vice president, and Habré as minister of defense in the government. An African peacekeeping force composed of units from Benin, Congo, and Guinea was also scheduled to be sent to Chad. The units from Benin and Guinea failed to arrive, however, and the 600 Congolese who appeared in January 1980 were withdrawn three months later without becoming involved in any military action.

The formation of GUNT did not end conflict among the factional armies. Both Goukouni's FAP and Habré's FAN occupied parts of N'Djamena during the negotiations of 1979 and after the coalition government was installed, maintaining separate spheres of influence radiating from their respective headquarters. When skirmishes broke out in the capital in March 1980, fighting between FAP and FAN gradually escalated. In spite of brief cease-fires and efforts at mediation, the struggle persisted for nearly nine months without much change in the positions of the combatants. Artillery exchanges reduced much of the capital to rubble. Civilian casualties were high, even though most of the remaining population had taken refuge in nearby towns in Cameroon and Nigeria. Under Kamougué FAT cooperated with Goukouni's GUNT coalition, but its attacks from the east on FAN failed. Despite FAT's attacks, FAN managed to preserve its supply lines from Sudan by maintaining control over the N'Djamena-Abéché road.

Although French troops were still present, they did not intervene. They deferred willingly to the efforts of the African nations to restore peace and at Goukouni's request departed in May 1980. FAN's superior firepower and discipline, however, was gradually imperiling the GUNT coalition and led Goukouni to turn to Libya for help. GUNT and Libya signed a treaty of friendship and cooperation on June 15, 1980.

Under the treaty, the Chadian government had the right to call upon Libya should Chad's independence, territorial integrity, or internal security be threatened. Armed with this legal pretext, Libya sharply increased its involvement in the country. After Habré resumed his offensive against GUNT in October 1980, Goukouni shifted the FAP's operations to Borkou-Ennedi-Tibesti Prefecture, where, stiffened by Libya's backing, his force ousted FAN from the main settlements. In the meantime, a substantial Libyan force of 7,000 to 9,000 troops accompanied by tanks and self-propelled artillery was transported southward from assembly points in southern Libya. With military advisers from the German Democratic Republic (East Germany) and the Soviet Union coordinating its movements, FAP seized the town of Ati on the N'Djamena-Abéché road, cutting Habré's supply line to the east. The Libyan army, which included 4,500 to 5,000 members of the Islamic Legion, was then moved into position for a strike at N'Djamena. After a week of intensive shelling, FAN was forced to evacuate the capital on December 15, 1980.

With the Libyans present in force, a period of relative calm ensued, although the various regions of the country remained divided under the control of rival military factions. The Libyan army occupied N'Djamena and was posted at bases in northern Chad alongside Goukouni's FAP; the latter's strength was estimated at over 5,000. Kamougué's FAT, comprising some 3,000 to 5,000 troops, occupied the south. The pro-Libyan Democratic Revolutionary Council (Conseil Démocratique Révolutionnaire—CDR), led by Acyl Ahmat, had about 3,000 men in Arab areas of the east. Habré's defeated FAN, numbering no more than 4,000 troops, had retreated to its original stronghold in Biltine Prefecture and along the Sudanese border.

On January 6, 1981, Goukouni signed an accord with Qadhafi to merge Chad and Libya, evoking a highly negative reaction among the Chadian factions and other African states. Under sustained pressure from African nations and from France to sever his dependence on Libya, Goukouni in effect later renounced the plan of unification and called for the withdrawal of the Libyan forces. Although Qadhafi's army had become highly unpopular and hundreds of his soldiers had become casualties of guerrilla activity, the haste with which he pulled back the Libyan units within a two-week period in November 1981 came as a surprise.

The Libyans were replaced by an OAU peacekeeping force, the Inter-African Force (IAF), consisting of 2,000 Nigerians, 2,000 Zairians, and 800 Senegalese. Originally, seven African governments had promised contributions, but disputes over financing limited the OAU operation. Because of the vague mandate of the peacekeeping force and the determination of all three countries to avoid combat, the IAF made no effort to block Habré's military comeback after the departure of the Libyans.

Habré's Return to Power and Second Libyan Intervention, 1982–84

Goukouni's army, weakened by defections and dissension and no longer benefiting from Libya's help, could not prevent Habré's advance. By the end of 1981, Habré had retaken Abéché, Faya Largeau, and other key points (see fig. 10). Following sharp fighting in the outskirts of N'Djamena, Habré entered the capital on June 7, 1982.

After initially fleeing the country, Goukouni returned to gather his forces around Bardaï in the far north. Numbering some 3,000 to 4,000, his troops included the remnants of the CDR, FAP, FAT, the First Liberation Army, the Volcan Forces, and the Western Armed Forces (Forces Armées Occidentales—FAO) (see Appendix B). Regrouped as the National Liberation Army (Armée Nationale de Libération—ANL), they were trained and equipped by the Libyans. Negué Djogo, a French-trained officer from the south, was placed in command.

When formed in January 1983, Habré's new FANT had an estimated strength of 10,000; the force consisted of a core of 6,000 members from FAN and 4,000 troops absorbed from other factions. Arrayed against it were Goukouni's coalition forces buttressed by Libyan units and the Islamic Legion, which had crossed back into northern Chad. Together, these forces amounted to about 12,000 troops. Returning to the offensive, Goukouni's army was able to take Faya Largeau in June 1983, following a devastating Libyan air bombardment. Continuing southward, Goukouni's army captured Kalait and Oum Chalouba; however, by the time it reached Abéché on July 8, 1983, severing Habré's supply line to Sudan, it had become overextended.

As the rebels advanced, aided by the poorly concealed participation of Libya, Habré made insistent appeals for international help. Rejecting direct intervention, France was prepared to go no further than airlifting arms and fuel. Zaire flew in a detachment of paratroopers, eventually furnishing about 2,000 men. Deployed chiefly around N'Djamena, they freed Chadian troops to fight the rebels. The United States announced that US$25 million in critically needed equipment would be provided (see United States Military Aid, this ch.). In a desperate effort to turn the tide, Habré took personal command of FANT, driving Goukouni's army out of Abéché four days after the city's fall, recapturing Faya Largeau on July 30, 1983, and sweeping on to retake other points in the north.

Faced with the collapse of the offensive spearheaded by Goukouni's army, Qadhafi increased his commitment of forces in Chad. Preceded by intensive strikes by ground attack fighters and bombers, a large Libyan armored force drove FANT out of Faya Largeau on August 10. The Libyan contingent of 4,000 to 5,000 troops was heavily equipped and included tanks and armored personnel carriers, supported by long-range self-propelled artillery and multiple rocket launchers.

In response to the introduction of the Libyan mechanized battalions, which led to the fall of Faya Largeau, the French reluctantly agreed to a renewal of direct involvement. They contributed a round-the-clock airlift of supplies and 180 French military advisers. A much larger troop commitment soon followed. The French force eventually totaled 3,500 air force, Foreign Legion, and airborne personnel in what was designated as Operation Manta (Stingray). The first contingents were deployed north of N'Djamena at points on the two possible routes of advance on the capital. Fighter aircraft and antitank helicopters were dispatched to Chad to discourage an attack on N'Djamena. As the French buildup proceeded, forward positions were established roughly along the parallel of 16° north latitude, which the French tried to maintain as the line separating the combatants.

In 1983 Goukouni's forces and their Libyan allies continued to occupy virtually all of Borkou-Ennedi-Tibesti Prefecture. Meanwhile, Libya was rapidly building new airstrips in southern Libya and in the Aozou Strip to provide support to Libyan forces and its Chadian allies. Protracted bilateral and multilateral negotiations eventually were successful in producing agreement on a simultaneous withdrawal of French and Libyan forces. Within the

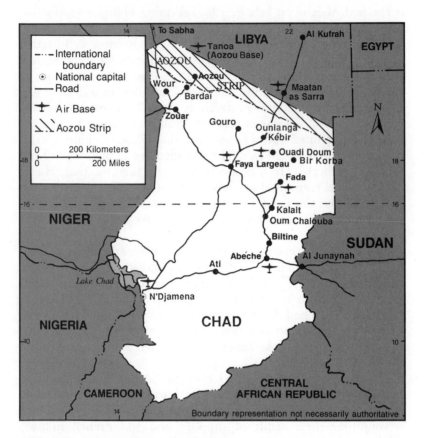

Figure 10. Areas of Fighting, 1980–87

stipulated period of two months, on November 10, 1984, the French withdrawal was completed. But evidence provided by United States satellite photographs made it apparent that Qadhafi had violated his commitment by not removing his troops from Borkou-Ennedi-Tibesti Prefecture. Although French president François Mitterrand confronted Qadhafi over his actions at a hastily arranged conference, he failed to obtain the Libyan leader's compliance.

Repelling Libya's Occupying Force, 1985–87

Although French negotiating efforts had failed to dislodge the Libyans from their foothold in northern Chad, Habré continued to consolidate his military situation during 1985 and 1986. At the same time, Goukouni's forces were becoming debilitated because of defections and internal dissension. Rebellion in the south by *codos* had virtually ceased by the summer of 1986, as increasing numbers of *codos* yielded to the Habré government. According to Colonel Alphonse Kotiga, the former *codo* leader who had become reconciled with Habré in 1986, as many as 15,000 had accepted offers of compensation and training to become reintegrated into civil or military life. Only about 10 percent could be absorbed as recruits by FANT, but the end of the revolt permitted the redeployment of FANT units from the south to face Goukouni's Libyan-backed forces in the north.

Goukouni's GUNT, reequipped by Libya and now numbering 4,000 to 5,000 men, was concentrated in the Tibesti region and at Fada and Faya Largeau. In addition to these forces, about 5,000 Libyan troops remained in northern Chad. At Ouadi Doum, near Faya Largeau, the Libyans had constructed a new air base to handle bombers and air resupply operations. A GUNT offensive in February and March 1986 ended the military stalemate that had prevailed through most of 1985. The GUNT drive, heavily supported by Libya, triggered a return of French forces, called Operation Epervier (Sparrowhawk). Initially involving about 1,400 men, by early 1987 when Libya appeared to be massing for a new thrust, the French deployment had mounted to 2,500 and included, in addition, a detachment of Jaguar and Mirage aircraft.

Differences within GUNT reached a critical stage in August 1986. Acheikh ibn Oumar, who had succeeded the deceased Acyl Ahmat as leader of the pro-Libyan CDR, had become Goukouni's adversary. The followers of Goukouni, essentially the former FAP, were increasingly resentful of Libya's domination in the north and were reluctant to renew their offensive against FANT. When fighting broke out between FAP units and the CDR at Fada, Libya intervened with armor and air power. As a result, Goukouni's men, constituting about two-thirds of the GUNT army, were forced to take refuge in the surrounding mountains.

A cease-fire was arranged in October 1986 between the government's FANT and the mutinous FAP units, although Goukouni himself was reportedly under house arrest at the Libyan capital of Tripoli. Provided by FANT with rations and military supplies, FAP troops set out to harass Libyan and CDR concentrations. But, under pressure from Libyan air strikes, most of FAP gradually made its way to traditional strongholds in the mountainous Tibesti region or slipped southward to be absorbed into FANT.

In mid-December 1986, three Libyan armored columns attacked the main settlements occupied by FAP in the Tibesti region. They forced the Chadians to retreat from the towns of Zouar and Wour into the nearby mountains; at Bardaï, however, the tide turned, and the Chadians repelled the Libyans, who suffered heavy losses. In the meantime, FANT troops had assembled at Kalait to prepare an assault on Fada, which was occupied by 1,200 Libyan and 400 CDR soldiers. FANT units had been equipped by France and the United States with light armored vehicles, all-terrain pickup trucks, and antitank and antiaircraft missile launchers.

The tactics employed by FANT at Fada became a model for subsequent attacks on Libyan garrisons. In a series of swiftly executed pincer movements, successive barriers of Libyan tanks and armored vehicles defending the desert track south of Fada were breached in the early hours of January 2, 1987. The fast-moving FANT columns would leave the road to outflank the entrenched Libyan armor, which was protected by mine fields, then open fire with antitank missiles and recoilless rifles, at times from ranges as close as fifty meters. In some cases, the destruction of one Libyan tank induced the others to flee. The final two Libyan tank barriers, twenty and ten kilometers south of Fada, were hurriedly withdrawn and regrouped around the headquarters and airstrip northwest of the oasis; by noon, however, both strongpoints had fallen. Most of the Libyan command escaped by air, but the Libyan death toll was more than 700, and 150 prisoners were taken. A considerable arsenal of weapons, armor, and munitions, as well as armed trainer aircraft, was captured (see table 10, Appendix A).

Striving to reestablish his position and salvage the reputation of his army, Qadhafi built up his troop strength in the region from 6,000 at the end of 1986 to 11,000 by March 1987. Offensive operations were resumed in late February 1987 against several oases. Two Libyan columns attempted to drive south from Ouadi Doum toward Fada, but each was routed by elements of FANT near Bir Korba on March 19 and 20. Pursuing the retreating Libyans, FANT units caught the defenders of Ouadi Doum unprepared and succeeded in capturing the base after a twenty-five-hour battle on March 22–23. Libyan casualties were especially heavy; reportedly, over 1,200 were killed and about 450 taken prisoner. At both Bir Korba and Ouadi Doum, FANT units captured large amounts of equipment intact, including 50 tanks, more than 100 other armored vehicles, and additional aircraft.

The fall of Ouadi Doum was a severe setback for Libya. Deserted by most of their Chadian allies, Libyan forces found themselves isolated in alien territory, and the loss of the main Libyan air base in Chad prevented Libya from providing close air cover to its troops. In general, the offensive against FANT had exposed the vulnerability of Libya's heavy armor to a more mobile enemy. Libya's combat performance reflected growing discouragement and a sapping of the will to fight. On Qadhafi's orders, a general withdrawal was undertaken from Borkou-Ennedi-Tibesti Prefecture, beginning with Faya Largeau, which had served as the main Libyan base during the preceding four years. Its garrison of 3,000 troops, together with the survivors of Bir Korba and Ouadi Doum, retired toward the Libyan base at Maatan as Sarra, north of the Chadian border. Subsequently, Libya mounted bombing raids from bases in its southern region in an effort to keep FANT from using the abandoned equipment.

In August 1987, the Chadians carried their offensive into the disputed Aozou Strip, occupying the town of Aozou following another battle in which the Libyans suffered severe losses in troops and abandoned equipment. In retaliation Libya intensified its air bombardments against towns in the north, usually from altitudes beyond the range of FANT's shoulder-fired missiles. Appeals by Habré for French air missions to defend the area against the bombing were rejected. President Mitterrand distanced himself from the advance into the Aozou Strip, calling for international mediation to settle competing claims to the territory.

After a succession of counterattacks, toward the end of August the Libyans finally drove the 400 Chadian troops out of the town of Aozou. This victory—the first by Libyan ground forces since the Chadian offensive had gotten under way eight months earlier— was apparently achieved through close-range air strikes, which were followed by ground troops advancing cross-country in jeeps, Toyota all-terrain trucks, and light armored vehicles. For the Libyans, who had previously relied on ponderous tracked armor, the assault represented a conversion to the desert warfare tactics developed by FANT.

Habré quickly reacted to this setback and to the continued bombing of FANT concentrations in northern Chad. On September 5, 1987, he mounted a surprise raid against the key Libyan air base at Maatan as Sarra. Reportedly, 1,000 Libyans were killed, 300 were captured, and hundreds of others were forced to flee into the surrounding desert. Chad claimed that its troops destroyed about thirty-two aircraft—including MiG-21 and MiG-23 fighters, Su-22 fighter-bombers, and Mi-24 helicopters—before the FANT column withdrew to Chadian soil.

The fighting was at least temporarily suspended on September 11, 1987, when both leaders accepted a cease-fire proposed by the OAU. Chadian efforts to regain the Aozou Strip were halted, and Libyan bombings were terminated. As of early 1988, the OAU Ad Hoc Committee on the Border Dispute was continuing to seek a peaceful resolution of the conflict, but prospects for success were not considered to be bright.

Foreign Military Cooperation

Since Chad's independence, France has exercised a preeminent role in the military sphere, sustaining both ground and air forces by providing the bulk of the equipment and training needs of the country. French military contingents have either been present in Chad or poised in nearby countries for rapid deployment during periods of instability. Aside from Libya, which had provided massive help to the forces arrayed against Habré, the United States was the only other country that had supplied military equipment. The rate of arms transfers to FANT from both France and the United States mounted sharply in 1986 and 1987 as the conflict with Libya intensified. During this phase, the value of the equipment supplied by the two countries was roughly the same, although the ongoing burden on France—including support for the defense budget, training, construction, and French troop operations—was much higher.

The French Military Role in Chad

Upon achieving independence in 1960, Chad joined former AEF members Central African Republic, Gabon, and Congo in a multilateral military assistance agreement with France. The agreement provided France with use of a major military base outside N'Djamena (then called Fort-Lamy), as well as with automatic transit and overflight rights. In return, France not only was to provide defense against external threats but also was to assist in maintaining internal security in the four countries. Under this clause, Chad or any other signatory could automatically request direct French intervention to ensure the security of its government in the face of insurgency or coup attempts. The French government, however, had the right to honor or refuse requests as it saw fit. Chad also signed a bilateral military technical assistance agreement under which France continued to provide equipment, training, and French advisers in Chadian uniforms. Fort-Lamy continued to serve as a combined army and air base and was one of the main French installations in Africa from which troops and aircraft could be rapidly deployed to any of the former French African colonies.

Finding it increasingly difficult to stem the rebellion that had broken out in 1965, President Tombalbaye sought French intervention to help restore order. From April 1969 until September 1972, the Foreign Legion and other French units supplied 2,500 soldiers, who joined in operations against the rebels. A mixed regiment was permanently stationed near Fort-Lamy. A limited number of ground attack aircraft, transports, and helicopters supported the Franco-Chadian forces facing the insurgents. As regular Chadian units were formed and exposed to French training, the French forces were gradually reduced.

After Tombalbaye was overthrown in 1975, France's disagreements with the new Malloum government resulted in withdrawal of the remaining French combat forces, although more than 300 advisers to the ground and air forces remained. In 1976 another series of military accords was negotiated covering future French military aid and the transfer of equipment left behind by the French. In 1978 Malloum invoked the guarantee clause of these agreements to ask for renewed French help in stabilizing his regime against the revitalized FROLINAT. French paratroopers and Foreign Legion units returned to Chad in response to Malloum's request but were evacuated two years later at Goukouni's insistence.

In spite of the decisive commitment of Libyan forces in the GUNT offensive of mid-1983, the French were at first reluctant to respond to Habré's urgent request for direct intervention. After further appeals from other francophone heads of state in Africa and from the United States, however, the French launched Operation Manta, a task force of ground troops accompanied by fighter aircraft and air defense systems. Except for several retaliations against Libyan incursions to the south, France avoided direct contact with GUNT insurgents and their Libyan allies. The French presence, however, protected Habré by deterring a GUNT-Libyan offensive south of 16° north latitude, where the French forward positions were established.

Libya's failure to honor its commitment to remove its troops, followed by a Libyan air attack across 16° north latitude in February 1986, triggered a new French deployment, Operation Epervier. The operation initially consisted of about 1,400 troops, backed by air units; continued replenishment brought the total to about 2,500 in early 1987. As of late 1987, most of the remaining French troops were grouped around the capital and at Abéché. The only French forces in Borkou-Ennedi-Tibesti Prefecture were a group of 150 engineers engaged in land mine disposal at Faya Largeau. The French aircraft were based at N'Djamena and protected by batteries of Crotale and Hawk surface-to-air missiles; radar units were installed at Abéché and Moussoro to provide early warning.

Although official data were not available, according to one estimate the value of French military assistance to FAN and FANT between 1983 and 1987 was about US$175 million. During the first six months of 1987 alone, all forms of aid, including the expense of Operation Epervier, amounted to nearly US$100 million. This figure included a US$12 million construction program that would enable the N'Djamena air base to handle Boeing 747 cargo aircraft and a project to harden the runway at Abéché to permit its use by fighter aircraft.

United States Military Aid

Until the early 1980s, United States aid to Chad had been restricted to shipments of food and development assistance. The United States had declined to become involved on behalf of any of the Chadian factions and had no desire to supplant France, which had shouldered the principal Western responsibility in Chad.

Military equipment valued at US$10 million reportedly was delivered in 1981 and 1982, mainly from Sudanese and Egyptian stocks (later replenished) to enable Habré to regroup and rearm after his forces had been driven into eastern Chad by the combined forces of GUNT and Libya. The United States also offered US$12 million to the IAF in 1980, but only 75 percent of that amount was spent. The United States viewed Libyan expansionism as the cause of the Chadian crisis of 1983 and sought to check Libyan involvement. Accordingly, in April 1983 Washington negotiated an agreement with N'Djamena to provide training in the United States for Chadian personnel in a number of military specialties. In July of the same year, the Mutual Defense Assistance Agreement was signed, which provided for sending military equipment to Chad.

In August 1983, Washington authorized US$25 million emergency aid package to help the Habré government, including the delivery of Redeye antiaircraft missiles and missile launchers. Three United States specialists visited Chad briefly to train Chadians in the use of the equipment. As a further symbol of American concern, two Airborne Warning and Control System (AWACS) aircraft, with support crews and fighter escorts, were sent to Sudan for possible deployment in conjunction with French combat aircraft. The AWACS aircraft, however, were not deployed and were withdrawn after about two weeks.

In United States fiscal years (FY) 1984 through 1987, United States military aid to Chad totaled about US$70 million; an additional US$9 million was proposed for FY 1988. Expenditures for training were about US$200,000 annually. Most of the assistance consisted of transport aircraft and aircraft maintenance, small arms, ammunition, trucks, jeeps, antiaircraft and antitank weapons, uniforms, first aid kits, and food rations. The United States also cooperated with France in the air delivery of items deemed critical. For example, in January 1986 the United States Air Force ferried a Hawk missile battery from France to N'Djamena.

Internal Security and Public Order

During more than twenty years of domestic conflict, the agencies of public order and the judiciary in Chad were severely disrupted. In areas of rebel activity in the south and in regions of the north under Libyan domination, the forces of civil protection and the system of criminal justice disintegrated. Where the national government was able to reimpose its authority, harsh and arbitrary martial law often resulted in mistreatment, torture, and extrajudicial detentions and executions. By 1986 efforts were under way to rebuild the civilian legal system, although long periods of detention without trial were still common, and the rights of accused persons were not fully respected during court proceedings (see Judicial System, ch. 4). The various elements of the police responsible for domestic security continued to reflect the strong influence of the military. Abuses by unsupervised military authorities, however, had diminished as a result of the Habré government's attempt to impose greater discipline and control.

Police Services

Police functions in Chad were the responsibility of the National Military Police (Police Militaire Nationale—PMN), the Territorial Military Police (Police Militaire Territoriale—PMT), and the National Security Police, known as the Sûreté. Certain internal security, intelligence, and antiterrorism operations were conducted by the Presidential Guard (Sécurité Présidentielle—SP). The Bureau of Documentation and Security (Direction de la Documentation et de la Sécurité—DDS) was a separate intelligence organization and political police force that sometimes engaged in covert operations against opponents of the government. The Special Rapid Intervention Brigade performed similar functions within the military, although it was controlled by the DDS and was not formally part of FANT.

The Sûreté was originally part of a unified force that, until 1961, served all four countries of the former AEF. With about 800 agents, the Sûreté constituted the national civil police and the municipal police force of the major towns. Its duties included maintenance of law and order, crime prevention, maintenance of criminal records and identification files, investigations and arrests, and traffic control.

Until 1979 the National Gendarmerie, a paramilitary body created in 1960, had primary responsibility for maintaining order in the countryside. The force had remained under the command of a French officer until 1971. Later, in 1979, headed by Habré's political rival, Kamougué, and composed mainly of southerners, the National Gendarmerie had been involved in the fighting around N'Djamena. It remained active as part of the southern resistance to Habré after the overthrow of the Malloum regime. The National Gendarmerie's basic units were twenty-five-man mobile platoons, which had responsibility for internal security and crowd control, and "brigades" (squads) of four to eight gendarmes, who performed ordinary police work in small towns and rural areas. Another force, the paramilitary Chadian Security Companies (Compagnies Tchadiennes de Sécurité—CTS), organized by Tombalbaye in 1967, performed mainly constabulary functions in eastern Chad against smugglers, cattle rustlers, and dissidents. The CTS resisted the 1975 coup that overthrew Tombalbaye, and it was subsequently disbanded.

To replace the National Gendarmerie, the 1979 GUNT coalition formed a police unit of soldiers drawn from FAN and FAP, with token contributions from the other military factions. Mixed military patrols attempted to maintain order in the capital among the contending factions. After the Habré government had been installed in 1982, most of the previous functions of the National Gendarmerie were entrusted to the newly created PMT. Many of the latter's personnel were southerners who had rallied to the government; it was often popularly referred to as the "gendarmerie."

In 1987 the PMT had an authorized strength of 1,600, but its personnel were poorly equipped, often armed with weapons confiscated from former *codos*. The PMT was nominally subject to the Ministry of Interior, and its field units were subject to the local prefect. In practice, the force came under military authority, and individual units were under jurisdiction of FANT military zone and subzone commanders.

The PMN, which in 1987 was under a military commander, Youssef Galmaye, was a branch of FANT; the force performed regular military police duties, assisted in control of prisoners of war, provided route and rear area security, and often took part in combat operations. Its authorized strength was 1,900, and the soldiers serving in it were better equipped than those of the PMT. Training was provided at a military police school organized by the French in 1986.

The Criminal Justice System

The Chadian judicial system and the criminal code were based on the French criminal justice system. The traditional system of

Presidential guard officers in Presidential Palace compound
Courtesy Joseph Krull

law presided over by local chiefs and sultans, however, has been preserved for property and family affairs and for cases of local petty crime. These customary courts, as they were called, have been described as generally effective and fair in rendering sentences. In theory, decisions of the customary courts were subject to appeal to the regular courts.

Normal protections against arbitrary arrest, as well as restraints on the actions of police and judicial authorities, were embodied in the criminal code statutes. Detention without being charged was permitted only for persons under suspicion of having committed a crime. In theory, the rights of detainees included access to counsel and prompt notification of the charges under which they were being held. The death penalty could only be imposed after a competent court had established guilt and rendered a verdict. In actual practice, the judicial system was severely undermined by the breakdown of local government throughout much of the country. According to human rights reports of the United States Department of State, most Chadians did not get speedy trials, and many were held for extended periods before being released without trial. There were only a few trained lawyers, judges, and other court personnel in the country, and law books were not widely available. Although in the late 1980s the Habré government was trying to rebuild the judicial system, the lack of individuals with the necessary legal training hampered the appointment of judges and examining magistrates.

All judges and judicial officers were appointed by the president. The courts were subject to the influence of the executive branch, especially in political and internal security cases, and individuals regarded as endangering the security of the state were subject to indefinite detention without trial. In 1987 the independent human rights group, Amnesty International, reported the detention of several former Chadian exiles upon their return to Chad, as well as the detention of relatives of government opponents. Although there were no reports of disappearances, nor confirmed reports of torture in 1987, Amnesty International expressed concern over the government's failure to account for a number of people who had disappeared after being detained in earlier years.

The Department of State and other groups have described Chadian prison conditions as primitive. To some extent, the conditions were a reflection of the general poverty of the country rather than a deliberate policy. The scanty prison rations made it necessary for prisoners to have a source of food outside the prison; food was usually supplied by the prisoners' families. Most prison personnel had no professional training, and many prisoners complained of beatings and other forms of abusive treatment. Conditions in government detention centers for political prisoners, where outside visitors were not permitted, were worse than those in the regular prisons. Those prisoners of war to whom the International Committee of the Red Cross had access (mostly Chadians captured before early 1986) were reported to be receiving adequate treatment. As of late 1987, the Chadian government was continuing to deny the Red Cross access to an estimated 2,000 Libyan prisoners of war captured since 1986 because the Libyans had refused the Red Cross access to FANT prisoners held in Libya.

Internal Security Conditions

Following his assumption of power in 1982, Habré faced both Goukouni's GUNT forces in the north and resistance by armed dissidents in the south, principally former gendarmes and soldiers of FAT. Government troops trying to establish control in the south were attacked, as were people and installations connected with the government and the state cotton company, Cotontchad. In response to these attacks, government forces adopted harshly repressive tactics. Reprisals were taken, often against innocent civilians. Suspected sympathizers of the dissidents were likely to be executed or to disappear.

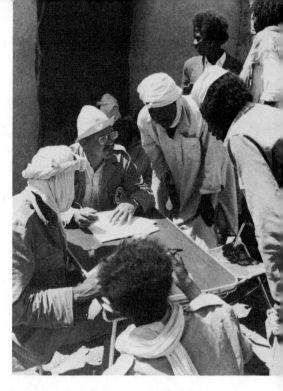

*A representative
of the International Committee
of the Red Cross visits prisoners
of war in the Tibesti Mountains
Courtesy International
Committee of the Red Cross
(Claire Bellmann)*

The violence in the south diminished for a time after the government adopted more conciliatory tactics beginning in late 1983. In
mid-1984, however, the guerrilla groups known collectively as *codos*
launched a new series of attacks. During this period, many civilians
were attacked by both government and rebel forces. Villagers suspected of complicity with the insurgents were often executed without
trial, or they suffered the destruction of their homes and crops.
There were also reports of *codo* atrocities against local officials or
civilians cooperating with the government. Under conditions of de
facto martial law, government troops exercised little restraint in
their efforts to curb the rebellion.

Numerous incidents of noncombatant deaths and detentions were
also reported in the northern battle zone, as control over towns
shifted between FANT and the forces of GUNT. Both armies were
accused of executions and detentions of private citizens suspected
of collaboration with opposing forces.

By 1986 most of the *codos* had accepted government offers of
amnesty, and the turmoil in the south had been replaced by a calmer
atmosphere. In addition, the enforcement of a military code of
justice and strict punishment of undisciplined soldiers had helped
to curb the political killings and disappearances. Many earlier
political detainees who could not be found, however, were assumed
to have been killed without trial.

As of 1988, most of the contending factions that had kept Chad

205

in a state of turmoil and instability had been assimilated into the unified military establishment of FANT. Under these circumstances, and with the activities of former rebels subject to scrutiny by various intelligence networks within the military, incipient defections could be kept in check. Moreover, Habré was placing increasing reliance on the well-equipped and trusted Presidential Guard to maintain internal control.

The only outbreak of dissidence had occurred among the Hajerai ethnic group from the Guéra Massif, who had been prominent in the original rebellion of the mid-1960s and in the ranks of Habré's FAN (see Languages and Ethnic Groups, ch. 2). In late 1986, after a series of incidents between Toubou troops and Hajerai soldiers, a group of Hajerai who felt that they were being pushed out of positions of influence formed the underground Movement for the National Salvation of Chad (Mouvement pour le Salut National du Tchad—MOSANAT). Its head was an army lieutenant and former prefect of Guéra Prefecture, Boda Maldoun.

Following the harassment of many Hajerai by the military police in mid-1987, MOSANAT armed insurrection in Guéra was restrained by the Presidential Guard. As of early 1988, MOSANAT reportedly was operating from bases in western Sudan, in alliance with the remnants of other rebellious Chadian factions that had formed part of GUNT. The Habré regime faced no immediate danger from the group, but the uprising underscored the fact that failure to accommodate the various ethnic and regional interests in the army could lay a foundation for renewed domestic instability and violence.

* * *

The monthly *Afrique défense* (available in English as *African Defence Journal*) regularly treats military developments in Chad. Its accounts of the fighting in northern Chad in 1986 and 1987 are fairly comprehensive, covering the tactics employed, the equipment used, and the size and caliber of the forces involved. Reports in *Jeune Afrique* and the *New York Times* also provide details on the main engagements. In the *CSIS Africa Notes* series, William J. Foltz appraises the politico-military situation in Chad in the latter part of 1987, in the wake of the Chadian successes. A study by Alex Rondos in the same series assesses earlier phases of the Chadian Civil War.

A concise military history of Chad between 1960 and early 1986 can be found in an article by Bernard Lanne in *Africa South of the Sahara, 1987. Conflict in Chad* by Virginia M. Thompson and

Richard Adloff interprets the sources of the struggle among the Chadian armed factions preceding the Libyan intervention of 1980. Additional and more recent analysis is included in a survey by Michael P. Kelley. An article by David S. Yost examines the French perspective on the warfare in Chad before 1983. *Opération manta,* a book by the pseudonymous French officer, "Colonel Spartacus," provides detail on the political and military aspects of French involvement in 1983 and 1984. Samuel Decalo's *Historical Dictionary of Chad* provides useful information on the various armed factions and their leaders. (For further information and complete citations, see Bibliography.)

Appendix A

Table 1. Metric Conversion Coefficients and Factors

When you know	Multiply by	To find
Millimeters	0.04	inches
Centimeters	0.39	inches
Meters	3.3	feet
Kilometers	0.62	miles
Hectares (10,000 m²)	2.47	acres
Square kilometers	0.39	square miles
Cubic meters	35.3	cubic feet
Liters	0.26	gallons
Kilograms	2.2	pounds
Metric tons	0.98	long tons
	1.1	short tons
	2,204	pounds
Degrees Celsius (Centigrade)	9 divide by 5 and add 32	degrees Fahrenheit

Table 2. Primary-School Enrollment by Prefecture, 1986–87

Prefecture	Enrollment	Percentage of Primary-School-Aged Children Enrolled
Batha	4,861	8.0
Biltine	4,401	14.5
Borkou-Ennedi-Tibesti	2,542	16.7
Chari-Baguirmi	39,440	33.4
Guéra	25,124	70.7
Kanem	4,898	14.6
Lac	2,441	10.6
Logone Occidental	35,852	70.0
Logone Oriental	43,414	82.1
Mayo-Kebbi	44,510	37.3
Moyen-Chari	64,789	71.6
Ouaddaï	7,653	13.0
Salamat	6,523	35.5
Tanjilé	19,594	37.6
TOTAL	306,042	40.3

Table 3. Cotton Production, 1960–87

	Area Under Cultivation (hectares)	Average Yield (kilograms per hectare)	Total Production (metric tons)
1960	260,000	152	39,600
1961	288,000	340	97,900
1962	300,000	155	46,700
1963	338,900	278	94,500
1964	286,900	365	104,900
1965	289,200	342	99,100
1966	294,100	295	86,800
1967	303,100	404	122,700
1968	241,000	421	101,600
1969	296,600	500	148,500
1970	292,200	399	116,700
1971	303,000	312	94,600
1972	304,300	356	108,400
1973	273,100	380	104,000
1974	265,000	431	114,400
1975	269,800	532	143,600
1976	332,000	524	174,000
1977	318,800	462	147,300
1978	284,000	441	125,000
1979	267,300	511	136,800
1980	179,800	507	91,300
1981	166,500	514	85,700
1982	133,900	533	71,400
1983	137,700	741	102,100
1984	176,100	900	158,500
1985	141,900	693	98,400
1986	147,300	674	99,400
1987	125,400	713	89,400

Table 4. Production of Selected Agricultural Products, Selected Years, 1961–85
(in thousands of metric tons)

	Millet, Sorghum, and *Berbere*	Wheat	Rice	Corn	Tubers	Peanuts
1961	715	2 [1]	21 [1]	7 [1]	201	130
1965	614	3	38	12	232	150
1970	610	n.a.	37	n.a.	303	96
1975	522	n.a.	n.a.	n.a.	337	82
1980	450	6 [2]	53 [2]	27 [2]	431	100
1985	526	1	21	48	563	90

n.a.—not available.
[1] 1953–57 average.
[2] 1979–81 average.

Source: Based on information from United Nations, Food and Agriculture Organization, *Food and Agriculture Organization Yearbook,* Rome, 1985.

Table 5. Direction of Trade, 1979–85
(in millions of United States dollars)

	1979	1980	1981	1982	1983	1984	1985
Exports (f.o.b.) [1]							
Portugal	9.0	14.9	12.7	10.9	13.9	25.7	15.8
West Germany	9.3	10.1	14.1	5.5	13.9	17.7	10.1
Cameroon	4.9	9.1	16.2	7.1	7.8	8.2	7.8
Spain	12.4	6.2	3.5	1.8	2.2	11.2	5.7
Benelux countries ..	2.5	2.1	2.0	1.7	0.7	2.2	2.8
France	10.6	11.5	5.2	4.8	5.4	10.5	2.1
Italy	1.1	1.0	3.2	1.4	2.8	2.0	1.3
Other	38.5	16.1	26.5	24.5	43.5	32.2	42.0
Total exports ...	88.3	71.0	83.4	57.7	90.2	109.7	87.6
Imports (c.i.f.) [2]							
France	35.1	12.6	19.1	24.6	25.8	43.4	48.5
United States	3.0	2.0	0.7	1.9	13.8	19.1	27.7
Cameroon	7.3	12.7	21.8	14.3	15.8	16.6	15.7
Italy	2.4	0.3	1.4	2.5	7.0	6.6	13.4
Benelux countries ..	2.2	1.5	2.9	4.7	4.2	8.3	15.1
West Germany	5.8	3.5	5.0	3.4	5.0	3.3	5.5
Other	29.4	40.9	57.1	57.2	85.7	73.9	90.4
Total imports ...	85.2	73.5	108.0	108.6	157.3	171.2	216.3

[1] f.o.b.—Free on board.
[2] c.i.f.—Cost, insurance, and freight.

Source: Based on information from International Monetary Fund, *Direction of Trade Statistics Yearbook, 1986,* Washington, 1987, 133.

Table 6. Balance of Payments, 1978–84
(in millions of United States dollars) [1]

	1978	1979	1980	1981	1982	1983	1984
Current account (excluding exceptional financing)							
Export of all goods [2]	99.0	88.3	71.0	83.4	57.7	78.2	109.7
(Export of cotton)	67.1	71.5	56.8	52.0	34.9	60.6	96.3
Import of goods [2]	-163.4	-64.1	-55.3	-81.2	-81.7	-99.1	-128.3
Merchandise trade balance	-64.4	24.2	15.7	2.2	-24.0	-20.9	-18.6
Other goods, services, income (including shipping) net	-87.1	-58.4	-27.5	-22.3	-18.8	-52.4	-60.4
Private transfers	-11.4	-9.3	-4.1	-0.6	-0.7	-2.8	-1.7
Official transfers, (including development grants, emergency relief, budget subsidies, military grants)	116.6	35.2	24.5	41.1	61.9	114.1	87.6
Current account balance	-46.3	-8.3	8.6	20.4	18.4	38.0	6.9
Capital account							
Long-term capital	36.8	-3.9	-4.2	-2.1	-1.2	-17.8	4.7
(Direct investment)	35.2	-1.3	-0.4	-0.1	-0.1	-0.1	9.2
Short-term capital	-3.3	-0.3	0.0	0.0	1.2	-3.8	-9.5
Counterpart items (including valuation changes in reserves)	0.7	2.3	2.0	2.6	3.2	-1.7	-0.2
Exceptional financing (including overdrafts with French Treasury, Stabex grants, etc.)	19.8	27.5	18.7	-16.4	-2.0	10.0	8.8
Errors and omissions	-12.8	-17.3	-28.1	-3.5	-14.0	-8.6	8.6
Total capital account	41.2	8.3	-11.6	-19.4	-12.8	-21.9	12.4
Total changes in reserves [3]	5.3	-0.1	3.1	-0.9	-5.5	-16.0	-19.2

[1] Converted from International Monetary Fund Special Drawing Rights.
[2] Free on board.
[3] Because of rounding, total changes in reserves plus total capital account may not equal current account balance.

Source: Based on information from International Monetary Fund, *Balance of Payments Yearbook*, 36, Pt. 1, Washington, 1985, 122–25.

Table 7. External Debt, 1980–85
(in millions of United States dollars)

	1980	1981	1982	1983	1984	1985
Long-term	191.8	173.9	144.7	148.1	140.0	149.6
Short-term	5.0	5.0	5.0	3.0	1.0	3.0
International Monetary Fund credit	6.9	8.3	7.8	7.4	4.4	8.7
TOTAL	203.7	187.2	157.5	158.5	145.4	161.3

Table 8. Major Equipment of Chadian National Armed Forces, 1987

Type	In Inventory *	Country of Manufacture
Armored vehicles		
Panhard ERC-90 armored cars with 90mm gun	4	France
AML-90 light armored cars, some with 90mm gun	50	–do–
AML-20 light armored cars	6	–do–
V-150 Cadillac Gage armored cars with 90mm gun	8	United States
Artillery		
M-101 105mm howitzers	5	–do–
60mm, 82mm, 106mm mortars	n.a.	n.a.
Antitank weapons		
Rocket launchers 68mm, 89mm	n.a.	n.a.
106mm recoilless rifles	n.a.	United States
112mm APILAS recoilless rifles	n.a.	France
Milan wire-guided missiles	50	–do–
LAW M-72 launchers	n.a.	United States
Air defense weapons		
20mm, 30mm guns	n.a.	France
Redeye, Stinger shoulder-fired missiles	n.a.	United States
SA-7 shoulder-fired missiles	n.a.	Soviet Union
All-terrain vehicles		
Toyota 4 x 4; AM General 4 x 4; Sovamag TC-10	400	Japan, United States, and France
Trucks		
2½ ton cargo	n.a.	France and United States

n.a.—not available.
* Estimated.

Source: Based on information from *The Military Balance, 1987–1988,* London, 1987,124.

Table 9. Major Equipment Items Captured from Libya, 1987

Type	Number	Country of Manufacture
Armored vehicles		
T-54 tanks	3	Soviet Union
T-55 tanks	113	-do-
T-62 tanks	12	-do-
Tank transporters	10	-do-
Cascavel armored cars	8	Brazil
AML-90 armored vehicles	4	France
BMP personnel carriers	146	Soviet Union
BRDM armored reconnaissance vehicles ...	10	-do-
BTR personnel carriers	10	-do-
Weapons systems		
14.5mm heavy machine guns	50	-do-
23mm air defense guns	16	-do-
106mm recoilless rifles	60	n.a.
107mm recoilless rifles	4	n.a.
122mm field howitzers	22	n.a.
SA-6 batteries (tracked missile launcher .... accompanied by radar on tracked carriage)	12	Soviet Union
SA-13 batteries (launcher and radar on tracked carriage)	4	-do-
Vehicles		
Toyota all-terrain mounted with 14.5mm guns	60	Japan and Soviet Union
Toyota troop transporters	194	Japan
Jeeps mounted with 106mm recoilless rifles .	30	United States
Land Rovers	24	Britain
Mercedes heavy transport trucks	228	West Germany
Mercedes repair vehicles	12	-do-
Mercedes tank trucks	43	-do-
Aircraft		
L-39 Albatros jet trainers	11	Czechoslovakia
SF-260 Marchetti light trainers	9	Italy
Mi-24 helicopters	3	Soviet Union

n.a.—not available.
Source: Based on information from Chad, *Kadafi/Tchad: Ingérence, agression, occupation: Livre blanc,* N'Djamena, Chad, 1987, 109-10.

Table 10. *Major Air Force Equipment, 1987*

Type	In Inventory *	Country of Manufacture
C-130 Hercules transport	2	United States
C-47 transport	3	–do–
DC-4 transport	1	–do–
CASA 212 Aviocar transport	1	Spain
Pilatus PC-7 trainer	2	Switzerland
SF-260 Marchetti trainer	n.a.	Italy

n.a.—not available.
* Estimated.

Source: Based on information from *The Military Balance, 1987–1988*, London, 1987, 124.

Appendix B

Principal Armed Factions, 1975-87

ANL—see National Liberation Army.

Armed Forces of the North (Forces Armées du Nord—FAN)—
Composed of FROLINAT (*q.v.*) units that remained loyal to
Habré following his break from Goukouni Oueddei in 1976. Consisting at first of only a few hundred Toubou and some Hajerai
and Ouaddaïan fighters, FAN began its operations from bases
in eastern Chad, where it received help from Sudan. Driven from
N'Djamena back to its eastern refuge after the Libyan incur-
sion of 1980, FAN scored a series of victories over Goukouni's
GUNT (*q.v.*) forces in 1982, which culminated in the recapture
of N'Djamena and Habré's assumption of the presidency. FAN
became the core of the new national army, FANT (*q.v.*), in January 1983.

CCFAN—see Second Liberation Army of FROLINAT.

CDR—see Democratic Revolutionary Council.

Chadian Armed Forces (Forces Armées Tchadiennes—FAT)—
The army of the central government of President Félix Malloum
until his downfall in 1979, when the head of the gendarmerie,
Wadel Abdelkader Kamougué, assumed command. Joined by
gendarmerie units, FAT became a regional force representing
primarily the Sara ethnic group of the five southern prefectures.
It joined with GUNT (*q.v.*) forces fighting against Hissein Habré
and was a recipient of aid from Libya. FAT began to disinte-
grate during 1982 as a result of defeats inflicted by Habré's FAN
(*q.v.*). Most remaining soldiers accepted integration into FAN
or resumed their insurgency as *codos*.

Chadian National Armed Forces (Forces Armées Nationales
Tchadiennes—FANT)—The army of the central government
since January 1983, when pro-Habré forces were merged. Consisting of about 10,000 soldiers at that time, it swelled with the
assimilation of former FAT (*q.v.*) and *codos* rebels from the south
and, in 1986, with the addition of GUNT (*q.v.*) soldiers who
had turned against their Libyan allies. Freshly outfitted by France
and the United States, FANT drove Libyan troops from their
bases in northern Chad in a series of victories in 1987.

codos—see commandos.

commandos (*codos*)—Southern guerrilla groups, active from 1983
to 1986, that resisted domination of their region by Habré's army.

Many were veterans of the government army of the 1970s or Kamougué's FAT (*q.v.*). Totaling as many as 15,000, they operated independently under such names as "Red Codos," "Thunder Red Codos," "Coconut Palms," "Hope," and "Green Eagles." The Red Codos under Colonel Alphonse Kotiga were the most effective. Kotiga exercised some influence over the other groups and was instrumental in persuading them to abandon their insurgency by promises of rewards and rehabilitation. About 1,500 had been assimilated into FANT (*q.v.*) as of 1986.

Democratic Revolutionary Council (Conseil Démocratique Révolutionnaire—CDR)—Members were Chadians of Arab origin, most originating in Ouaddaï Prefecture or Batha Prefecture, with close ties to Libya and receptive to some of the ideological precepts of Muammar al Qadhafi. After the death of its founder, Acyl Ahmat, the CDR was headed by Acheikh ibn Oumar. The most pro-Libyan faction in GUNT (*q.v.*), it fought to prevent the defection of FAP (*q.v.*) units from Libya in 1986. Believed to number up to 3,000 at its peak in the early 1980s, the CDR dwindled to fewer than 1,000 adherents before it was battered by FANT (*q.v.*) attacks in 1987.

FAN—see Armed Forces of the North.

FANT—see Chadian National Armed Forces.

FAO—see Western Armed Forces.

FAP—see People's Armed Forces.

FAT—see Chadian Armed Forces.

First Liberation Army of FROLINAT—Operated in eastern Chad as one of the original armies of the FROLINAT insurgency under General Mohamed Baghlani. After Baghlani's death in 1977, its personnel gravitated to the First Volcan Army of Adoum Dana or Acyl Ahmat's New Volcan (see Volcan Forces). The First Liberation Army reemerged under Mahamat Abba Said in 1984, joining the GUNT (*q.v.*) coalition against Habré, but was one of the factions disapproving dependence on Libya.

FROLINAT—see National Liberation Front of Chad.

GUNT—see Transitional Government of National Unity.

MPLT—see Third Liberation Army of FROLINAT.

National Liberation Army (Armée Nationale de Libération—ANL)—The military wing of the GUNT coalition under Goukouni that had been formally constituted in October 1982 (see Transitional Government of National Unity).

National Liberation Front of Chad (Front de Libération Nationale du Tchad—FROLINAT)—See First Liberation Army of FROLINAT, Second Liberation Army of FROLINAT, and Third Liberation Army of FROLINAT.

People's Armed Forces (Forces Armées Populaires—FAP)—
Composed of followers of Goukouni after the schism with Habré
in 1976. With an ethnic base in the Teda clan of the Toubou
from the Tibesti area of northern Chad, the force was armed
by Libya and formed the largest component of the GUNT (*q.v.*)
coalition army opposing Habré's rule. FAP troops rebelled
against their Libyan allies in the latter part of 1986. Many of
them were subsequently integrated into the national army, FANT
(*q.v.*), and participated in the 1987 attempt to drive Libya out
of Chadian territory.

Popular Movement for the Liberation of Chad (Mouvement Populaire pour la Libération du Tchad—MPLT)—see Western
Armed Forces.

Second Liberation Army of FROLINAT—One of the original
groups in rebellion against the regime of François Tombalbaye.
The Second Liberation Army was composed of the Toubou active
in Borkou-Ennedi-Tibesti Prefecture, first under Goukouni's
command and later under Habré's command. Renamed the
Command Council of the Armed Forces of the North (Conseil
de Commandement des Forces Armées du Nord—CCFAN), it
was in a bitter struggle with the First Liberation Army in the
early 1970s. After the rift between Habré and Goukouni in 1976,
Habré's followers adopted the name of Armed Forces of the
North (Forces Armées du Nord—FAN), and Goukouni's followers adopted the name of People's Armed Forces (Forces
Armées Populaires—FAP).

Third Liberation Army of FROLINAT—A small group from among
the Kanembu people of western Chad, the Third Liberation Army
splintered off from FAP (*q.v.*) in 1977; initially headed by Abou-
baker Abderrahmane, it later became known as the Popular Movement for the Liberation of Chad (Movement Populaire pour la
Libération du Tchad—MPLT). In a subsequent split, part of the
MPLT became the Western Armed Forces (*q.v.*).

Transitional Government of National Unity (Gouvernement
d'Union Nationale de Transition—GUNT)—A coalition of factions occupying the north with the aid of Libya, GUNT formed
the principal opposition to Habré after 1981. Its component factions (*q.v.*) included initially FAP, FAT, the CDR, the FAO, and
Volcan Forces. The National Liberation Army (Armée Nationale
de Libération—ANL) was formally constituted as the military
arm of GUNT in October 1982. Although Goukouni served as
commander in chief, the various GUNT military factions
remained as distinct units under their individual commanders.
In general usage, the term GUNT continued to be used to refer

to the northern rebel army. After Goukouni's FAP mutinied against Libyan domination in 1986 and Goukouni was removed as head of GUNT, the remaining GUNT contingents under the CDR's Acheikh ibn Oumar were sometimes referred to as "Neo-GUNT" or "GUNT/CDR."

Volcan Forces—The First Liberation Army of FROLINAT (*q.v.*) split up in 1977 into two Volcan (volcano) armies. The First Volcan Army of Adoum Dana was an ethnic Arab force receiving support from Sudan. It was absorbed into GUNT (*q.v.*) in 1981 and fought against Habré. New Volcan, the predecessor of the CDR (*q.v.*), was commanded by Acyl Ahmat, a protégé of Libya. Acyl aligned his followers with Goukouni against Habré in 1979. Although initially among the smallest elements (400 to 500 men), New Volcan constituted a corps of shock troops who were among the most resolute fighters in GUNT.

Western Armed Forces (Forces Armées Occidentales—FAO)— An offshoot of the MPLT (*q.v.*), the FAO recruited its forces mainly among the Kanembu group located along the shores of Lake Chad and enjoyed support from some political elements in Nigeria. Initially part of GUNT (*q.v.*), the FAO had reportedly divided into pro- and anti-Goukouni factions. Its leader, Moussa Medela, rejected Acheikh ibn Oumar as head of GUNT after Goukouni was deposed at the close of 1986.

* * *

Additional background on the rivalry between the numerous armed factions in Chad during the 1970s and early 1980s can be found in Virginia M. Thompson and Richard Adloff's *Conflict in Chad* and in *Why Chad?*, a monograph by Alex Rondos in the *CSIS Africa Notes* series. Each of the groups, together with its antecedents, is briefly sketched in *Peut-on encore sauver le Tchad?* by Michel N'Gangbet. Samuel Decalo also provides sketches of most factions in *Historical Dictionary of Chad*. (For further information and complete citations, see Bibliography.)

Bibliography

Chapter 1

Bjørkelo, Anders J. *State and Society in Three Central Sudanic Kingdoms: Kanem-Bornu, Bagirmi, and Wadai.* Bergen, Norway: University of Bergen, 1976.

Brenner, Louis. *The Shehus of Kukawa.* Oxford: Clarendon Press, 1973.

Buijtenhuijs, Robert. *Le Frolinat et les révoltes populaires du Tchad, 1965-1976.* The Hague: Mouton, 1978.

Cordell, Dennis D. *Dar al-Kuti and the Last Years of the Trans-Saharan Slave Trade.* Madison: University of Wisconsin Press, 1985.

_____. "Extracting People from Precapitalist Production: French Equatorial Africa from the 1890s to the 1930s." Pages 137-52 in Dennis D. Cordell and Joel W. Gregory (eds.), *African Population and Capitalism: Historical Perspectives.* Boulder, Colorado: Westview Press, 1987.

Curtin, Philip, Steven Feierman, Leonard Thompson, and Jan Vansina. *African History.* Boston: Little, Brown, 1978.

Decalo, Samuel. *Historical Dictionary of Chad.* (2d ed.) Metuchen, New Jersey: Scarecrow Press, 1987.

_____. "Regionalism, Political Decay, and Civil Strife in Chad," *Journal of Modern African Studies* [London], 18, No. 1, March 1980, 23-56.

Fisher, H.J. "The Central Sahara and Sudan." Pages 58-141 in Richard Gray (ed.), *The Cambridge History of Africa,* 4. Cambridge: Cambridge University Press, 1975.

_____. "The Eastern Maghrib and Central Sudan." Pages 232-330 in Roland Oliver (ed.), *The Cambridge History of Africa,* 3. Cambridge: Cambridge University Press, 1977.

Foltz, William J. *Chad's Third Republic: Strengths, Problems, and Prospects.* (CSIS Africa Notes, No. 77.) Washington: Center for Strategic and International Studies, 1987.

July, Robert W. *A History of the African People.* New York: Scribner's, 1980.

Kelley, Michael P. *A State in Disarray: Conditions of Chad's Survival.* Boulder, Colorado: Westview Press, 1986.

Lanne, Bernard. *Tchad-Libye: La querelle des frontières.* Paris: Karthala, 1982.

Le Cornec, Jacques. *Histoire politique du Tchad de 1900 à 1962.* Paris: Libraire générale de droit et de jurisprudence, 1963.

Lemarchand, René. "Chad: The Misadventures of the North–South Dialectic," *African Studies Review*, 29, No. 3, September 1986, 27–41.

Levtzion, Nehemia. "The Sahara and the Sudan from the Arab Conquest of the Maghrib to the Rise of the Almoravids." Pages 637–84 in J.D. Fage (ed.), *The Cambridge History of Africa*, 2. Cambridge: Cambridge University Press, 1978.

Rondos, Alex. *Why Chad?* (CSIS Africa Notes, No. 18.) Washington: Center for Strategic and International Studies, 1983.

Thompson, Virginia M., and Richard Adloff. *Conflict in Chad.* Berkeley: University of California Press, 1981.

_____. *The Emerging States of French Equatorial Africa.* Stanford: Stanford University Press, 1960.

Weinstein, Brian. *Eboué.* New York: Oxford University Press, 1972.

Zeltner, Jean-Claude. *Pages d'histoire du Kanem: Pays tchadien.* Paris: L'Harmattan, 1980.

Chapter 2

Bouquet, Christian. *Tchad: La genèse d'un conflit.* Paris: L'Harmattan, 1982.

Bret, René-Joseph. *Vie du Sultan Mohamed Bakhit, 1856–1916: La pénétration française au Dar Sila, Tchad.* Paris: Editions du centre national de la recherche scientifique, 1987.

Britannica Book of the Year, 1988. (Eds., Daphne Daume and Louise Watson.) Chicago: Encyclopaedia Britannica, 1988.

Cabot, Jean. *Atlas pratique du Tchad.* Paris: Institut de géographie national, 1972.

Cabot, Jean, and Christian Bouquet. *Le Tchad.* Paris: Presses universitaires de France, 1973.

Chad. Ministry of Planning and Reconstruction. *Tchad: Relance économique en chiffres.* N'Djamena, Chad: 1983.

Chapelle, Jean. *Nomads noirs du Sahara.* Paris: Plon, 1958.

_____. *Le peuple tchadien: Ses racines et sa vie quotidienne.* Paris: L'Harmattan, 1980.

Christopher, John. *Islamic Civilization.* New York: Harper and Row, 1971.

Cordell, Dennis D. "The Awlad Sulayman of Libya and Chad: Power and Adaptation in the Sahara and Sahel," *Canadian Journal of African Studies* (Revue canadienne des études africaines) [Montreal], 19, No. 1, 1985, 319–43.

_____. *Dar al-Kuti and the Last Years of the Trans-Saharan Slave Trade.* Madison: University of Wisconsin Press, 1985.

_____. "Extracting People from Precapitalist Production: French Equatorial Africa from the 1890s to the 1930s." Pages 137–52 in Dennis D. Cordell and Joel W. Gregory (eds.), *African Population and Capitalism: Historical Perspectives.* Boulder, Colorado: Westview Press, 1987.

_____. "The Savannas of North-Central Africa." Pages 30–74 in David Birmingham and Phyllis Martin (eds.), *History of Central Africa.* London: Longman, 1983.

Decalo, Samuel. *Historical Dictionary of Chad.* (2d ed.) Metuchen, New Jersey: Scarecrow Press, 1987.

Dumas-Champion, Françoise. *Les Masa du Tchad: Bétail et société.* Paris: Maison des sciences de l'homme, 1983.

Greenberg, Joseph. *The Languages of Africa.* Bloomington: Indiana University Press, 1966.

Hiernaux, J. *Les populations du Moyen-Chari.* Fort-Lamy, Chad: Institut national tchadien des sciences humaines, 1967.

Jaulin, Robert. *La mort sara.* Paris: Plon, 1971.

Lange, Dierk. *Chronologie et histoire d'un royaume africain.* Wiesbaden: Franz Steiner, 1977.

Lebeuf, Annie M.D. *Les principautés Kotoko.* Paris: Centre national de la recherche scientifique, 1969.

Le Rouvreur, Albert. *Sahéliens et sahariens du Tchad.* Paris: Berger Levrault, 1962.

Lovejoy, Paul. *Salt of the Desert Sun: A History of Salt Production and Trade in the Central Sudan.* Cambridge: Cambridge University Press, 1985.

Magnant, Jean-Pierre. *La terre sara, terre tchadienne.* Paris: L'Harmattan, 1986.

Murphy, Elaine M. *World Population: Toward the Next Century.* Washington: Population Reference Bureau, 1985.

Ouaidou, Nassour G. *Situation démographique des états membres du CILSS.* Bamako, Mali: Institut du Sahel, 1984.

Population Reference Bureau. *World Population Data Sheet, 1987.* Washington: 1987.

Sautter, Gilles. "Notes sur la construction du chemin de fer Congo-Océan (1921–1934)," *Cahiers d'études africaines* [Paris], 7, No. 26, 219–99.

Sillans, Roger. *Les savanes de l'Afrique centrale.* Paris: Chevalier, 1958.

Tubiana, Marie-José. *Survivances préislamiques en pays zaghawa.* Paris: Institut d'ethnologie, 1964.

Works, John A., Jr. *Pilgrims in a Strange Land: Hausa Communities in Chad.* New York: Columbia University Press, 1976.

Zeltner, Jean-Claude. *Les Arabes dans la région du Lac Tchad.* Sarh, Chad: Collège Charles Lwanga, 1977.

Chapter 3

Assegninov, S., and J. Hervieu. *Mils et Sorghos du Tchad.* (Report No. 7.) N'Djamena, Chad: Centre ORSTOM de N'Djamena, 1975.

Azevedo, Mario J. "Foreign Assistance and Dependence: Post-Colonial Chad, 1960–85," *Journal of African Studies,* 13, No. 3, 1986, 102–10.

Banque des Etats de l'Afrique Centrale. *Etudes et Statistiques* [Yaoundé, Cameroon], No. 128, January 1986, 3–14.

Banque des Etats de l'Afrique Centrale. *Etudes et Statistiques* [Yaoundé, Cameroon], No. 120, March 1985, 55–98.

Bouquet, Christian. *Tchad: La genèse d'un conflit.* Paris: L'Harmattan, 1982.

Brandily, M. "Le Tchad face nord, 1978–1979," *Politique africaine* [Paris], No. 16, December 1984, 45–65.

Buijtenhuijs, Robert. "Le Frolinat à l'épreuve du pouvoir," *Politique africaine* [Paris], No. 16, December 1984, 15–29.

Cabot, Jean, and Christian Bouquet. *Le Tchad: Que sais-je?* Vendôme: Presses Universitaires de France, 1978.

Caprile, J.P. *L'homme et le milieu, aspects du développement au Tchad.* N'Djamena, Chad: Annales de l'Université du Tchad, 1975.

Chad. Ministry of Planning and Reconstruction. *Tchad: Relance économique en chiffres.* N'Djamena, Chad: 1983.

————. Ministry of State for Agriculture and Rural Development. *Bilan programme des productions végétales pluviales et irriguées du Tchad.* N'Djamena, Chad: 1984.

"Chad." Pages 350–69 in *Africa South of the Sahara, 1988.* London: Europa, 1987.

"Chad." Pages B201–12 in Colin Legum (ed.), *Africa Contemporary Record, 1985–1986.* New York: Africana, 1987.

"Chad—Country Report," *Courier* [Brussels], No. 102, 1987, 36–43.

Chapelle, Jean. *Le peuple tchadien: Ses racines et sa vie quotidienne.* Paris: L'Harmattan, 1980.

Cornu, A. *Les ressources en protéines au Tchad: Disponibilités et orientations nouvelles.* N'Djamena, Chad: Centre ORSTOM de N'Djamena, 1975.

Fieldhouse, D.K. "The Economics of French Empire," *Journal of African History* [London], No. 27, 1986, 169–72.

France. Institut d'élevage et de médicine vétérinaire des pays tropicaux. *Pâturages du Batha.* Paris: 1975.

————. *Pâturages du Kanem.* Paris: 1975.

Gatta, Gali Ngothé. *Tchad: Guerre civile et désagrégation de l'état.* Paris: Présence africaine, 1985.

International Monetary Fund. *Annual Report on Exchange Arrangements and Exchange Restrictions, 1987.* Washington: 1987.

————. *Balance of Payments Yearbook,* 36, Pt. 1. Washington: 1985.

————. *Direction of Trade Statistics Yearbook, 1986.* Washington: 1987.

————. *International Financial Statistics.* Washington: February 1986.

————. *International Financial Statistics.* Washington: June 1987.

Kelley, Michael P. *A State in Disarray: Conditions of Chad's Survival.* Boulder, Colorado: Westview Press, 1986.

Lanne, Bernard. "Le sud, l'état, et la révolution," *Politique africaine* [Paris], No. 16, December 1984, 30–44.

Organisation for Economic Co-operation and Development. *Geographic Distribution of Financial Flows to Developing Countries, 1982–85.* Paris: 1987.

Stürzinger, Ulrich. "Au Tchad: Coton et développement," *Revue tiers-monde* [Paris], 24, No. 95, July–September 1983, 643–52.

Tobias, C. *Utilisation du sol et possibilités d'irrigation dans la région de N'Djamena.* (Report No. 13.) N'Djamena, Chad: Centre ORSTOM de N'Djamena, 1976.

United Nations. Department of International Economic and Social Affairs. *Handbook of International Trade and Development Statistics, Supplement 1986.* New York: 1987.

————. Food and Agriculture Organization. *Country Tables, 1987: Basic Data on the Agriculture Sector.* Rome: 1987.

————. Food and Agriculture Organization. *Food and Agriculture Organization Yearbook.* Rome: 1985.

————. Food and Agriculture Organization. *Yearbook of Fishery Statistics, 1985.* 61. Rome: 1987.

————. Food and Agriculture Organization. *Yearbook of Forest Products, 1974–85.* Rome: 1986.

————. International Labour Office. *Economically Active Population: Estimates and Projections, 1950–2025,* Geneva: 1986.

United States. Agency for International Development. *Annual Budget Submission, FY 1986: Chad.* Washington: 1984.

————. *Annual Budget Submission, FY 1987: Chad.* Washington: 1985.

————. *Annual Budget Submission, FY 1989: Chad.* Washington: 1987.

————. *Chad: Country Development Strategy Statement, FY 1986.* Washington: 1984.

————. *Famine Early Warning System Country Report: Chad.* (Report No. 12.) Washington: 1987.

World Bank. *Chad: Economic Situation and Priorities*. (Report No. 6785–CH.) Washington: 1987.

_____. *World Debt Tables: External Debt of Developing Countries, 1986–87*. Washington: 1987.

(Various issues of the following publications were also used in the preparation of this chapter: *Africa Economic Digest* [London]; *Bulletin de l'Afrique noire* [Paris]; *Economie développement* [N'Djamena, Chad]; Economist Intelligence Unit, *Country Report: Cameroon, CAR, Chad* [London]; and *Marchés tropicaux et méditerranéens* [Paris].)

Chapter 4

Aurillac, Michel. "France-Tchad: L'Afrique au coeur," *Politique internationale* [Paris], No. 39, Spring 1988, 157–63.

Azevedo, Mario J. "The Post-Ahidjo Era in Cameroon," *Current History*, 86, No. 520, May 1987, 217–20, 229–30.

Azevedo, Mario J., and Gwendolyn Prater. "Foreign Assistance and Dependence: Post-Colonial Chad, 1960–1985," *Journal of African Studies*, 13, No. 3, Fall 1986, 102–10.

Azonga, Tikum Mbah. "Back to Square One?" *West Africa* [London], No. 3689, April 25, 1988, 730.

_____. "A New Dimension," *West Africa* [London], No. 3655, August 31, 1987, 1678–79.

Bach, David. "Le Nigéria et le Tchad," *Politique africaine* [Paris], No. 16, December 1984, 125–28.

Buijtenhuijs, Robert. "L'Art de menager la chèvre et le chou: La politique tchadienne de François Mitterrand," *Politique africaine* [Paris], No. 16, December 1984, 86–101.

_____. *Le Frolinat et les révoltes populaires du Tchad*, 1965–1976. The Hague: Mouton, 1978.

"Chad." *Africa Economic Digest* [London], 9, No. 23, June 17, 1988, 10.

"Chad." Pages B201–12 in Colin Legum (ed.), *Africa Contemporary Record, 1985–1986*, New York: Africana, 1987.

"Chad: Carrot and Stick," *Africa Confidential* [London], 28, No. 17, August 17, 1987, 5–6.

"Chad: Habré and the Hadjerai," *Africa Confidential* [London], 29, No. 2, January 22, 1988, 7.

"Chad: Out with the New, In with the Old," *New African* [London], No. 227, August 1986, 26.

"Chad: The Last Round," *Africa Confidential* [London], 28, No. 4, February 18, 1987, 1–2.

Clements, John. *Clements' Encyclopedia of World Governments, 7.* Dallas: Political Research, 1986.

Daddieh, Cyril Kofie, and Timothy M. Shaw. "The Political Economy of Decision-Making in African Foreign Policy." Pages 61–85 in Bahgat Korany (ed.), *How Foreign Policy Decisions Are Made in the Third World.* Boulder, Colorado: Westview Press, 1986.

Decalo, Samuel. *Historical Dictionary of Chad.* (2d ed.) Metuchen, New Jersey: Scarecrow Press, 1987.

Diallo, Siradiou. "Tchad: Houphouët s'en mêle," *Jeune Afrique* [Paris], No. 1382, July 1, 1987, 28–32.

Diamond, Larry, Juan J. Linz, and Seymour Martin Lipset. *Democracy in Developing Countries, 2: Africa.* Boulder, Colorado: Lynne Rienner, 1988.

Doornbos, P. "La révolution dérapée," *Politique africaine* [Paris], No. 7, September 1982, 5–13.

Doucet, Lyse. "Trying to Put the Pieces Together Again . . .," *West Africa* [London], No. 3638, May 4, 1987, 862–64.

El-Kikhia, Mansour O. "Chad: The Same Old Story," *Journal of African Studies,* 10, No. 4, Winter 1983–84, 127–35.

Foltz, William J. *Chad's Third Republic: Strengths, Problems, and Prospects.* (CSIS Africa Notes, No. 77.) Washington: Center for Strategic and International Studies, 1987.

Gatta, Gali Ngothé. *Tchad: Guerre civile et désagrégation de l'état.* Paris: Présence africaine, 1985.

Gérard, Alain. "Nimeiry face aux crises tchadiennes," *Politique africaine* [Paris], No. 16, December 1984, 118–24.

Gibour, Jean. "Le conflit du Tchad," *Défense nationale* [Paris], June 1985, 127–38.

Hoche, Christian. "Tchad: L'Allié déchainé," *L'Express* [Paris], September 18, 1987, 16–17.

Jackson, Robert H., and Carl G. Rosberg. *Personal Rule in Black Africa.* Berkeley: University of California Press, 1982.

James, Franziska. "Habré's Hour of Glory," *Africa Report,* 32, No. 5, September–October 1987, 20–23.

"Le jardin privé du 'camarade president'," *Jeune Afrique* [Paris], No. 1367, March 18, 1987, 28–29.

Kelley, Michael P. *A State in Disarray: Conditions of Chad's Survival.* Boulder, Colorado: Westview Press, 1986.

Lafaye, Jean-Jacques. "Consolider la victoire (Entretien avec le President Hissène Habré)," *Politique internationale* [Paris], No. 35, Spring 1987, 7–19.

Lanne, Bernard. "Les causes profondes de la crise tchadienne," *L'Afrique et l'Asie modernes* [Paris], No. 140, Spring 1984, 3–14.

_____. "Chad—Recent History." Pages 350-63 in *Africa South of the Sahara, 1988*. London: Europa, 1987.

_____. "Quinze ans d'ouvrages politiques sur le Tchad," *Afrique contemporaine* [Paris], No. 144, October–December 1987, 37-47.

_____. *Tchad-Libye: La querelle des frontières*. Paris: Karthala, 1982.

Lemarchand, René. "Chad: The Misadventures of the North-South Dialectic," *African Studies Review*, 29, No. 3, 1986, 27-41.

_____. "Chad: The Road to Partition," *Current History*, 83, No. 491, March 1984, 113-16, 132.

_____. "The Crisis in Chad." Pages 239-56 in Gerald J. Bender, James S. Coleman, and Richard L. Sklar (eds.), *African Crisis Areas and U.S. Foreign Policy*. Berkeley: University of California Press, 1985.

_____. "Republic of Chad." Pages 184-88 in George E. Delvry (ed.), *World Encyclopedia of Political Systems and Parties*, 1. (2d ed.) New York: Facts on File, 1987.

LeVine, Victor T. "African Patrimonial Regimes in Comparative Perspective," *Journal of Modern African Studies* [London], 18, No. 4, 1980, 657-73.

"Libya/Chad: A Fragile Peace," *Africa Confidential* [London], 28, No. 19, September 23, 1987, 2-4.

Michaud, Paul. "French Africa Policy: Continuity with Change," *New African* [London], No. 227, August 1986, 18-19.

Nelson, Harold (ed.). *Libya: A Country Study*. Washington: American University, 1979.

_____. *Sudan: A Country Study*. Washington: GPO, 1982.

Neuman, Stephanie G. "Arms, Aid, and the Superpowers," *Foreign Affairs*, 66, No. 5, Summer 1988, 1044-66.

Ngansop, Guy Jérémie. *Tchad: Vingt ans de crise*. Paris: L'Harmattan, 1986.

"OAU Summit Conference—'Col. Gaddafy's Initiative'," *African Research Bulletin* [Exeter, Devon, United Kingdom], 25, No. 5, June 15, 1988, 8865.

Oded, Arye (ed.). *Africa and the Middle East Conflict*. Boulder, Colorado: Lynne Rienner, 1987.

Olufemi, Kola. "Chad: From Civil Strife to Big Power Rivalry," *India Quarterly* [New Delhi], 41, July–December 1985, 376-89.

Piro, Timothy J. "France." Pages 226-49 in Bernard Reich (ed.), *The Powers in the Middle East*, New York: Praeger, 1987.

Qadhafi, Muammar. "Qadhafi Versus Christianity in Africa: Colonel Muammar Qadhafi's Speech in Kigali, Rwanda, as Broadcast by Radio Tripoli on May 17, 1985, at the Opening of the Muslim Center." Pages 227-30 in Arye Oded (ed.), *Africa and the Middle East Conflict*. Boulder, Colorado: Lynne Rienner, 1987.

Robinson, Pearl T. "Playing the Arab Card: Niger and Chad's Ambivalent Relations with Libya." Pages 171–84 in Bruce E. Arlinghaus (ed.), *African Security Issues: Sovereignty, Stability, and Solidarity,* Boulder, Colorado: Westview Press, 1984.

Soudan, François, and Jean-Marc Zaidi. "Tchad: Habré et la France," *Jeune Afrique* [Paris], 1385, July 22, 1987, 22–26.

Tarantino, Mark. "Chad." Pages i–xvi, 1–12 in Albert P. Blaustein and Gisbert H. Flanz (eds.), *Constitutions of the Countries of the World,* 3. Dobbs Ferry, New York: Oceana, 1983.

Thompson, Virginia M., and Richard Adloff. *Conflict in Chad.* Berkeley: University of California Press, 1981.

" 'We May Be at War, But We Are Still Trying to Improve Our Standard of Living'. An Interview with President Hissène Habré," *Courier* [Brussels], No. 102, March–April 1987, 32–35.

Whiteman, Kaye. "Chad—Down But Not Out," *West Africa* [London], No. 3703, August 1, 1988, 1387–88.

———. "Chad 1987—The Year of Pushing North," *West Africa* [London], No. 3673, January 11, 1988, 34–35.

Yakpo, E.K.M. "Who Owns Aouzou?" *West Africa* [London], No. 3694, May 30, 1988, 964–65.

Zartman, I. William. "Africa and the West: The French Connection." Pages 39–58 in Bruce E. Arlinghaus (ed.), *African Security Issues: Sovereignty, Stability, and Solidarity,* Boulder, Colorado: Westview Press, 1984.

(Various issues of the following publications were also used in the preparation of this chapter: *Africa Economic Digest* [London]; *Africa Report; African Research Bulletin* [Exeter, Devon, United Kingdom]; *Africa Today;* Economist Intelligence Unit, *Country Report: Cameroon, CAR, Chad* [London]; Foreign Broadcast Information Service, *Daily Report: Near East and South Asia; Guardian* [London]; *Marchés tropicaux et méditerranéens* [Paris]; *Le Monde* [Paris]; *New York Times; Politique africaine* [Paris]; *Politique internationale* [Paris]; and *Washington Post.*)

Chapter 5

Amnesty International. *Detentions and Arbitrary Killings in the Republic of Chad, 1982–83.* London: 1983.

———. *Emprisonnements et assassinats politiques dans le sud du Tchad, août-septembre 1984.* Paris: 1984.

Chad. *Kadafi/Tchad: Ingérence, agression, occupation. Livre blanc.* N'Djamena, Chad: 1987.

"Chad." Pages B357-68 in Colin Legum (ed.), *Africa Contemporary Record, 1982-1983.* New York: Africana, 1984.

"Chad." Pages B348-64 in Colin Legum (ed.), *Africa Contemporary Record, 1983-1984.* New York: Africana, 1985.

"Chad." Pages B125-32 in Colin Legum (ed.), *Africa Contemporary Record, 1984-1985.* New York: Africana, 1986.

"Colonel Spartacus" (pseud.). *Opération manta: Tchad, 1983-84.* Paris: Plon, 1985.

Cowell, Alan. "The Bitter Life of Chad," *New York Times Magazine,* September 4, 1983, 24, 26, 28-31.

Decalo, Samuel. *Historical Dictionary of Chad.* (2d ed). Metuchen, New Jersey: Scarecrow Press, 1987.

Foltz, William J. *Chad's Third Republic: Strengths, Problems, and Prospects.* (CSIS Africa Notes, No. 77.) Washington: Center for Strategic and International Studies, 1987.

Gibour, Jean. "Au Tchad, trois mois pour reconquérir le BET (Borkou-Ennedi-Tibesti)," *Afrique défense* [Paris], No. 113, August 1987, 40-47.

_____. "Le conflit du Tchad," *Défense nationale* [Paris], June 1985, 127-38.

Kelley, Michael P. *A State in Disarray: Conditions of Chad's Survival.* Boulder, Colorado: Westview Press, 1986.

Laipson, Ellen. "Chad Crisis: Background and U.S. Policy." (Library of Congress, Congressional Research Service.) Washington: 1983.

Lanne, Bernard. "Chad—Recent History." Pages 353-60 in *Africa South of the Sahara, 1987.* London: Europa, 1986.

Lemarchand, René. "Chad: The Road to Partition," *Current History,* 83, No. 491, March 1984, 113-16, 132.

_____. "Chad: The Roots of Chaos," *Current History,* 80, No. 470, December 1981, 414-18, 436-38.

_____. "The Crisis in Chad." Pages 239-56 in Gerald J. Bender, James S. Coleman, and Richard L. Sklar (eds.), *African Crisis Areas and U.S. Foreign Policy.* Berkeley: University of California Press, 1985.

_____. "Putting the Pieces Back Together Again," *Africa Report,* 29, No. 6, November-December 1984, 60-67.

Matthews, Lloyd. "Chad." Pages 102-104 in John Keegan (ed.), *World Armies.* (2d ed.). Detroit: Gale Research, 1983.

The Military Balance, 1987-1988. London: International Institute for Strategic Studies, 1987.

Neuberger, Benyamin. *Involvement, Invasion, and Withdrawal: Qadhafi's Libya and Chad, 1969-1981.* (Occasional Papers, No. 83.) Tel Aviv: Tel Aviv University, 1982.

N'Gangbet, Michel. *Peut-on encore sauver le Tchad?* Paris: Karthala, 1984.

Rondos, Alex. "Civil War and Foreign Intervention in Chad," *Current History,* 84, No. 502, May 1985, 209–12, 232.

_____. *Why Chad?* (CSIS Africa Notes, No. 18.) Washington: Center for Strategic and International Studies, 1983.

Sada, Hugo. "Habré cherche la guerre totale," *Jeune Afrique* [Paris], No. 1393, September 16, 1987, 17–19.

"Tchad: Le face-à-face franco-libyen." Pages 228–32 in *L'Année stratégique.* Paris: Editions maritimes et d'outre-mer, 1985.

"Tchad-Libye: La bataille de Fada," *Jeune Afrique* [Paris], No. 1366, March 11, 1987, 10–16.

Thompson, Virginia M., and Richard Adloff. *Conflict in Chad.* Berkeley: University of California Press, 1981.

United States. Congress. 97th, 1st Session. House of Representatives. Committee on Foreign Affairs. Subcommittee on Africa. *Libya-Sudan-Chad Triangle: Dilemma for United States Policy.* (Hearings held October 29 and November 4, 1981.) Washington: GPO, 1982.

_____. Department of State. *Country Reports on Human Rights Practices for 1986.* (Report submitted to United States Congress, 100th, 1st Session, Senate, Committee on Foreign Relations, and House of Representatives, Committee on Foreign Affairs). Washington: GPO, February 1987.

_____. Department of State. Bureau of Public Affairs. *Chad: U.S. Policy.* (GIST Series). Washington: 1987.

_____. Department of State. Bureau of Public Affairs. *The Libyan Problem.* (Special Report No. 111.) Washington: Department of State, 1983.

Yost, David S. "French Policy in Chad and the Libyan Challenge," *Orbis,* 26, No. 4, Winter 1983, 965–97.

(Various issues of the following publications were also used in the preparation of this chapter: *Africa Confidential* [London]; *African Defence Journal* [Paris]; *Africa Report; Africa Research Bulletin* [Exeter, Devon, United Kingdom]; Economist Intelligence Unit, *Country Report: Cameroon, CAR, Chad* [London]; Foreign Broadcast Information Service, *Daily Report: Near East and South Asia; Frères d'Armes* [Paris]; *Jane's Defence Weekly* [London]; *Jeune Afrique* [Paris]; *Keesing's Contemporary Archives* [London]; *Le Monde* [Paris]; *New York Times; Washington Post;* and *West Africa* [London]).

Decalo, Samuel. *Historical Dictionary of Chad*. (2d ed.) Metuchen, New Jersey: Scarecrow Press, 1987.

N'Gangbet, Michel. *Peut-on encore sauver le Tchad?* Paris: Karthala, 1984.

Rondos, Alex. *Why Chad?* (CSIS Africa Notes, No. 18.) Washington: Center for Strategic and International Studies, 1983.

Thompson, Virginia M., and Richard Adloff. *Conflict in Chad*. Berkeley: University of California Press, 1981.

Glossary

Aozou Strip—A disputed section of northern Chad, running the length of the border with Libya and extending south to a depth of about 100 kilometers into Borkou-Ennedi-Tibesti Prefecture. Libya based its claim to the area on an unratified 1935 treaty between France and Italy, the colonial powers of Chad and Libya, respectively. Libya occupied some areas of the strip beginning in 1972 and remained there as of 1988.

barrels per day (bpd)—Production of crude oil and petroleum products is frequently measured in barrels per day. A barrel is a volume measure of forty-two United States gallons.

CFA franc—The African Financial Community (Communauté Financière Africaine) franc, the currency of the organization of former French colonies, often referred to as the Franc Zone. The CFA franc was guaranteed by the French treasury and pegged to the French franc, into which it was freely convertible. In December 1988 the exchange rate was CFA F298 to US$1.

French Equatorial Africa (Afrique Equatoriale Française—AEF)—The former colonial federation of areas that later became the independent states of Chad, Gabon, Central African Republic, and Congo. A history of French rule and missionary involvement forged organizational ties connecting these areas. The AEF was dissolved in 1958, but upon gaining independence in 1960, Chad joined former AEF members in a multilateral military assistance agreement with France.

gross domestic product (GDP)—A value measure of the flow of domestic goods and services produced by an economy over a period of time, such as a year. Only output values of goods for final consumption and intermediate production are assumed to be included in the final prices. GDP is sometimes aggregated and shown at market prices, meaning that indirect taxes and subsidies are included; when these indirect taxes and subsidies have been eliminated, the result is GDP at factor cost. The word *gross* indicates that deductions for depreciation of physical assets have not been made. *See also gross national product.*

gross national product (GNP)—Gross domestic product (*q.v.*) plus the net income or loss stemming from transactions with foreign countries. GNP is the broadest measurement of the output of goods and services by an economy. It can be calculated at market prices, which include indirect taxes and subsidies.

Because indirect taxes and subsidies are only transfer payments, GNP is often calculated at factor cost, removing indirect taxes and subsidies.

International Monetary Fund (IMF)—Established along with the World Bank (*q.v.*) in 1945, the IMF is a specialized agency affiliated with the United Nations and is responsible for stabilizing international exchange rates and payments. The main business of the IMF is the provision of loans to its members (including industrialized and developing countries) when they experience balance of payments difficulties. These loans frequently carry conditions that require substantial internal economic adjustments by the recipients, most of which are developing countries.

Lomé Convention—The first Lomé Convention (Lomé I) came into force in 1976, Lomé II came into effect in 1981, and Lomé III came into force in 1986. The convention covers economic relations between the members of the European Economic Community (EEC) and their former colonies in Africa, the Caribbean, and the Pacific (ACP). The convention allows most ACP exports to enter the EEC duty-free or at special rates and, among other things, provides funds through the Stabex system (*q.v.*) to offset adverse fluctuations in the prices of ACP exports.

polders—Areas of low-lying land reclaimed from a sea, lake, or river by the protection of dikes. In Chad polders have been created along the southeastern shores of Lake Chad and are used for the production of wheat and corn.

Sahel—The subarid climatological zone located south of the Sahara Desert that stretches from east to west across Africa. In Chad the Sahel, also called the *sahelian* zone, forms roughly the central third of the country and supports subsistence farming and livestock raising.

Stabex system—A system of export earnings stabilization set up by the European Community (EC) in accordance with the African, Caribbean, and Pacific (ACP) states. Under the system, the EC helps developing countries withstand fluctuations in the price of their agricultural products by paying compensation for lost export earnings.

World Bank—Informal name used to designate a group of three affiliated international institutions: the International Bank for Reconstruction and Development (IBRD), the International Development Association (IDA), and the International Finance Corporation (IFC). The IBRD, established in 1945, has as its primary purpose providing loans to developing countries for productive projects. The IDA, a legally separate loan fund but administered by the staff of the IBRD, was set up in 1960 to furnish credits to the poorest developing countries on much easier terms than those of conventional IBRD loans. The IFC, founded in 1956, supplements the activities of the IBRD through loans and assistance specifically designed to encourage the growth of productive private enterprises in the less-developed countries. The president and certain senior officers of the IBRD hold the same positions in the IFC. The three institutions are owned by the governments of the countries that subscribe their capital. To participate in the World Bank group, member states must first belong to the International Monetary Fund (IMF—*q.v.*).

Index

Abatcha, Ibrahim, 20
Abd al Karim, 10
Abdullah IV (Bagirmi), 10
Abéché, 18, 30, 36, 45, 52, 77, 105, 113, 117, 119, 150, 192–93, 199
Abou Charib people, 51
acquired immune deficiency syndrome (AIDS), 83
Action Committee of the Democratic Revolutionary Council (Comité d'Action et de Concertation du Conseil Démocratique Révolutionnaire: CAC-CDR), 152
Acyl Ahmat, 30, 153, 161, 191, 195
Adamawa, 7
Administrative Reform Mission (Mission de Réforme Administrative: MRA), 21
AEF. *See* French Equatorial Africa (Afrique Equatoriale Française: AEF)
Africa (*see also* Central, or Equatorial, Africa; North Africa; Northeast Africa; West Africa), 4
African Democratic Assembly (Rassemblement Démocratique Africain: RDA), 15
African Financial Community franc (Communauté Financière Africaine: CFA), 124, 160
Africanization policy (*see also authenticité* movement), 18, 19, 23
African religions (*see also* animism), xiii, xxi, 66–70
Afro-Asiatic language family, 47, 54–58
Afro-Malagasy and Mauritian Common Organization (Organisation Commune Africaine, Malgache, et Mauricienne: OCAMM), 22
agriculture (*see also* cotton production; drought; food production; herding; land reclamation; Operation Agriculture; rainfall), xiv, xxi, 42, 51, 52, 53, 55, 58, 59, 63, 89–90; areas under cultivation for, 92–98, 102–5; labor force participation in, 92
AID. *See* United States Agency for International Development (AID)
AIDS. *See* acquired immune deficiency syndrome (AIDS)
Air Afrique, 118–19

air force, xvi, 186–87
airports, xiv, 119
Air Sudan, 119
Air Tchad, 119
air transport, 118–19, 164
Air Transport Union (Union des Transports Aériens: UTA), 119
Al Azhar University, 72
Algeria, 140, 166, 167, 171, 176
Algiers, 20
Alifa of Mao, 49
Al Kufrah, 10
Alooma, Idris (king). *See* Aluma, Idris (king)
Aluma, Idris (king), xx, 8–9, 17
Amnesty International, xiv, 204
Am Timan, 18, 117
animism, 67
ANL. *See* National Liberation Army (Armée Nationale de Libération: ANL)
Annakaza people, 48
Aozou Strip, 14, 20, 27, 90, 112, 138, 142, 159, 161, 166, 167, 171, 193, 197
Aozou (town), 197
Arabic language (*see also* Chadian Arabic language), 28, 57–58
Arabic-speaking groups, 5
Arab League. *See* League of Arab States (Arab League)
Arab migration, xx, 6
Arabs (*see also* Sahel; seminomadic people), xiii, 28, 60, 63–65; influence in Chad of, 64–65
archeological sites, 4–5
armed forces, xvi, xxiii
Armed Forces of the North (Forces Armées du Nord: FAN) (*see also* Second Liberation Army (FAN)), xv, xxii, 21, 27, 28, 30, 144, 154, 175, 177, 180, 181, 189–91, 192, 206, 219
armies of factional groups, 171, 174
army, national (*see also* Chadian Armed Forces (Forces Armées Tchadiennes: FAT); Chadian National Armed Forces (Forces Armées Nationales Tchadiennes: FANT)), 178, 180; after independence, 171, 176; consolidation by Habré

Published Country Studies

(Area Handbook Series)

550-65	Afghanistan	550-153	Ghana
550-98	Albania	550-87	Greece
550-44	Algeria	550-78	Guatemala
550-59	Angola	550-174	Guinea
550-73	Argentina	550-82	Guyana
550-169	Australia	550-151	Honduras
550-176	Austria	550-165	Hungary
550-175	Bangladesh	550-21	India
550-170	Belgium	550-154	Indian Ocean
550-66	Bolivia	550-39	Indonesia
550-20	Brazil	550-68	Iran
550-168	Bulgaria	550-31	Iraq
550-61	Burma	550-25	Israel
550-37	Burundi/Rwanda	550-182	Italy
550-50	Cambodia	550-30	Japan
550-166	Cameroon	550-34	Jordan
550-159	Chad	550-56	Kenya
550-77	Chile	550-81	Korea, North
550-60	China	550-41	Korea, South
550-26	Colombia	550-58	Laos
550-33	Commonwealth Caribbean, Islands of the	550-24	Lebanon
550-91	Congo	550-38	Liberia
550-90	Costa Rica	550-85	Libya
550-69	Côte d'Ivoire (Ivory Coast)	550-172	Malawi
550-152	Cuba	550-45	Malaysia
550-22	Cyprus	550-161	Mauritania
550-158	Czechoslovakia	550-79	Mexico
550-36	Dominican Republic/Haiti	550-76	Mongolia
550-52	Ecuador	550-49	Morocco
550-43	Egypt	550-64	Mozambique
550-150	El Salvador	550-88	Nicaragua
550-28	Ethiopia	550-157	Nigeria
550-167	Finland	550-94	Oceania
550-155	Germany, East	550-48	Pakistan
550-173	Germany, Fed. Rep. of	550-46	Panama

550–156	Paraguay	550–89	Tunisia
550–185	Persian Gulf States	550–80	Turkey
550–42	Peru	550–74	Uganda
550–72	Philippines	550–97	Uruguay
550–162	Poland	550–71	Venezuela
550–181	Portugal	550–32	Vietnam
550–160	Romania	550–183	Yemens, The
550–51	Saudi Arabia	550–99	Yugoslavia
550–70	Senegal	550–67	Zaire
550–180	Sierra Leone	550–75	Zambia
550–184	Singapore	550–171	Zimbabwe
550–86	Somalia		
550–93	South Africa		
550–95	Soviet Union		
550–179	Spain		
550–96	Sri Lanka		
550–27	Sudan		
550–47	Syria		
550–62	Tanzania		
550–53	Thailand